CREATING CASUAL GAMES
FOR PROFIT & FUN

CREATING CASUAL GAMES
FOR PROFIT & FUN

ALLEN PARTRIDGE

CHARLES RIVER MEDIA
Boston, Massachusetts

Cover Design: Tyler Creative
Cover Art: Michael S. Link

CHARLES RIVER MEDIA
25 Thomson Place
Boston, Massachusetts 02210
617-757-7900
617-757-7969 (FAX)
crm.info@thomson.com
www.charlesriver.com

This book is printed on acid-free paper.

Allen Partridge. *Creating Casual Games for Profit & Fun.*
ISBN: 1-58450-519-2
ISBN-13: 978-1-58450-519-8

Library of Congress Cataloging-in-Publication Data
Morales, Carlos, 1972-
  Mobile 3D game development : from start to market / Carlos Morales and
David Nelson.
     p. cm.
  Includes index.
  ISBN 1-58450-512-5 (pbk. with cd : alk. paper)
  1. Computer games--Design. 2. Computer games--Programming. 3.
Computer games--Authorship. 4. Pocket computers--Programming. 5.
Mobile computing. 6. Three-dimensional imaging. I. Nelson, David,
1983- II. Title.

  QA76.76.C672M648 2007
  794.8'1536--dc22
2007000007

Printed in the United States of America
07 7 6 5 4 3 2 First Edition

For Mary and Lily.

Contents

Acknowledgments

A tremendous number of people make books like this possible. Their contributions are constant, generous, and selfless. I am deeply indebted to them not just for helping me better produce this book, but also for helping me better understand the field of casual games.

Michael Link has provided substantial support in the form of graphics for games in the book and ideas about the functionality and usability of those games. Dan Allen helped enormously with the acquisition of rights to show you many of the wonderful images on the book and CD-ROM. Mary Partridge provided editorial and research assistance as well as physical and mental support. Adam Altemus eagerly read chapters and tested the exercises to make certain they could be easily followed and performed as expected.

Brian Robbins was a guardian of truth and merit who kept me on target and constantly thinking about the best way to adequately capture the amazing work being done every day by specialists in this field. Margaret Wallace, Andy Phelps, and Adriano Parrotta were incredible sources of information and wisdom. Their commitment to openness and sharing among the casual games community is a model for us all to follow. The entire casual games community, especially those who contribute regularly to the casual games mailing list hosted by the IGDA Casual Games Special Interest Group, were a tremendous source of information and generously offered advice and insight.

Jenifer Niles and Jen Blaney at Charles River Media were incredible supporters and provided me with constant feedback and insight. The kind folks at PopCap, Sandlot, Gamehouse, Sprout, Big Fish, Skunk, Oberon, Electronic Arts, Reflexive RealArcade and Boonty, all granted us permission to show screen captures of their amazing games and portals. Together they represent the best and brightest in the industry, and their contributions have been significant both directly and via their contributions to the active and generous casual games development community.

I have been the beneficiary of enormous support from the DirGames-L and Dir3D-L mailing lists. I would be remiss not to mention the ever-present support of industry giants such as Danny Kodicek, James Newton, Barry Swan, Tom Higgins, NoiseCrime, and the dozens of other developers whose constant feedback and discussion keeps me learning.

Dr. Kurt Dudt, Dr. Mary Beth Leidman, Dr. Mary Ann Rafoth, Dr. Ed Nardi, and Lloyd Onyett all provided support for this project and all of my activities. Mary Ann Rapach and Jill Sweeney were consummate beta testers. All of my students are constantly willing to test games, read sample chapters, and even change their plans in order to help accommodate my crazy writing schedule.

Special thanks to Third Eye Software and Meliora Software, who provided some excellent goodies for the CD-ROM.

Introduction

As I talk to people who are first discovering an interest in video games, they invariably work their way to the same question: "How do I learn to make games?" It's a sort of guilty, hesitant request. Is this something I'm allowed to pursue? Is this a real job or career option? I think some would rather tell their parents that they had committed murder or were addicted to cocaine than admit that they are secretly studying video game design or development. The industry remains a mystery. It can be difficult to locate video game companies in your community and even more difficult to locate video game development courses at your local college or university.

The fact that the industry seems almost hidden to newcomers stands in stark contrast to reports from the NPD group and the U.S. Department of Labor Statistics suggesting that the size and growth rate of the industry continue to climb at a rate that outpaces virtually every other profession and industry. Clearly there are opportunities in this industry. It is less clear how exactly a person can embark on such a career.

WHO IS NPD?

The NPD Group is the world's largest independent provider of consumer retail information for a huge range of industries. They have been collecting and reporting data about consumer purchasing trends for about 50 years. The NPD Group is one of a handful of consumer auditing organizations that have begun following the fast-growing sector of the games industry known as casual games.

One of the reasons the terrain is difficult to tread is that it is in nearly constant motion. The types, levels, technologies, and methods of game design have all evolved at an equally staggering pace. When I first became enamored of computer games only 25 years ago, Asteroids and Pong were state-of-the-art games. Back then, I gladly sat in front of black screens, enthralled by a single white blinking cursor prompting me to make a simple choice between heading left or right in an entirely imagined dungeon.

Today, we've come to expect full-motion video, detailed 3D graphics, and slickly produced images and animations. Every aspect of video games evolves at a pace so rapid that people who haven't played in a while are often overwhelmed by the available selection, complexity, and sophisticated production techniques. Among the most recent evolutions in the video game design landscape is the growing subindustry of casual games.

NEW OPPORTUNITY FOR INDEPENDENT DEVELOPERS

- Low development cost
- High return on investment
- Explosive growth rates
- Short development cycles
- Substantially broader audience
- World's largest video game audience
- Expanding distribution options

WHY CASUAL GAMES?

Thousands of game enthusiasts and would-be developers search constantly for an opportunity to expand their knowledge of games. Whether they're clicking through Amazon® or browsing Barnes and Noble®, they are all looking for a path to their dream, a secret door into the games industry. The casual games market provides that secret passage.

The industry features online downloadable games delivered through distribution portals like Real-One Arcade®, Shockwave.com®, MSN Games Center, and Pogo. It has experienced explosive growth over the past five years, moving from essentially nothing in 2001 into a projected multibillion dollar annual marketplace within the decade. Independent developers have rapidly discovered the field as one of the last remaining venues to break into the public eye. It is now the single most attractive opportunity available to anyone who wants to become a game developer.

It is appealing because the games are basic enough to be within the reach of small developers, and the profit potential is substantially higher than the profit potential of traditional CD-ROM–based software distribution. Games within this market conform to very specific conventions and are rapidly setting the standard that will likely be used to ease the transition from a world dominated by casual players to one dominated by serious game enthusiasts. Essentially, casual game players need their hands held as they encounter any new conventions in game play. In an effort to capture and hold this massive new audience, developers have launched and enhanced a series of interface and gameplay conventions that are rapidly becoming the accepted norm for all video games.

Every new type of media begins as an innovation. It is launched on the world, and entrepreneurs struggle to find a reliable method for generating a profit from the new media form. An examination of the video games industry reveals a pattern that suggests that this period of entrepreneurship is coming to a close as paradigms for profiting from the media become more and more stable. It now appears that the online distribution system will be at least one of the major ways that people profit from electronic games in the future.

MANY PEOPLE WILL FIND HELPFUL INFORMATION IN THIS BOOK

- Enthusiasts
- Developers
- Publishers
- Managers
- Producers
- Teachers
- Students
- Parents
- Artists
- Designers
- Players
- Advertisers
- Marketers
- Promoters

Is Casual Game Development Different?

While there are many similarities between casual game development and traditional game development, the audiences are radically different, and this combined with smaller budgets and tighter timelines leads to a remarkably different approach to the development of the games.

- Development cycles are accelerated.
- Budgets are lower.
- Technology requirements emphasize optimization.
- Performance platforms are more diverse and less powerful.
- The audience expects facilitation and accommodation.

When combined, these factors create a fast-paced, creative, and exciting new landscape for developers to explore their creative options. The field is exploding as hundreds of millions of players flock to online portals to experience the immediate, on-demand satisfaction of a casual game. In many ways this is the obvious expansion of games into the mainstream audience. People who don't want to be burdened by awkward gameplay mechanics but want to join in the fun are demanding an ever-expanding array of easy-to-learn, tough-to-master distractions in the form of these games.

Who Should Read this Book?

This book is ideal for virtually anyone with an interest in games, regardless of their expertise or prior experience, because it deals with the industry and development issues in everyday language. This information is useful for independent and amateur game developers and for programmers and game enthusiasts who hope to expand their role to that of game developer, publisher, producer, or designer. This book is for mainstream multimedia developers, game developers, software developers, game enthusiasts, business persons, and even hobbyists who just want an easy way to learn more about this booming industry.

This book could easily be used for courses in multimedia game development. Current texts focus on so much specific technology and such a broad range of games that beginning students are often overwhelmed. This book allows nonprogrammers to access the fundamental concepts behind game development. (Casual games are authored in everything from Adobe® Flash® to Microsoft Visual C++®, Adobe Director®, and Visual Basic®.)

This book is also for casual game enthusiasts and developers, people who want to learn how to make these games, and people who want to know how the industry works. Finally it is for those interested in learning more about casual games in general.

WHAT IS IN THIS BOOK?

This casual games handbook is divided into two parts: Part 1, "Designing and Developing a Casual Game," and Part 2, "Understanding the Market and the Business Model."

Part 1, "Designing and Developing a Casual Game," focuses on the genres and formats common in the market today. It includes an examination and analysis of current hit games and generally successful genres and an introduction to the basic model used by game developers to create casual games. The reader will learn how to implement a casual game, from initial treatment to installation. Casual Games contain many special techniques that are demonstrated in the book using Adobe Flash and Director. Common game development methods will also be demonstrated.

TOP FIVE DEVELOPMENT ENVIRONMENTS FOR CASUAL GAMES

- C++ (often paired with Simple DirectMedia Layer [SDL])
- Adobe Director
- Adobe Flash
- PopCap Games Framework
- Torque Game Builder

The final section, "Understanding the Market and the Business Model," focuses on the demographics of the audience and their preferences in game play. It includes an overview of the market and an explanation of current opinions about player preferences. This section also contains sample instruments for beta testing games and an explanation of the process that developers use to integrate user experiences into their game design.

This section examines the current business practices of the industry's largest distribution portals, RealOne Arcade, Shockwave.com, Pogo Games, Yahoo® Games, Big Fish Games™, and MSN Games. It provides a guide to submitting games to portal and distribution sites and an overview of common business practices. Throughout the book there are interviews and case studies from independent developers, industry leaders, and experts, illustrating professional practices and industry conventions.

SCOPE AND LIMITATIONS OF THIS BOOK

Game development is a complex, ever-changing, and thrilling process that cannot and should not be fully understood or mastered by reading a single book. No one expects to become a brain surgeon or nuclear physicist after browsing a few hundred pages of text, but I meet people all the time who are convinced that they can master game development in a few weekends.

This is a journey that will take even the most gifted student quite a long time to master, but the rewards can be genuinely exhilarating. There are opportunities to focus on virtually any field within games, and there is room in the industry for practically anyone who is willing to work.

I fell into game design a little more than a decade ago. As a student, I focused on journalism, television, theater, and film. My father worked for Big Blue (IBM) in the days of walk-in main frames, so I had plenty of early exposure to computers and an unnatural "knack" for understanding code and programming. I think it's only fair to disclose that I have always found computers and programming very simple and logical. I believe that recognizing this has helped me realize that many people do not adjust so easily and as a result find the whole development process intimidating.

This book reveals trends in the management, distribution, and development of casual games. The information can be used to do anything from learning to submit games to online portals, to mastering developmental approaches. It is not a fundamental programming book or a step-by-step tutorial collection. The information is designed to help the readers learn how to make their own casual games based on guiding principles. Add creativity and perseverance, and the book should prove useful to anyone interested in the industry.

Code samples in the book are intended to provide a base for developers to work from. Just as it isn't reasonable to exactly copy the functions and interface of someone else's game, it isn't wise to depend on other people's code to create your own games. The code should be used as a guide and motivator. Readers should find inspiration where they can and then create their own code to drive their own games.

WHAT TOOLS OR TECHNOLOGIES ARE USED?

Code samples in the book make use of Adobe (formerly Macromedia) Flash, Adobe (formerly Macromedia) Director, and several small applications used for general development. Each of these applications are available either for free or as free time-limited downloads over the Internet.

The primary development environments used to demonstrate casual games in this book are Flash and Director. Flash is the most ubiquitous Web plug-in, with virtually universal reach. Its client-based application engine is slightly less versatile and powerful than Director, which is the longest-lived and potentially the most powerful multimedia development environment available today.

These basic engines enable the reader to repeat the exercises and code samples that are included without requiring a substantial investment in learning to program. Game development always requires some programming, but it also involves a substantial number of other skills. Using these technologies will allow the reader to focus on all of the skills used by a game developer.

About the Author

D r. Allen Partridge is director of the Applied Media and Simulation Games Center at Indiana University of Pennsylvania. Partridge is the founder and co-owner of Insight Interactive games and has developed a myriad of interactive 2D and 3D games.

Partridge's casual games have been featured on Reflexive® Arcade, Pogo™ Games, Oberon™ Games, and dozens of other distribution portals worldwide. He has written several articles and a book on Shockwave 3D games and was the technical editor for Paul Catanese's *Director's Third Dimension*. Partridge is the host of the popular dirGames-l and dir3d-l mailing lists.

Part

I

Designing and Developing a Casual Game

A variety of genres and formats are now commonplace in the newly emerging casual games market. This part of the book includes an examination and analysis of hit casual games and successful genres as well as an introduction to the basic model used by game developers to create casual games (Figure 1.1).

FIGURE 1.1 Mystery Case Files: Prime Suspects. © Big Fish Games. All Rights Reserved.

You will learn to implement a casual game, from initial treatment to final installation, in this part of the book. Casual games typically feature many special techniques that are detailed and demonstrated in Adobe Flash and Adobe Director. Common game development methods are also demonstrated in this section.

1 Casual Game Design Basics

In This Chapter

- Easy to Learn, Tough to Master
- Qualities of a Casual Game
- Integrated Context-Based Help
- Navigation Conventions
- Bells and Whistles
- Project 1: Make a Match-Three Puzzle

One mixed blessing of casual games is that they have rapidly fallen into several common conventions for better appeal to the mass market. The market for casual games is substantially larger than that of hard-core games. It is flooded with people just beginning to master the use of their personal computers.

In some ways this normalization or standardization of games in the industry is helpful to developers, because it clarifies exactly what tasks need to be completed for your game. On the other hand, it can be a real creativity killer, tempting developers to fall into the fold, pressing out an endless array of *Tetris*® descendents.

Originally released in 1986, Tetris was created by Alexey Pajitnov, Dmitry Pavlovsky, and Vadim Gerasimov. The trio of Russian computer programmers was fascinated by the burgeoning computer games industry and hatched a plan to create several hit games. Tetris was not the one they expected to flourish, but it quickly demonstrated that elusive power to addict its audience. The game's name is a combination of tetramino (four boxes arranged in varied patterns, see Figure 1.2) and tennis.

→

FIGURE 1.2   Tetramino are the four block combination shapes featured in *Tetris*.

In this chapter you will learn how to:

- Design a game that is accessible to a mass audience and that excites players
- Design rules and puzzles for a game that reward players effectively
- Explain the science behind a games challenge/reward model to producers and clients.
- Plan a strategy for hooking your audience in the first few minutes of play
- Design integrated help systems to guide your audience through your game

- Develop reward systems that provide constant reassurance and satisfaction as well as escalating rewards that motivate continued play
- Tease, tempt, and promise bigger and better rewards and features
- Emulate standard industry navigation conventions
- Apply these skills to the development of a game

Industry analysts have predicted that the worldwide market for casual games will be 1.2–1.5 billion dollars by 2007. Approximately 50% of industry profits come from advertising while players are enjoying the game online at portal sites.

EASY TO LEARN, TOUGH TO MASTER

When asked to define casual games, the phrase *easy to learn, tough to master* generally comes to mind. In some ways it sums up the concept beautifully. It's such a universal truth that you'll find the phrase in the ad campaigns and mission statements of countless games and game companies in the casual games industry. It means these games are based on simple, universally understandable conventions. They combine a model of constant enticement and reward with an increasingly complicated puzzle or problem. The objective provides just the right amount of stimulation for people to enjoy. While this definition is at the heart of casual games, it can also be found at the heart of many games. A casual game is easy to learn and hard to master, but it is also something more.

Players access casual games using popular portals (Figure 1.3). Portals are online retail outlets and distribution centers. These often provide a sense of community for game players, allowing members to write reviews of their favorite

→

games and providing a nonstop stream of new online and downloadable casual games.

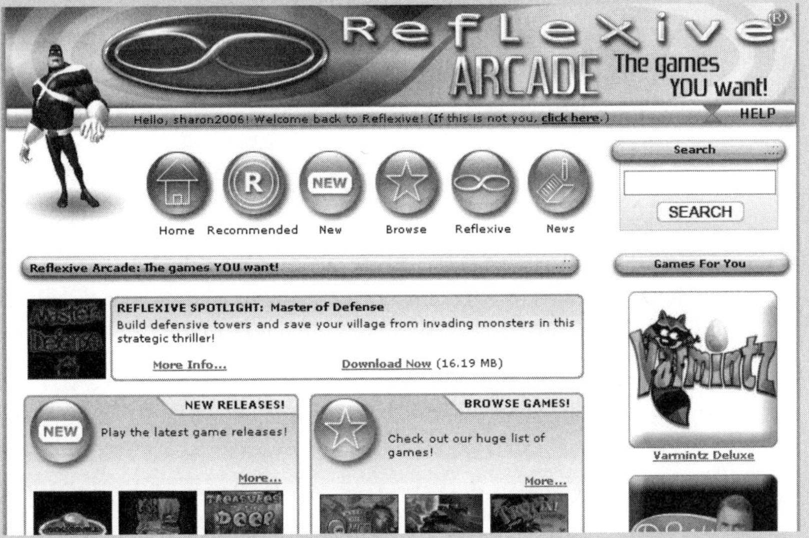

FIGURE 1.3   Reflexive Arcade® is one of several popular casual game portals.
© Reflexive Entertainment. All Rights Reserved.

The term *casual* is a description of the audience, not the games. A casual game shouldn't be nonimmersive or nonengaging. Casual game players can be as heavily involved in any given moment of game play as a hard-core gamer. The difference is largely that they probably wouldn't define themselves as gamers if you asked. They are looking for a game experience that does not require a significant investment. Ironically it doesn't mean they aren't going to make one.

QUALITIES OF A CASUAL GAME

- Easy to learn, tough to master
- Audience does not consider themselves gamers
- Broad appeal and inoffensive content
- Easily acquired, typically via Internet download

A casual game is easy to learn to play and it never makes the player feel threatened or inadequate. Another characteristic of a casual game is that it appeals to the target demographic: a forty-year-old woman with an interest in travel, pets, and gardening. She has disposable income and plays casual games quite regularly on the Internet. It's important to note that this audience is widely regarded as an expanding market, so it is likely that the demographics will continue to evolve over the next decade.

Casual games are benign and have a broad appeal. They feature subjects, characters, and gameplay that are never offensive. While they are clean enough for kids, they are not juvenile or childish. The subjects are not conflict-oriented (war games) or adult in nature. The games can be played by anyone and witnessed by anyone and are easily understood by everyone.

Finally, a casual game uses a customer-friendly, easy-to-acquire sales model. It isn't generally sold in stores. It's available online for free and then after a time asks the player to purchase a license in order to keep playing. The purchase process, handled through digital rights management (DRM) tools, is as simple and as reassuring as possible for the customer. This is critical because it introduces a fact about casual games that is often overlooked. They are impulse purchases, made because the player feels a need to keep playing that game (Figure 1.4).

Boonty is one of the largest casual games platforms in the world, operating in more than 25 countries. Since its launch in 2001, the company's customized end-to-end solutions have been implemented by major publishers, Internet portals, ISPs, mobile phone operators, advertisers, Internet communities, and PC manufacturers globally.

How many entertainment products can you think of that let you take them home and try them for an hour or two before you decide whether to buy them? The standard for top-10 *hits* in casual games is insanely high. It is not uncommon for dozens of new casual games to

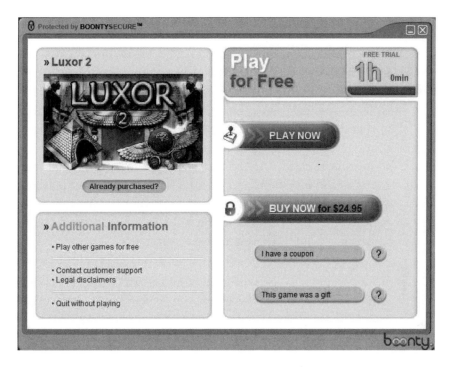

FIGURE 1.4   A Boonty digital rights management/up-sell pop up. © 2004 Boonty.
All Rights Reserved.

appear on the portals every week, so catching the attention of a large audience is very challenging. Ultimately it doesn't matter if an enormous number of people play the game, if very few of them actually pay to own the game. A developer could easily create a game that more than 100,000 people will play, but never earn a profit from the title. However, a developer can create a game that over a year could generate half a million dollars or more (just for the developer) and over its lifespan could net millions. This topic is discussed in Part 2 of this book, which deals with the market and the industry.

> The term *success* is used to describe any game that makes a profit. The term *hit* is commonly used to describe a game that achieves substantial ubiquity and enjoys a long run at the top of ratings charts.

COGNITIVE PROCESS OF CHALLENGE AND REWARD

People are constantly learning. It's an absolutely essential part of human nature. We all are built to be curious and to learn from the investigations that this inherent curiosity launches. We see this all the time in our daily lives. You may meet friends in the shopping mall and note that one seems distracted or evasive. Generally we try to explore and examine such irregular behavior. Sometimes we ask direct questions, such as, "Are you okay?" At other times we simply explore the question internally and wonder what might have distracted them. If we see a simple math problem, we often solve it without being asked. This is an obvious truth, but its easier to see in the young, as once we are older, there are fewer unknowns.

We play games, watch murder mysteries, explore caverns, even travel because it stimulates our minds and satisfies our insatiable appetite to learn. There are limits to the size of puzzle or challenge that we like to encounter. Music provides a fine example of this cognitive limit. We like music that we can easily follow and that challenges or surprises us in some way.

When we are young, the surprise need not be sophisticated. The Barney® song for example, "I love you, you love me. . . ," is perfectly acceptable to a young toddler, but will quickly irritate most adults. "Get it out of my head!" Adults find the music repetitive and annoying almost beyond their limit to endure. It isn't challenging enough to interest them, so it frustrates them. Likewise, if the music were too complex, full of discordant harmonies or complex rhythmic patterns, the adult would also find the music frustrating, not because it's too simple, but because it's too complex (Figure 1.5).

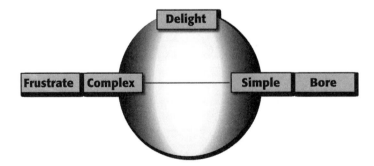

FIGURE 1.5 Delighting an audience requires the right amount of challenge.

If you think about it, effective games must fall in the middle of this cognitive range: between too simple (boring) and too difficult (frustrating). If they do, the player finds them delightful. This, of course, raises two obvious problems. First, the player will get better at solving the game's puzzles, so the range of the target changes grows more sophisticated over time. Second, all players have different starting points, so they will all have slightly different ranges that they find satisfying.

The result is that all games are a delicate balance of challenges to stimulate the player's need to learn and rewards to motivate the player to continue facing more challenges. Good games quickly allow players to identify the right starting level to challenge them and strongly reward the player for significant growth. If a game is tough to learn, players are less motivated to invest time in the experience. If a game is easy to master, players lose interest too quickly and are unlikely to purchase the game.

Any functional version of the game that is ready for evaluation and testing is called a beta. Versions that are unfinished (lack some of the planned functions) but demonstrate essential functions are called alphas.

Listening to Your Audience

One way to stay in tune with the cognitive challenge your game is providing for your audience is simply to ask them and listen to them. Developers often poll players in the form of beta tests to find out what they think about the various challenges and rewards in a new game. You can even take this step further by enlisting the advice of your audience earlier in the development process, thereby getting a sense of their likes and dislikes before precious development time is wasted on features that are of little benefit. Regardless of how you learn your audience's tastes, it's important that you identify the characteristics of a given audience and work with representative members of that audience to make a game they enjoy.

To do this you have to first understand who that audience really is. This can be tough for developers. The casual gamer is often referred to as *stupid* and casual games labeled as games for *stupid people*. This is, first, nonproductive and, second, not at all correct. Casual game players are not stupid. They are just not the sort of people who would think of themselves as gamers. They often don't have a lot of experience playing games and they aren't always very familiar with computers, especially computer interfaces for games. It would never occur to them to press keys to jump, run, or steer a game character. They don't immediately see what people with a lifetime of game experience see.

> A *release candidate* is a postbeta functional version of the software that is stable and believed ready for release. Only a *stop ship* or *showstopper* bug (something that would render the software unusable) is sufficient to make changes to the software at this point.

A great first-hand reminder of this was provided when *Podz* was presented to a typical casual gamer to test. This game player is an office worker by day, exposed to computers and used to playing casual games on them, but not at all accustomed to "new game paradigms." In retrospect, she was the project's best beta tester. Immediately she had dozens of questions, many of which were literally dumbfounding. "How do I start?" she asked, staring at a screen with a bright green arrow (Figure 1.6).

> Most portals expect a *release candidate* or *gold* version of the software to be ready by the time you start working with them. They do not want to spend expensive time waiting for last-minute changes.

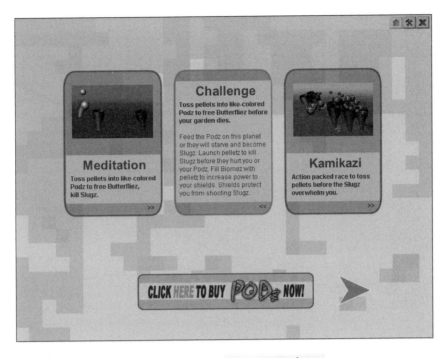

FIGURE 1.6   An early interface that was far too complex.

Based on comments from the beta testers, we made the arrow flash brightly, and it was the only motion on the screen. We removed the up-sell button and removed the three mode-setting buttons, including their *huge* expandable descriptions. We worked for months to figure out what exactly the player needed to know to play the game and concluded that there were only two critical concepts required to start (remember, easy to learn—no novella required). Those concepts are summed up in the final launch screen, which reads simply, "Feed Podz" and "Kill Slugz" (Figure 1.7).

Too much text on the screen frustrates and confuses many casual game players. They want to get to the fun, and don't generally like to read lengthy instructions. They will often ignore text, refusing to read lengthy instructions.

FIGURE 1.7   The final interface for *Podz* requires much less thought.

We added a prescreen pop up to gather the player's name before a new player even reaches this screen. The result allowed us to create a drop-down menu, preset to the player's name, right next to a bright blue flashing arrow. After this change, players were no longer confused about how to begin the game. Much of the confusion of the original interface can clearly be attributed to information overload. Remember, a casual game player doesn't want to have to work to figure out how to play the game (Figure 1.8).

FIGURE 1.8   This basic window appears first, to gather the player's name.

Most casual game *launch screens* use text-based buttons to give users choices. This is probably to ensure that the players are absolutely certain of what will happen when they make a choice. Generally these choices avoid unusual words to describe choices, using words such as *timed* and *story* rather than descriptive or themed terms that might be less clear.

We still let people play the game in the untimed and noncolor matching modes, but we simplified the interface to allow the player to toggle time and color modes on and off using the buttons on the bottom left. Clicking the clock button disables the game timers, and a bright red NOT symbol appears over the clock. Clicking again toggles the button back to timed mode. Clicking the button on the right toggles off the color-matching feature (all the balls match all the cones). Like the timer button, clicking it again sets it back to the original, multicolor mode (Figure 1.9).

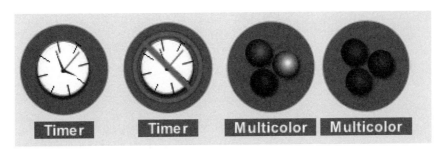

FIGURE 1.9   Labels appear when the mouse is over the buttons. Icons indicate button state.

It's difficult for developers to imagine that you need more than a green arrow to know what to do, but the casual gamer doesn't want to have to think (or more importantly, worry) about what to do. This tester helped us realize that we needed a whole new definition of what kinds of things needed explanation. We couldn't rely on conventions of design or gameplay to teach the player how to interact with the game. This is why casual gamers have so much trouble with new game paradigms and why they need so much hand-holding to find their way through your puzzles.

> Visual feedback is essential in casual games. Players are often tentative, and it is essential to do things like reinforce the idea that an object is a button by making it glow.

Developing Extensible Puzzles

Another essential way to respond to the needs of your audience is to design puzzles and challenges that may be easily modified and complicated to maximize their usefulness while minimizing development costs. Profit margins for game developers in the casual games industry are not huge. If you are going to be successful, you'll need to keep development costs as low as you can. Designing and developing puzzles that can easily be reused simply by changing the rules of play slightly will greatly reduce your costs.

> Typical casual games are produced by teams of 5–10 developers. Insight Interactive Games produces them with only two developers and one artist.

In a practical sense this means doing things like creating a color-matching game that uses the same basic logic throughout but adds a few elements (rewards such as bombs and chain reactions or punitive elements such as blocked paths and time limits) to complicate your puzzle without draining your limited development budget. A common and easy-to-implement example of this is timers. By simply decreasing the amount of time available to solve your puzzle, you can create a great sense of excitement for the player, with almost no additional programming.

Zuma Deluxe provides a great example of how even a simple device like a timer can delight the player. As balls pile up and the player is in danger of losing to the cave, the mouth of the demon starts to open slowly, and an audible timer ticks faster and faster. A simple graphical representation combined with compelling audio creates the combination of time pressure (the balls pushed out over time) and distance from the cave. The players can literally feel the pressure as the gates open and feel the relief if they manage to eliminate enough balls to close them.

Time, Complication, and Nesting Goals

Designers use several basic methods to create engaging and self-complicating puzzles. Developers learn to use these puzzle complication strategies to create great games. It's important to remember that no matter which of these strategies you use, casual game players do not like to lose. They are interested in a casual, fun experience. They want to enjoy their time without significant investment and without arbitrary or unproductive distractions such as losing the game.

Many casual games don't even include a lose screen or option (Figure 1.10). Failure to accomplish a goal simply results in the player repeating the current level or area.

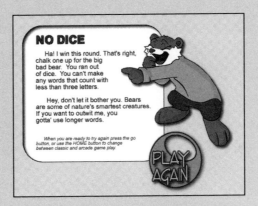

FIGURE 1.10   A lose screen from *Word Whacky* lets the player start again.

The first method is to manipulate time. There are a couple of ways to do this. Limit the amount of time a player has to solve a puzzle. Increase or decrease the speed at which a given element of the puzzle moves or interacts. Using these strategies you can easily reward the player by adding time or adjusting the rate of game elements or challenge the player by reducing available time or adjusting the rate of game elements in a manner that makes the game more difficult (Figure 1.11).

FIGURE 1.11   Time is an ever-present force in *MCF: Prime Suspects*. © Big Fish Games. All Rights Reserved.

The second puzzle enhancement method is to complicate the puzzle. This can also be accomplished in a variety of ways. The number of tasks that must be completed can be increased, the rules for completing a task can be adjusted, and the environment in which the game is played can be made more complex.

> ### Puzzle Enhancement and Extension Methods
> - Manipulate time
> - Complicate the puzzle
> - Change the goals or rules

Designers can also make changes to the goals of the game that will entice the player to continue. This is generally done by nesting a new goal inside a perceived reward. In other words, the player accomplishes a task or solves a puzzle and is rewarded with a new, different puzzle. This is often the strategy of games that include substantial *story* elements (Figure 1.12).

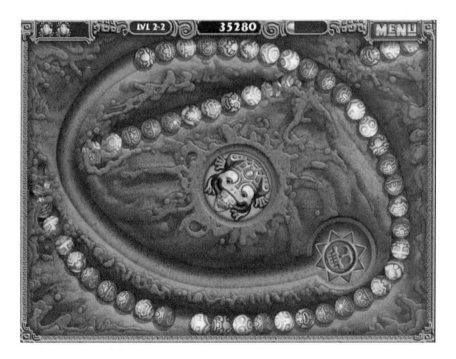

FIGURE 1.12   A complication in *Zuma Deluxe* puts balls beneath parts of the map. © PopCap Games, Inc. PopCap Games, Zuma, Feeding Frenzy, Bookworm, Bejeweled, and Diamond Mine are registered trademarks or PopCap Games, Inc. All Rights Reserved.

> Games like PopCap's *Zuma Deluxe* are generally catego-
> rized as arcade or action games because the objectives em-
> phasize shooting and fast-paced action. There are also
> strong puzzle elements to many of these games, most no-
> tably the need to *match three* tokens.

HOOK TO SELL

Ultimately, to profit from a casual game, a developer must include a
substantial hook. Most developers agree that the key to hooking an
audience on a new game is in that mysterious and elusive quality, *addictiveness*. If there were a simple formula that could be used to identify or design addictive games, every game on the planet would be
hopelessly addictive. It just isn't that easy. Still, some qualities are
consistently present in addictive games. It is reasonable to conclude
that designing games that make use of these aspects commonly ob-
served in addictive games could help make a game more successful
and perhaps even make it slightly more addictive.

> While addictiveness is necessary to turn a game download
> into a sale, it is not by itself sufficient to make a casual game
> a success. Casual game players generally know almost im-
> mediately if they are going to buy a game. The addictiveness
> is important, but it is also important that the players feel
> that the game has something else to offer them.

Five-Minute Window

The most addictive games generally convince the player to purchase
within the first five minutes. If your game hasn't hooked the audience within about five minutes, they are likely to shut it down at the
next convenient spot. Players often play every game for quite a while,

but if they come back to a game, they are much more likely to pay the upgrade cost. The experience for the player during this initial five minutes is crucial.

You need to make certain that every aspect of their experience feels slick and professional, that they have no doubt that the product performs well. Most developers feel that the challenge here is to create lots of cool features and gadgets. The truth is that the only thing enticing players to buy is that they are having a good time.

This means the game must be learned almost immediately and that the initial experience must be very pleasant (Figure 1.13). People don't like to lose. They must not lose right out of the gate, or there must be some potential to see progress, during the first few minutes of game play.

FIGURE 1.13 *Feeding Frenzy® 2* is very addictive and requires virtually no explanation. © PopCap Games, Inc., PopCap Games, *Zuma, Feeding Frenzy, Bookworm, Bejeweled,* and *Diamond Mine* are registered trademarks or PopCap Games, Inc. All Rights Reserved.

In *Feeding Frenzy 2* the reward for purchase is in part immediately apparent. Players who purchase the game and continue playing will be able to experience many additional fish and environments.

Casual Means Trauma Free

It is nearly impossible to overestimate the amount of timidity and outright fear common among the audience of casual games. This group is often concerned that they will break or disable their computers. They are reticent to explore or play, so they will often just close a new game, quitting before play if any element is unclear.

One of the biggest frustrations of developing for this audience has been that they often get addicted to our games when introduced to them by one of the developers, but similar testers would panic and bail out when asked to play the game without any *live person* helping them as they learned the rules. This is actually a great way to understand and anticipate the concerns and fears of your audience. You won't always be around to explain *how* to play the game, so you need to develop a perfect virtual guide that can hold the hands of the nervous players as they slowly encounter every new button, bomb, and barrier.

Many casual game developers spend more time *tweaking*, manipulating the difficulty levels, challenges, and rewards in the game than they do creating the game's essential functions.

Of course, one of the problems in developing casual games is that some people, including virtually every developer on the planet, find this sort of handholding and nurse-maiding very irritating. First, remember that the larger portion of your audience falls in the *guide me* category. Second, you can always find ways to disable your help services, letting advanced users avoid this kind of detailed instruction (Figure 1.14). Above all, the experience must be free of trauma. The player is in search of a pleasant, fun overall experience, so frustration should never overtake challenge. It's fun to be challenged; it isn't fun to be frustrated.

FIGURE 1.14   Players are often able to disable help using a button on the tips.

So far, although these games are downloaded online, the players and portals have tended to avoid the multiplayer arena. Some portals insist that the game have absolutely no code that enables the game to perform any functions over the Internet, including things like online scoreboards and communities.

Understanding the Demographic

According to a June 2006 survey by Macrovision®, the average casual gamer is a woman, in her early 40s, playing at night. She's on a broadband connection, which also implies that she has disposable income. Her hobbies include pets, travel, arts and crafts, shopping, and gardening. She sits down to play more than once a day on average and she sticks to it for at least an hour when she does. She also likes to play when she has the house to herself, which is pretty often because there's a 60% chance that no children under 18 are living with her.

Her favorite games by far are puzzles, followed fairly closely by card games. She'll occasionally download and play a strategy game (like Mahjong) or an action game. Perhaps most importantly, she has downloaded games online and has purchased at least one already this year.

Some of the more common puzzle games in recent years have been descendents of tangrams. Tangrams are a form of dissection puzzle originally created in China (Figure 1.15).

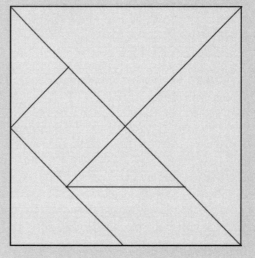

FIGURE 1.15 Dissection puzzle games ask players to match shapes to a pattern.

Anticipating Frustration

Because this audience is known to be easily put off, developers must anticipate both their audience's tolerance level for frustration and the symptoms that show they have reached that level. All games have some challenging components. It is part of the fun of playing a game. The major battle for the developer of casual games is in finding exactly the right balance between challenging the player with potentially frustrating puzzles and rewarding the player with victories.

One way to become aware of the level of frustration experienced by a player is to integrate monitoring or tracking functions into beta tests of a game. Developers can monitor things like the number of successful attempts versus failed attempts at each task over a broad group of testers within the intended demographic and then make better informed decisions about setting difficulty levels in the game.

Monitoring or tracking player interaction can be useful for more than figuring out when to provide help. Developers often program the game to watch for inactivity. If the player is distracted or called away, an inactive game can be paused so that the player's work is saved and timers do not run out when no one is actually playing the game.

Many of the conventions used in today's casual games were common in children's games for the past decade. While casual games are seldom targeted at young audiences, many of the conventions that made children's games easy to use have been adopted and improved for casual games. Notable examples include the use of detailed, learn-as-you-play help systems and constant and consistent feedback associated with every player interaction.

This strategy can also be implemented dynamically in some cases. The same tracking functions can watch a player's success-to-failure ratio and then offer assistance or dynamically alter the difficulty level based on the player's success or failure. This method can be quite tricky, as it's also possible to make changes that the players notice and in so doing, further frustrate them.

INTEGRATED CONTEXT-BASED HELP

One mechanism that has become common in casual games, probably because of its ability to respond to the frustrations and concerns of casual gamers, is integrated, context-sensitive help. Casual game developers now generally include extensive features aimed at guiding the player through the game. Some estimate that as much as 30% of casual game development time can be spent creating help features that are intended to put casual gamers at ease and meet their every need. To understand these tools and features, you need to start thinking like a casual gamer.

SPARE ME THE QUESTION

The first rule of casual game help systems could be described as *spare me the question.* Why should the player have a question in the first place? If you label everything clearly and give context clues and feedback for everything, the players won't have any questions (Figure 1.16). They will simply understand what kind of interaction is expected and then proceed to playing the game.

FIGURE 1.16   A context-based help screen from *Podz* is called after a few misses.

Feedback is any reassurance provided by interface items that an interaction element will behave the way that the player expects. A good example is a button that appears to glow when the player moves the mouse over it, appears depressed when the player selects it, and appears raised or unaffected when it is not selected.

The idea here is that you should at least be able to separate the mechanics of the computer from the actual game. This manifests itself in all kinds of ways, including things such as save and load game features that automatically do the work that in typical hard-core games require significant user participation. In a typical hard-core game, user customization is king. If the player wants to save a game, it is presumed that he will want to be able to save under various names and have all sorts of information about the game available. In a typical casual game, the save and load features are simply done for the player.

Context clues provide information to the player based on what the player seems to be doing. A common example is a pop-up help tip. If a player holds the mouse over an interface element for a period of time (usually a second or so) without doing anything, a help item can appear to tell the player about the function of the button or interface element.

The game will usually save automatically, similar to the way a word processor saves your document periodically. To casual gamers, it often appears that the game simply recognizes them and remembers where they left off in the game. The practice of assigning human characteristics to their computers is typical, and thinking in this way can help you understand the viewpoint of the primary audience.

Anthropomorphism, the practice of assigning human qualities to inanimate or nonhuman entities, is not at all unique to casual game players. It is a natural byproduct of explaining complex computer behavior by relating it to things that we think of as human. Sometimes this tendency makes it a bit more difficult to figure out how to make parts of a game, because the developer must first refute the supposition that the computer behaves in some way and then design the specific interactions that result in the perceived behavior.

Anticipating the Player's Experience

Anticipating what the player will experience during every stage of interaction with your game is a fundamental part of game design, regardless of the game's classification. This generally takes the form of a "walkthrough" in a treatment or a storyboard or flow diagram. We'll talk more about creating a game treatment in Chapter 2. The walkthrough is a description of a typical player's experience, generally from the moment they begin the game through the first level of game play. Figuring out what their experience will be can help developers discover elements that may be confusing or unusual and to plan and implement tools that will reduce or eliminate potential road blocks.

Anticipating the Players' Needs

Casual games anticipate players' needs and include features designed to meet those needs. They anticipate the audience's questions and answer them even before they are asked. For example, most casual games include options to enable and disable the audio, to set the application to play full screen or in windowed mode, and other controls to make the game conform to the needs and expectations of the player. Often small accommodations are made, such as pausing and player time-outs to account for players being unexpectedly interrupted and walking away from the game for a period of time (Figure 1.17).

FIGURE 1.17   In Skunk Studios'® *Sveerz* players pause using the universal pause symbol. © Skunk Studios, Inc.® All Rights Reserved.

In every case the player is not punished for such unexpected behavior. In other words, pausing the game doesn't lead to a lost round or level, nor does walking away for a short period. It's important to note here that casual gamers are just as likely to become hopelessly addicted to a game as a hard-core gamer, but as a general rule, they are much less likely to tolerate severe punishments, especially for incidental interruptions (Figure 1.18).

INSTANT GRATIFICATION

A good way to describe the ideal player experience in a casual game is that it provides instant or nearly instant gratification and assistance. It shouldn't take much to start feeling rewarded by a casual game. That means the game itself should be easily launched (not a lot

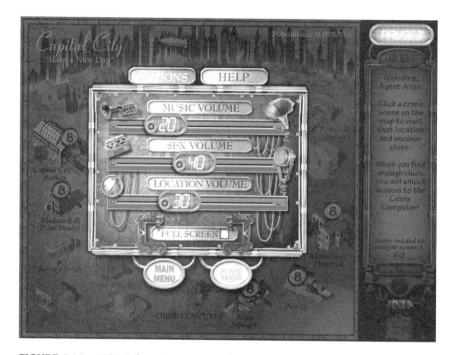

FIGURE 1.18 *MCF: Prime Suspects* combines pause with the options menu.
© Big Fish Games. All Rights Reserved.

of introductory or option screens). The act of solving a puzzle, de-feating a foe, or overcoming an obstacle within the game gives the player a reward, usually in the form of points or other in-game ma-terials, but more importantly it gives the player psychological plea-sure. It is fun and satisfying to win a game. It is also fun and satisfying to win small immediate rewards as individual parts of the puzzle or obstacle are solved and overcome.

Constant, Consistent, and Clear Feedback

Casual games provide constant, consistent, and clear feedback to the player (Figure 1.19). This does several things. It enhances the players' sense of satisfaction when the feedback confirms their belief that they are incrementally solving the puzzle and it reassures the players that the interaction they chose is having the effect they intended. Con-versely the feedback can show the player that a strategy for solving a puzzle or overcoming an obstacle is failing (Figure 1.20). It can also show that an interaction is not having the intended impact.

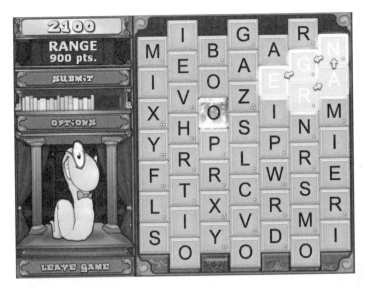

FIGURE 1.19 PopCap's *Bookworm* uses arrow feedback to show selection order. © PopCap Games, Inc., PopCap Games, *Zuma, Feeding Frenzy, Bookworm, Bejeweled,* and *Diamond Mine* are registered trademarks or PopCap Games, Inc. All Rights Reserved.

FIGURE 1.20 *Bejeweled 2* uses pop-up help to inform the player of a bad move. © PopCap Games, Inc., PopCap Games, *Zuma, Feeding Frenzy, Bookworm, Bejeweled,* and *Diamond Mine* are registered trademarks or PopCap Games, Inc. All Rights Reserved.

Nonstop and Escalating Rewards

In addition to providing rewards for the players' successful interactions, casual games often also increase the impact and value of the rewards over the whole game experience. This can be done by simply providing a greater number of points for progress in higher levels, for example. It can also be quite complex, providing increasing opportunities to acquire complex power upgrades, for example.

> Action- or arcade-style shooters (games that involve launching a ball or other projectile at a target) often use this approach. The players are generally given more and more powerful weapons as they improve their scores and move through game levels.

Just as players will rapidly grow bored solving the same puzzle over and over, they will rapidly grow bored with earning the same rewards throughout the entire game. In some cases this wouldn't matter, as the player is simply scratching an itch via the game play. In others it is a significant issue. This area is especially difficult to design for in casual games. There are plenty of examples, even among the most popular genre (puzzles), to suggest that players don't need any escalation in rewards. These players seem to gain almost unlimited satisfaction from solving the puzzles, even with only slight variations in the manner in which the puzzle is presented.

The *match-three game* (*Bejeweled*®-like game) is an obvious example. In this sort of game, players work to place three like objects in a horizontal or vertical row. There are literally hundreds of variants on this game, and many of them are popular. These games sometimes only offer points as a reward for progress in the game. No escalation is necessary, and very few complications are warranted.

Tease, Temptation and Promise

Ultimately the casual game has a built-in imperative to convince the player, the customer, to go ahead and pay for the right to play the game after the initial free trial. One common device used to accomplish this is to provide information about the extra functionality, features, levels, or gameplay opportunities that will become available to the player only after paying for the game. This is a delicate balancing act, as you want to make certain the customer finds the promise of more features tempting and not off-putting.

While at first pass it may seem ideal to restrict the coolest features and then use them to tease the player into upgrading, in practice it is preferable to include the bulk of the coolest features to sell the player on the game. For the most part, casual game purchasers view the value of their purchase as extended game play. While they may be encouraged to buy a game in order to accomplish a goal such as completing a world or winning the overall game, they will probably view feature or tool restrictions as a nuisance.

NAVIGATION CONVENTIONS

Some navigation conventions have become so common to casual game interfaces that it's tempting to believe they are a product of the industry. For the most part, the casual games industry did not invent these navigational approaches, but it has worked as a body to standardize them to a much higher degree than any other type of game. The similarities these interface conventions bear to the conventions seen in children's games during the 1990s is striking. Note here that we're not talking about the chrome or aesthetic qualities of the games—casual games rarely have any kind of juvenile or child-friendly look to them—but the user interaction and navigation qualities of the interfaces. Casual games typically use progress maps to provide a sort of visual narrative of overall success for the player. These maps are used to guide and motivate the player. Multiple modes of game play are also a mainstay. These modes can facilitate different levels of difficulty, narrative, or even varying game rules.

PROGRESS INDICATORS

Sprout Games' *Feeding Frenzy 2* includes a great example of the classic approach to a progress map. The basic idea is that the players can quickly see how much progress they have made toward beating or finishing the game. Progress indicators come in many different forms, including classic maps, rankings, gates, or other inhibitors that forbid the player to move on in the game without solving a given puzzle or round (Figure 1.21). Casual games often include clear, easy-to-follow images that represent these steps to solving the overall game. This creates an inherent sense of narrative and gives users an increasing sense of reward as they move farther and farther along the path.

> Some progress maps include animations and create a sort of narrative as the player witnesses a game character moving from one location to the next.

FIGURE 1.21   A progress map from *Feeding Frenzy 2* by Sprout Games.
© PopCap Games, Inc., PopCap Games, *Zuma, Feeding Frenzy, Bookworm, Bejeweled,* and *Diamond Mine* are registered trademarks or PopCap Games, Inc. All Rights Reserved.

Progressive Maps

Progress maps create a very clear indicator of the player's success in the overall game. The maps are often level selection interfaces as well.

The basic idea is that a spatial world is defined for the game and the map identifies places through which the player has traveled. In Sprout Game's *Feeding Frenzy 2*, for example, the players work their way through a series of underwater locations. Each location is noted like a city on a map, and once the players have completed a level they may click on the dot to return to that level at any time.

Dropping the Gates

Another approach to player progress is to provide gates or locks that prevent the player from moving forward in the game until they have accomplished a given task or solved a given puzzle. Games have used mechanisms of this sort nearly since their inception. The idea is that the player must defeat all of the enemies before the drawbridge falls or must find all of the gems before the key will appear. Keys and locks are the most obvious forms of gates in games, but in casual games they tend to be related quite clearly to clearing a level or accomplishing a goal (Figure 1.22). You can, of course, find some casual games that use literal locks and doors to accomplish this sort of progress indication.

FIGURE 1.22 A gate in *Tradewinds™ Legends* is locked until a power-up is acquired. All *Tradewind Legends, Westward,* and *Glyph* properties are trademarks, registered trademarks, or copyrights owned exclusively by Sandlot Games Corporation. All Rights Reserved.

There are several good reasons why game developers would choose to develop their games with this sort of gate, breaking the game into smaller chunks. In casual games, as in virtually all computer games, the player responds to a series of rewards and challenges. It is essential that these rewards and challenges are communicated clearly and simply for the messages to get clearly through to the player. The gates provide an opportunity to give new information to the player at predictable intervals. Many casual games take full advantage of these natural breaks to guide the player to supplemental information. A common system in casual games is to trigger guidance or help at these points in the game, essentially combining the fact that a new level is a complication, and it will require some new information to get beyond that complication.

Sprout Games' *Feeding Frenzy 2* provides a nice example of this sort of new concept narrative between levels (Figure 1.23). As the new player first encounters the game, no real instruction is required. Mouse movement causes a clear fish movement, so the player only needs to understand that the point is to eat smaller fish and avoid being eaten. At the first level completion, the player is given new information about gameplay. They learn that by pressing the mouse button, they can get a forward speed burst.

FIGURE 1.23 Players are taught how to dash between rounds in *Feeding Frenzy 2*. © PopCap Games, Inc., PopCap Games, *Zuma, Feeding Frenzy, Bookworm, Bejeweled,* and *Diamond Mine* are registered trademarks or PopCap Games, Inc. All Rights Reserved.

Earning Tools and Enhancing Powers

Sometimes the progress indicator in a casual game comes in the form of an earned tool or power-up. These take a variety of forms, but one good example is found in most match-three games. Many of today's puzzle games are descendents of a game developed by a trio of Russian students in the 1980s called *Tetris*. The wildly popular game is played by dropping shaped blocks into a glass or tray and rotating them in order to create horizontal rows of solid blocks. When an entire horizontal row is filled with solid blocks, the row is removed and the blocks fall downward. One evolution of this game genre is the match-three switching game, which became legend in the casual games industry with the release of *Diamond Mine™* (later called *Bejeweled*) from PopCap Games (Figures 1.24).

FIGURE 1.24 PopCap's *Diamond Mine* made the match-three a household game. © PopCap Games, Inc, PopCap Games, *Zuma, Feeding Frenzy, Bookworm, Bejeweled,* and *Diamond Mine* are registered trademarks or PopCap Games, Inc. All Rights Reserved.

In PopCap's original release, *Diamond Mine*, there are not power-ups for matching clusters of more than three gems, but in the retooled and massively successful *Bejeweled 2* the power-ups are a major part of gameplay. It is immediately clear when playing the game that these power-ups provide a much-needed internal reward. They explode, knocking out clusters of blocks or zap them with electric beams and create a more exiting game dynamic.

MODES OF PLAY

Another mainstay of casual games is the provision of various modes of gameplay, generally a manipulation of the rules, allowing a player to change the experience of the game to better suit player preferences (Figure 1.25). This makes the game more ubiquitous, as players with different likes and dislikes will be able to customize the game rules to their likings, but because the players in this group are fairly unlikely to seek out or make that sort of adjustment, it isn't clear that there is any real perceived additional value for the consumer in making additional options available. This leaves developers with a tough decision to make. Is it better to present players with a large list of

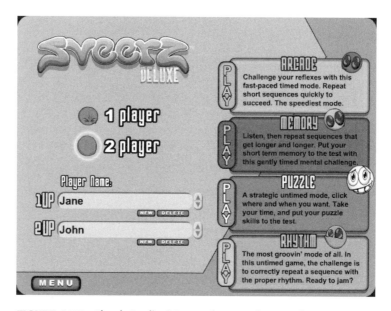

FIGURE 1.25 Skunk Studios' *Sveerz* features four modes of gameplay.

choices to launch various game modes, or is it better to simply get them playing and ignore game customization altogether?

If the developer chooses to provide these options, there are several different ways that the features may be implemented. The difficulty of the game can often be increased or decreased by changing variables in the programming. Another common option is to play a narrative-driven versus a basic arcade-style version of the game. The rules of play can also be varied, altering the overall experience within the shared conventions and interface. Finally, some casual games allow players to customize the game itself by changing fundamental elements within the game.

Difficulty

Adjusting the level of difficulty is a typical feature in many games, but it is not all that common in casual games. Often developers build this sort of function into a game simply because it is likely to be tweaked frequently during the beta testing. Some developers argue that finding the perfect level of difficulty for a game is more important than everything else. It's a very good point.

The casual game player does not like to lose. They aren't interested in an overly challenging or confrontational environment. Setting the level of difficulty too high is a common mistake. The audience for casual games is extremely broad, and often these players are struggling with basic interaction, so convoluted controls can be a real product killer. Likewise, experienced game players (and developers) tend to set the level of difficulty much too high. It's threatening to the players who don't consider themselves accomplished gamers and therefore affects sales negatively.

When working on our first casual game, *Word Whacky*, we struggled to understand and appreciate this concept. When conceptualizing the game, we didn't really understand the audience. We thought people addicted to word games would be interested in bigger, more exciting options. We designed a game that was faster, harder, and more sophisticated than any available casual word game. We began to realize that something was really wrong as we started to see who was buying the game.

The demographic of purchasers was loaded with highly skilled professionals such as doctors, lawyers, and psychologists. They were not a broad-based audience at all. Our beta testers tried to tell us that we had managed to squeeze all of the fun out of the game, but we just didn't listen. Had we listened to the audience, we would have quickly realized that they don't play word games because they want to challenge their mental acuity and expand their vocabulary. They play them because they provide the sort of reward for simple play that makes them happy. They play to have fun, not to work.

In retrospect it's easy to see that while *Word Whacky* is probably the most challenging word game available, it is also loaded with examples of what *not to do* to achieve success in the casual games industry.

In word games difficulty is managed in several ways. First, players are often given access to integrated hints that enable quick escape when they aren't finding the answer (Figure 1.26). They are also generally only challenged with short, simple words. *Word Whacky* uses one of the largest dictionaries available to find valid words, while typical word games use much smaller dictionaries that are limited to much more common words. Many word games further simplify things by providing definitions of target words.

FIGURE 1.26 Pixelstorm and Pogo's *Word Whomp* uses hints to guide players to potential answers. *Pogo*™ Images © 2007 Electronic Arts Inc. *Pogo, Pogo to Go,* and *Word Whomp* are trademarks or registered trademarks of Electronic Arts Inc. in the U.S. and/or other countries. All Rights Reserved. Used with permission.

Story and Arcade Games

Frequently the story of a game and the game itself may be easily separated. Some players find the narrative essential. It helps them keep track of progress, contextualize the problems, and appreciate the rewards. Other players find the story annoying. They don't want to take time to watch animation or read text; they just want to play the game. Typically a casual game that has story and arcade modes of play is attempting to address these disparate tastes by allowing players to choose whether or not to go through the narrative aspects of the game.

Rule Variation

Sometimes the rules of the game may be easily changed. This means the player can have an entirely different game-playing experience because the rules of play are different in different versions of the game. For example, changing the rules of Mahjong to force players to lift tiles off a conveyer belt before too many pile up is a way to change the rules of the game. It would also change the rules if you allowed tiles to relate to one another in nonstandard ways or created a poker game with different rules regarding the face value or playability of cards. Sometimes these differences can be slight enough changes that developers include them as optional modes of game play.

Game Customization

One element of game customization is standard practice in casual games. Players are usually asked at the beginning of the game to give their name. This device is no doubt common because it makes it possible for developers to automatically save information about the player's progress and success in the game. Casual game players don't usually like to save information manually, preferring to stay invested in the game or get to whatever real-world tasks are pending. *Word Whacky* and *Podz* provide good examples of the different ways of handling the saving and loading of casual games (Figure 1.27). In *Word Whacky* users were prompted to save their games by typing in a preferred name and pressing a button to save. Conversely they may load games from a menu of available saved games.

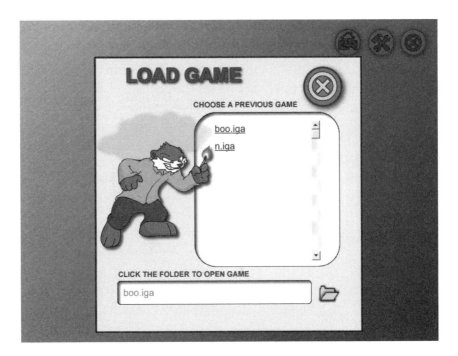

FIGURE 1.27   This load game screen forces players to search for old games.

Podz uses the more accepted method for casual games. It solicits the player's name immediately and then allows the player to create new profiles (or games) by using a drop-down menu available when starting the game (Figure 1.28).

FIGURE 1.28   This game uses profiles to automatically save and load.

In addition to this well-established approach to customization, casual games can also allow the players to further customize their game experience through a variety of other devices. Players may be asked to create a virtual representation of themselves, or an avatar, which can be customized to create a look and feel that they prefer. Players may also be invited to customize other aspects of the game, including the interface elements or colors, but keep in mind that this will probably not help make the game more marketable. This audience is unlikely to spend time on this sort of thing and could easily find a large set of options intimidating. Note that the most successful and universally adopted customization is only there to make the game's saving and loading features more transparent. The customization makes the experience easier for the players, who then can be called away at any time and never have to worry about how the game managed to *magically* remember where they left off, even if it was shut down with little warning.

BELLS AND WHISTLES

One nice thing about all of the standardization of features such as customizable profiles and automated file loading and saving is that these elements are often reusable. While the interface will generally change, the basic functions can usually be implemented in a way that allows developers to easily port the functions from one project to the next. The file save and file load features are generally integrated into the data design for the game. Top scores also are generally integrated into these functions.

FILE SAVE AND LOAD

Some of the basic functions and conventions of casual games are so ubiquitous that portals and distribution outlets literally require save and load integration as part of their beta test functions. Ultimately there are a few major questions you need to answer when designing a save and load file system for your game, and there are a few elements that must be built into your game to accommodate file loading. You must have some sort of data structure that allows you to start a game from various points with varied scores and other elements preloaded into the gameplay. You must be able to save the database on the player's computer, and be able to load the database from the player's computer.

Data Design and Storage

We usually build a text-only, flat file database to perform these functions for a game. There are some benefits and some drawbacks to this system. The nice thing about a flat text file is that it is small and requires no database support or binary manipulations. The data may be simply saved to a list or array, and then the array may be saved as a text file. It is important to note here that some languages will not easily support writing a text file with references to various types of data.

Essentially we create a list of key information for the game and store that list under the name of the player. For example we might make a list like the following:

CazPlayer

- `#roundComplete: 7`
- `#roundAttempt:8`
- `#score: 7465`
- `#powerups: [1,2,4,6]`
- `#obstacles: [#badStuff, #moreBadStuff]`
- `#money:5860`
- `#soundPref:180`
- `#musicPref:190`
- `#helpTipPref:1`
- `#fullscreenPref:1`

While these arrays might be configured and manipulated differently depending on the programming language used, the concepts are universal. Information about the player's progress is stored in the list. If the game is stopped, the data can easily be reloaded at startup and the players can return to the game with all of their power-ups and points and in the round of their preference.

We usually also store a separate list with information about the most recent player and a list of all the players who have ever used the game. It is also very useful to store information such as player preferences in these lists. That way the game can do things like recall and reset to the preferences of the last player, giving them the audio, full screen, and help tip settings that they chose the last time they played. Consider from the player's point of view how annoying it would be to have to reset the volume or disable help tips every time they play the game (Figure 1.29).

FIGURE 1.29 Save is not fully automatic in *Word Whacky*.

TOP SCORES

Most casual games allow the players to compare their scores to the scores of other players. Because online connections are not presumed to be active while playing and many portals discourage network-enabled features, most of these scoreboards are local. Sometimes they use the Internet to compare the scores to others online. The ones on the client machine are called local, and the ones online are often called global or online scoreboards.

Local Score Systems

The advantage of local scoreboards is that you don't have to worry about accessing the Internet or about what kind of language the players online might use to describe themselves. The disadvantage of local scoreboards is that the only players you can compare scores to are those who are playing on the same computer. Sometimes scores are included for fictional characters to try to give players a sense that they are competing with others.

Online Score Options

The advantage of online scoreboards is that the player can see how they stack up against others all over the planet in real time. The disadvantages include limitations from portals, loss of control over content displayed in your game, and connectivity issues. While online scoreboards are cool, there is very little evidence that they add any perceived value to the game in the eyes of the potential consumer.

PROJECT 1:   MAKE A MATCH-THREE PUZZLE

ON THE CD

In this project you will make a match-three puzzle. Use Adobe Director to complete the project steps. You'll find full source code and resources on the companion CD-ROM. In any project be certain to follow each step carefully.

If you find that the project isn't working as you expected, retrace your steps carefully and remember to pay attention to details such as the position of sprites and the association of scripts and look for errors in code.

The project can be divided into three basic steps:

1. Create a new package, game, project, or movie
2. Make graphics resources (six colored widgets and a selector)
3. Write code

It doesn't matter what tool or language you use to create a casual game like this match-three game, but it will matter what language you use to publish it. A casual game should be published at least as a downloadable self-contained executable application. It should also be published as a Web application. Ideally that Web application should run on Windows® and Macintosh® operating systems, but minimally it must run on all of the major versions of Windows dating back nearly a decade. Common solutions are Adobe Director, C++ using libraries like SDL, and Adobe Flash. Some are also developed using Java.

The following walk-through was created using Adobe Director, but you should easily be able to translate the interactions and code to any development environment in which you like to work. The programming language, Lingo, is quite commonly used as a good substitute for pseudo-code because it is very simple and uses common language conventions.

STEP ONE: OPEN DIRECTOR AND CREATE A NEW PROJECT FILE

Launch Adobe Director and choose File: New Movie either from the File menu or from the startup launcher. In Director a project file is called a *movie*. If you don't have a copy of Director, you can download a free demo from Adobe's Web site (Figure 1.30).

STEP TWO: CREATE GRAPHICS

Adobe Fireworks® was used to quickly create six differently colored circles for use as the primary puzzle pieces. You could do the same or make them using any graphics or vector editor. Your pieces don't have to be simple circles; you could just as easily make them fruit or coins or anything you can imagine. It is important, however, that you make six easily distinguishable images that are all the same size. If you like, you can use the ones included in the demo on the CD-ROM.

ON THE CD

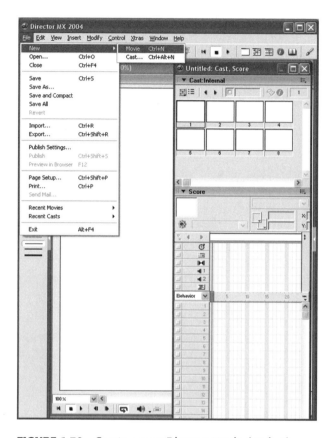

FIGURE 1.30   Create a new Director movie (project).

Once you have created the puzzle pieces, you'll need one additional graphic. A selector should appear to help the players know they've selected a given puzzle chip. We made another graphic, with no fill so that it could be placed above the circles without masking them from view. If you use a graphics application to build yours, remember to include an alpha channel so that you don't mask the tokens when the selector is positioned on top of them on the screen.

Import the Seven Graphics into the Cast

ON THE CD

1. Choose File: Import in Director and then import the graphics files that you created or the graphics on the CD-ROM (img01.png–img07.png in Chapter01).

2. They will appear in your cast.
3. Now select the six cast members and drag them onto the score, depositing them in the first 30 frames of channels 1–6. These are now sprites 1–6 (Figure 1.31).

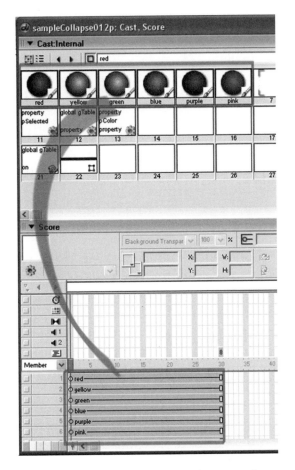

FIGURE 1.31   Drag the cast members onto the score.

4. Use the property inspector to move all six sprites to *x*: 44, *y*: 0. (Hint: You can select them all at once using the Shift key.)
5. Copy all six sprites in channels 1–6 and paste them into channels 7–12.

6. Copy all 12 sprites in channels 1–12 and paste them in channels 13–24.

7. Copy all 24 sprites in channels 1–24 and paste them in channels 25–48.

8. Copy sprites 1–42 (note that it's 42) and paste them in channels 49–90.

9. In this demo, we use a simple rectangle sprite to mask (cover up) the top row of the puzzle pieces. It helps with the illusion of falling.

10. Use the shape tool to draw a rectangle across the top of the stage that is about 60 pixels tall and the whole width of the stage.

11. Make the rectangle color match your stage color. Ours is white.

12. Drag your selector cast member into channel 100 of the score.

STEP THREE: WRITE THE CODE

Above all, if this is your first game, don't panic! We'll walk you through all of the code for the Director version of the game here. The code, along with a working sample, is included in the demo Director file matchThree.dir in the Tutorials\ch01media folder on the companion CD-ROM. You can download a free demo version of Director and Flash from the Adobe website. You can download the SDL libraries from the SDL organization website.

ON THE CD

1. Create a new behavior script by double-clicking in the frame script channel at frame 30 (Figure 1.32). Type the script in the behavior script editor exactly as it is shown in Figure 1.32. The most important thing that this script does is simply to keep the game running through its animation cycle. The command go the frame in Director is a way of telling the engine to keep repeating the basic commands found at this point in the timeline, over and over until told otherwise. The rest of the script just tells the engine that every 20 times it

runs through the animation cycle it should also run a command called `mCheckRowMates()`. You'll see how that command works a little later, but for now it's enough to know that it checks to make sure there are no unresolved matches on the screen.

Files with the extension *.dir are Director source files. These are editable project files, called movies, that allow you to work on your software and save or edit your code and changes. Eventually the project is converted into an executable application that cannot be edited and that can be distributed to potential customers.

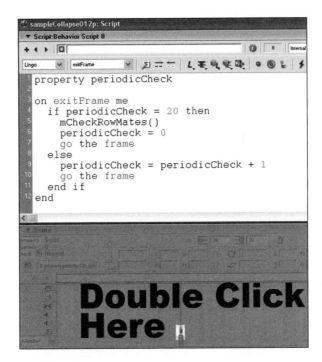

FIGURE 1.32 An empty behavior script will appear when you double-click.

2. Create another behavior script by clicking the + icon on the upper-left corner of the Script Editor Window.
3. Create a property called `pSelected` by typing the first line of code exactly as it appears in the figure: `property pSelected`.

4. This property, which will be used to identify which sprite the player chose for a potential match, is initially set to be VOID. Type the beginSprite handler as it appears in the figure.

5. Once you have finished typing the behavior, select the behavior from the cast. Ours is in member 11, shown selected in Figure 1.33. Drag the behavior member (not the script editor) to channel 100 in the score and drop it onto your selector sprite (Figure 1.33).

The beginSprite event is roughly equivalent to the onClipEvent(load) in ActionScript. Director uses an event-driven model to allow the engine to generate internal event notices when things happen, such as a new sprite being created on the screen.

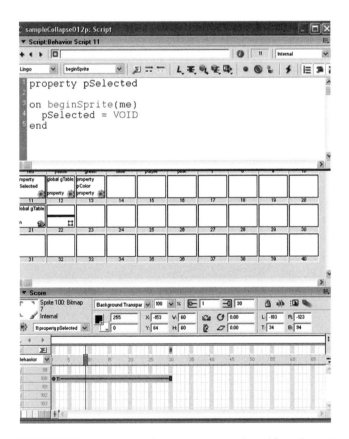

FIGURE 1.33 Associate the pSelected script with sprite 100.

6. In the Script Editor Window, press the + icon again to create a new blank behavior. This script will be used to respond to the player's mouse-click events. There are three events to which we will react: mouseUp (when the player releases the mouse), mouseDown (when the player presses the mouse), and mouseUpOutside (when the player releases the mouse outside the area of the sprite they were on when they first pressed the mouse).

7. Type the code in Listing 1.1 into your Behavior Window. Note that we've commented the code here to help you understand it as you work. Comments in Director are preceeded by two dashes. You don't need to type the comments, but they won't affect your code either.

LISTING 1.1   Global and Property Declarations, Shift/Select Token Behavior

```
global gTable
-- This declares a global (universally available) variable
-- (a container) called gTable that will store all of the
-- colors of the balls on the screen.

property pColor
property pStartPos
-- create two properties (variables that are tied to an
-- individual instance of an object. This script will be
-- attached to all 90 circle sprites, so the pColor of
-- each one can be different.
```

The mouseDown() handler (Listing 1.2) is called by the engine when the player presses the mouse button down while hovering over a sprite on the stage. If the selector sprite's pSelected property is VOID, it means the selector sprite is off the screen and this is the first selection of the player's match attempt. If the conditional statement in this mouseDown handler is met, the resulting commands move the selector sprite onscreen over the position of the selected ball and then sets the value of the property pSelected so that it may be used either on this mouseUp event or on the next mouseUp event.

LISTING 1.2   MouseDown() Event Handler, Shift/Select Token Behavior

```
on mouseDown(me)
  if voidP(sprite(100).pSelected) then
    sprite(100).loc = sprite(me.spritenum).loc
    sprite(100).pSelected = me.spriteNum
  end if
end
```

The mouseup() event (Listing 1.3) is called by the engine when the player releases the mouse. The property pSelected of sprite(100) has a value equal to the number of the sprite that the player initially selected. If the player hasn't actively selected a first token, then the value of sprite(100).pSelected is void.

LISTING 1.3   MouseUp() Event Handler, Shift/Select Token Behavior

```
on mouseUp(me)
  if NOT voidP(sprite(100).pSelected) then
    if (sprite(100).pSelected) <> (me.spriteNum) then
-- the previous line is an error check to make sure that
-- the player isn't trying to swap the item for itself.
      tGridPos = indexToGrid(sprite(100).pSelected)
```

Later you will see that there are some custom functions that convert an index token number to the equivalent column and row and visa versa. The next line in the mouseUp() handler calls this converter to get the row and column. Then the code makes sure the player has not attempted an illegal move (Listing 1.4). The rules of the game dictate that a player may only shift one slot up, down, left, or right. Note as you work on this section of the Select Token Behavior that the backslash character in Director indicates that the line continues onto the next one. You may type these all on one line without the backslash or use the backslash and then return to a new line.

LISTING 1.4   MouseUp() Grid Check, Shift/Select Token Behavior

```
tGridPosMatch = indexToGrid(me.spriteNum)
case TRUE of
```

```
    (tGridPos[1] - tGridPosMatch[1] = 1 \
    AND tGridPos[2] = tGridPosMatch[2]):
      clear = 1
    (tGridPosMatch[1] - tGridPos[1] = 1 \
    AND tGridPos[2] = tGridPosMatch[2]):
      clear = 1
    (tGridPos[2] - tGridPosMatch[2] = 1 \
    AND tGridPos[1] = tGridPosMatch[1]):
      clear = 1
    (tGridPosMatch[2] - tGridPos[2] = 1 \
    AND tGridPos[1] = tGridPosMatch[1]):
      clear = 1
    otherwise:
      beep()
      clear = 0
  end case
```

As the code checks to make certain the move was legal, it sets the value of the variable called clear to 1 (TRUE) if a legal move was made. The next section of the mouseUp() handler prepares to switch the tokens back if the move didn't result in a match. The index number of the manipulated tokens along with their color values are stored in the series of switchback variables. This essentially creates a memory of the state of the board before the change was made.

After the switchback variables store the original type and indices of the game tokens, the images are switched using the member-swapping command sprite(n).member = referenceToSomeMember (Listing 1.5). In Director a cast member is a resource file. Flash handles resources via the library, and other languages often simply call them resources.

LISTING 1.5   MouseUp() Switchback Prep, Shift/Select Token Behavior

```
  if clear then
      switchBackA = me.spriteNum
      switchBackB = sprite(100).pSelected
      switchBackAType = sprite(me.spriteNum).pColor
```

```
        switchBackBType =
          sprite(sprite(100).pSelected).pColor
    sprite(me.spritenum).member = \
  sprite(sprite(100).pSelected).member
      sprite(sprite(100).pSelected).member = \
      member(string(sprite(me.spriteNum).pColor))
      sprite(me.spriteNum).pColor = \
      symbol(sprite(me.spriteNum).member.name)
      sprite(sprite(100).pSelected).pColor = \
      symbol(sprite(sprite(100).pSelected).member.name)
      tGrid = indexToGrid(me.spriteNum)
      tGrid2 =
      indexToGrid(sprite(sprite(100).pSelected).spriteNum)
      gTable[tGrid[1]][tGrid[2]] =  \
  sprite(me.spritenum).pColor
      gTable[tGrid2[1]][tGrid2[2]] = \
  sprite(sprite(100).pSelected).pColor
```

Once the onscreen images of the tokens have been switched, some code is needed to delay the switch back to their original appearance (Listing 1.6). Without the delay, the code would execute so quickly that the player would probably not see a switch when the match was unsuccessful.

LISTING 1.6   mouseup() Delay Switchback, Shift/Select Token Behavior

```
repeat with q = 1 to 2000
  sprite(100).locH = -100
  updateStage()
end repeat
```

Finally we call the function to check for matches, mCheckRowMates() (Listing 1.7 and 1.8). The switchback variables are used as arguments for this function. The pSelected sprite is then released (reset to VOID) so that the process of initial selection may start all over again with the next mouse click.

LISTING 1.7   `MouseUp()` Check Matches, Shift/Select Token Behavior

```
        mCheckRowMates(switchBackA, switchBackAType, \
         switchBackB, switchBackBType)
        sprite(100).pSelected  = VOID
      end if
    end if
  end if
end
```

LISTING 1.8   `MouseUpOutside()`

```
-- This handler just calls mouse up. It helps make dragging
-- possible.
on mouseUpOutside(me)
  me.mouseUp()
end
```

8. When you finish typing the behavior script, choose the behavior script member from the cast (it will be the one that shows `global gTable` in the thumbnail preview.) Drag the script onto all 90 circle sprites. (Hint: You can select all 90 sprites and then drop the behavior member.)

9. In the Script Window use the + icon to create another script. This is the last one, and it's a little different. This script is going to be full of universally accessible functions, and not associated with any on-screen sprites or events.

10. In the Property Inspector Window change the script type from behavior to *movie*. This will make it possible for the handlers in this script to be called from any of the other scripts.

11. Type Listing 1.9 into this Movie Script Window.

The `startMovie()` script is a global script. Its handlers may be called from anywhere in any of your scripts. We'll need access to the data table from this script and from other scripts, so we declare it here as a global variable. The next line is the `startMovie` handler. The `startMovie` event is triggered one time only when the game engine starts.

Each of the commands that fall inside the `startMovie` handler calls a subroutine from those in this script. The first one makes sure all the sprites are visible and not faded out for testing. The `buildtable()` handler makes an array (a 2D list) that contains information about the tokens. The `randomizeDots` handler randomizes the circles. The `layoutDots` handler puts them out on the screen in columns and rows. Finally `checkRowMates` is a method that checks for matches and triggers the removal of match sets of three or more (Listing 1.9).

LISTING 1.9   `StartMovie()` Script

```
global gTable

on startMovie()
  mResetVisibility()
  mBuildTable()
  mRandomizeDots()
  mLayoutDots()
  mCheckRowMates()
end
```

A repeat loop (Listing 1.10) runs a set of commands a given number of times, in this case 100 times, each time changing the value of the iterating variable (a) to count incrementally. This steps through all of the sprites and resets their basic visibility and blend properties to the default values.

LISTING 1.10   `StartMovie()` Script

```
on mResetVisibility()
  repeat with a = 1 to 100
    sprite(a).visible = 1
    sprite(a).blend = 100
  end repeat
end
```

The `mBuildTable()` handler (Listing 1.11) makes a table with nine columns and ten rows of icons. This table provides the logical foundation for the position of each of the tokens in the game (Figure 1.34).

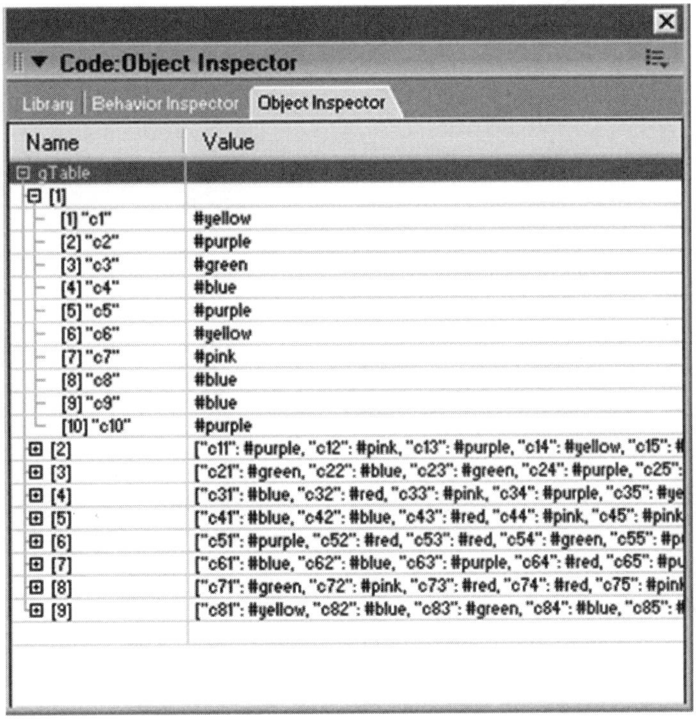

FIGURE 1.34   mBuildTable() creates a 2D array of nine columns and ten rows.

LISTING 1.11   Code for the mBuildTable Handler

```
on mBuildTable()
-- make a 2D array that represents the columns and rows
   onscreen
   index = 1
-- we need index to count the sprites (1-90)
   gTable = []
-- this makes an empty list to hold the rows
```

```
    repeat with column = 1 to 9
-- there are 9 columns
      tRow = [:]
-- make a blank property list for each row
      repeat with row = 1 to 10
-- there are 10 rows
        tRow.addProp("c"&index, #none)
-- adds a property value pair ["c1":#none]
-- this will eventually store the colors of each token
        index = index + 1
-- count to the next sprite
      end repeat
      gTable.add(tRow)
-- after each row is given color slots, then go to the next
   row.
   end repeat
end
```

The mLayoutDots() handler moves the sprites into position on the stage, providing the table of tokens with which the player may interact (Figure 1.35, Listing 1.12).

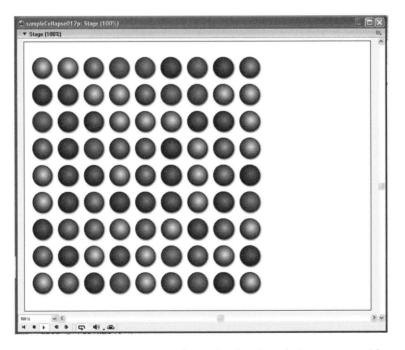

FIGURE 1.35 mLayoutDots() places the dots into their onscreen grid.

LISTING 1.12   Code for the `mLayoutDots` Handler

```
on mLayoutDots()
-- this records the startposition
  sprite(1).pStartPos = sprite(1).loc
-- do this next bit for each element in each row/column
  repeat with column = 1 to 9
    repeat with row = 1 to 10
      cell = gridToIndex([column,row])
      if cell > 1 then
-- move all but the first one.
-- move each one to a position based on its table column
-- / row 60 in this case represents a good width / height
-- for these images, usually this number would be relative
-- to the width / height of the image and not hard coded.
        sprite (cell).locH = sprite(cell).locH +
        (60 * (column - 1))
        sprite (cell).locV = sprite(cell).locV +
        (60 * (row - 1))
-- record the start position of each element
        sprite(cell).pStartPos = sprite(cell).loc
      end if
    end repeat
  end repeat
end
```

In order for the dots to be placed without a clear pattern, the assignment of tokens to cells within the table must be randomized. The `mRandomizeDots()` handler traverses through the list of all of the tokens and randomly assigns a color property to each one (Figure 1.36 and Listing 1.13). This way there will be no regular pattern to tokens on the screen.

LISTING 1.13   Code for the `mRandomizeDots` Handler

```
on mRandomizeDots()
  repeat with b = 0 to 89
-- this just chooses colors for each element at random and
-- documents the result in the main table.
    a = b+1
    sprite(a).member = member(random(6))
```

```
        pColor = symbol(sprite(a).member.name)
        sprite(a).pColor = pColor
        column = (b / 10)+1
        row = a - ((column-1)*10)
        gTable[column][row] = pColor
    end repeat
end
```

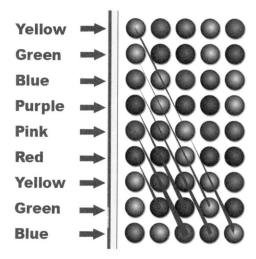

FIGURE 1.36   Randomizing dots prevents a pattern from appearing.

The next two handlers do conversions of grid position to index (sprite number) or visa versa (Listing 1.14). This way it is easy to figure out the cell index if you know the column and row position or to learn the column and row position if you know the index number of the cell.

LISTING 1.14   Code for the mRandomizeDots Handler

```
on indexToGrid(index)
  column = ((index-1) / 10)+1
  row = index - ((column-1)*10)
```

```
    RETURN [column, row]
end

on gridToIndex(grid)
  cell = (((grid[1] - 1)*10)+grid[2])
  RETURN (cell)
end
```

You may find it helpful to add a debug marker (just click on the blue bar to the left of a script on the line numbers.) If you add one in the mCheckRowMates handler, you can see more clearly how each property and variable is being tested in order to find matches in the table data (Figure 1.37).

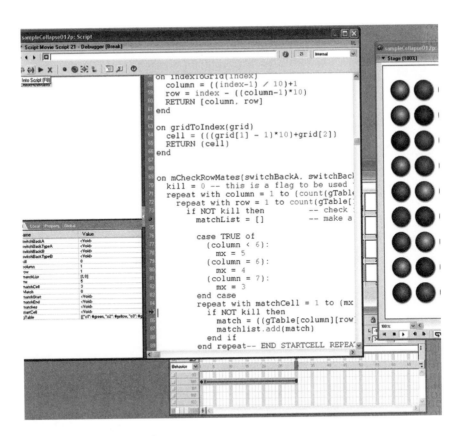

FIGURE 1.37   Try using the debugger to step through mCheckRowMates().

The next handler, mCheckRowMates(), is the main function of the game. The code passes through each row and checks for matches. If a match is found, it performs some animation (it would normally handle scoring here as well) and then calls itself again. The optional switchback arguments are used to restore the sprites from a mouse trigger if a match attempt fails.

Parsing each element in the list is a little problematic. We need to check for matches of five, four, and three tokens long. We know we might find a five-item match in a group 5–9, 4–8, 3–7 and so on. We also know that we'll not find a five-item match starting in any row above 5. The mx variable limits the length of the match string so we don't try to evaluate table positions such as column 20, row 15 when there aren't that many columns or rows (see Listing 1.15).

LISTING 1.15 Code for the mCheckRowMates() Handler

```
on mCheckRowMates(switchBackA, switchBackTypeA, \
switchBackB, switchBackTypeB)
  kill = 0 -- this is a flag to be used to stop the handler
  repeat with column = 1 to (count(gTable)-2)   -- FOR EACH
  COLUMN
      repeat with row = 1 to count(gTable[1])   -- FOR
      EACH ROW
        if NOT kill then
  -- check flag
          matchList = []
  -- make a blank list (will hold data for each row)
          case TRUE of
          (column < 6):
            mx = 5
          (column = 6):
            mx = 4
          (column = 7):
            mx = 3
        end case
```

In Listing 1.16 the code loops through each row and searches for possible sets of three or more matching tokens in a row. This is the first time we've used the syntax n=n=n to set the value of a variable. The idea behind it is simple. The expression to the right is evaluated first, so if the second token matches the first token, the value of the first variable, match, will be 1 (TRUE). This value is then added to a list for the row, which becomes a list of ones and zeros. Next, the number of consecutive 1s in the list are counted. If there are three or more 1s (TRUES) in the list, special subroutines are called to animate the match on the screen.

LISTING 1.16   mCheckRowMates Create List of Matched Tokens in a Row

```
--  repeat this next for each item in a potential match
    cluster
        repeat with matchCell = 1 to (mx)
            if NOT kill then
--  check for an actual color match (will be 1 (true) if
    matched)
                match = ((gTable[column][row] = \
        gTable[column+(matchCell-1)][row]))
                matchlist.add(match)
            end if
        end repeat
--  now look at the matches in the list to see if there's a
    set of 3
--  or more. This way we get the length of the match as
    well.
        matchStart = matchList.getPos(1)
        matchEnd = matchList.getPos(0)
        if matchEnd = 0 then
          matchEnd = matchList.count + 1
        end if
        matches = ((matchEnd - matchStart))
--  if there are 3 or more matches then call a subroutine
--  to animate the removal effect. Fix the switchback so it
--  won't fail.
        if matches > 2 then
          startCell = gridToIndex([column,row])
          mCallMatch(startCell, #row, (column), matches,
          row)
```

```
            kill = 1
            switchBackA = VOID
          end if
        end if
      end repeat
   end repeat   -- END COLUMN REPEAT
```

In the last section of the mCheckRowMates handler, found in Listing 1.17, the switchback variables are considered. If a match was found, the first switchback variable would have been set to VOID. If the first switchback variable is not void, then the attempt was not valid, and the tokens must be returned to their original positions. If no match was found, we move on to check for vertical matches.

LISTING 1.17   Code for the Final Switchback Evaluation of mCheckRowMates

```
  if NOT voidP(switchBackA) then
     mCheckColumnMates(switchBackA, switchBackTypeA, \
  switchBackB, switchBackTypeB)
   else
     mCheckColumnMates()
   end if
end
```

The mCheckColumnMates handler (Listing 1.18) is very similar to the row check system, except that it checks for vertical matches. Because there are different numbers of columns and rows, and because the tokens all fall downward, there are some slight differences between row handling and column handling, though the methods used to detect matches are virtually identical.

LISTING 1.18   Code for the mCheckColumnMates Handler

```
on mCheckColumnMates(switchBackA, switchBackTypeA, \
switchBackB, switchBackTypeB)
   kill = 0 -- this is a flag to be used to stop the handler
   repeat with column = 1 to count(gTable)  -- FOR EACH
   COLUMN
```

```
repeat with row = 1 to (count(gTable[1]))-2)   -- FOR
EACH ROW
  if NOT kill then            -- check flag
    matchList = []
    case TRUE of
      (row <= 6):
        mx = 5
      (row = 7):
        mx = 4
      (row = 8):
        mx = 3
    end case
    repeat with matchCell = 1 to (mx)
      if row <= (count(gTable[1])-(matchCell-1)) then
        cell = gridToIndex([column,row])
        match = ((gTable[column][row] = \
    gTable[column][row+(matchCell-1)]))
        matchlist.add(match)
      end if
    end repeat-- END STARTCELL REPEAT
    matchStart = matchList.getPos(1)
    matchEnd = matchList.getPos(0)
    if matchEnd = 0 then
      matchEnd = matchList.count + 1
    end if
    matches = ((matchEnd - matchStart) )
    if matches > 2 then
      kill = 1
      mCallMatch(cell, #column, column, matches, row)
      switchBackA = VOID
    end if
  end if
  end repeat
end repeat  -- END COLUMN REPEAT
if kill then
  kill = 0
  mCheckRowMates()
else
  if NOT voidP(switchBackA) then
```

```
    switchBack(switchBackA, switchBackTypeA, \
  switchBackB, switchBackTypeB)
     end if
   end if
end
```

The `switchBack` handler (Listing 1.19) switches the match attempt back in case of a failed match attempt (Figure 1.38). It has to switch back the visible member as well as fix the data table and the `pColor` properties of the sprites.

FIGURE 1.38   An invalid switch attempt results in a switchback.

LISTING 1.19   Code for the `switchBack` Handler

```
on switchBack(switchBackA, switchBackTypeA, \
switchBackB, switchBackTypeB)
  sprite(switchBackA).member =
  member(string(switchBackTypeA))
  sprite(switchBackA).pColor = switchBackTypeA
  sprite(switchBackB).member =
  member(string(switchBackTypeB))
```

```
    sprite(switchBackB).pColor = switchBackTypeB
    tGridA = indexToGrid(switchBackA)
    tGridB = indexToGrid(switchBackB)
    gTable[tGridA[1]][tGridA[2]] = switchBackTypeA
    gTable[tGridB[1]][tGridB[2]] = switchBackTypeB
  end
```

Balls don't actually fall. Sprites don't even actually keep moving further and further down the screen (Figure 1.39). All of these things are sleight of hand. While we will eventually move the sprites down a bit, they will quickly also be snapped back to their original positions. The mCallMatch handler reduces the opacity of a token slated to be removed and calculates the necessary changes for each ball in a row (Listing 1.20). Every ball inherits the color property of the ball above it. This makes it appear that the balls are falling when combined with a little bit of animation to suggest the motion.

FIGURE 1.39 Balls appear to fall
because sprites fade and move down.

In addition to changing the visible appearances of the tokens as they inherit the colors of the tokens above them in the column, the data table and individual sprite properties are updated to reflect the new values.

LISTING 1.20 Code for the `mCallMatch` Handler

```
on mCallMatch(startCell, direction, column, streak, row)
  -- for each item in the streak
  colStartCell = (startCell + (streak-1))
  if direction = #row then -- if it is a row match
    repeat with b = 1 to (streak)
      startIndex = startCell mod(10)
-- finds the position in the rowlist
-- vanish the cleared item
      sprite(startCell).blend = 30
-- drop the column down one position for each element in
   the column
      mAnimateFall(startCell, column)
      if startIndex = 1 then -- this is a problem
-- if it's in the first position, a parent will not exist
        subMatch(startCell)
      else
        if startIndex = 0 then startIndex = 10
        -- in the last position, so make it index 10 rather
        than 0
        repeat with changingToken = 1 to (startIndex)
          -- c = 1 to the number of falling items affected
          if startCell - changingToken < 1 then
-- subMatch chooses a color at random, because the call was to
-- a token at the top or bottom of the screen.
            subMatch(startCell)
          else
-- this group of code passes the properties of each
-- token in a column down the column so that they
-- may appear to fall.
            gridChild = indexToGrid(startCell-
            (changingToken-1))
            gridParent = indexToGrid(startCell-
            changingToken)
            parentColor =
            gTable[gridParent[1]][gridParent[2]]
            childSprite = gridToIndex(gridChild)
            sprite(childSprite).member = \
```

```
      member(string(parentColor))
      sprite(childSprite).pColor = parentColor
      gTable[gridChild[1]][gridChild[2]] =
      parentColor
      updateStage()
    end if
  end repeat
end if
sprite(startCell).blend = 100
column = column + 1
startCell = startCell + 10
  end repeat
end if
```

The `mCallMatch` handler responds to matches from both row matches and column matches. The section of the handler in Listing 1.21 is the part that responds to matches in columns.

LISTING 1.21   Remaining Code for the `mCallMatch` Handler

```
if direction = #column then
  -- direction = #column-----------
  startIndex = colStartCell mod (10)
  if startIndex = 0 then startIndex = 10
  repeat with b = 1 to startIndex
    sprite(colStartCell).blend = 30
    mAnimateFall(colStartCell, column)
    changingToken = startIndex
    if (changingToken = 1) then
      subMatch(colStartCell)
    else
      if startIndex-streak < 1  then
        subMatch(colStartCell)
      else
        gridChild = indexToGrid(colStartCell)
        gridParent = indexToGrid(colStartCell-streak)
        if gridParent[2] < 1 then
          subMatch(colStartCell)
```

```
--parentColor = symbol(member(random(6)).name)
        else
          parentColor =
          gTable[gridParent[1]][gridParent[2]]
        end if
        childSprite = gridToIndex(gridChild)
        sprite(childSprite).member =
        member(string(parentColor))
        sprite(childSprite).pColor = parentColor
        gTable[gridChild[1]][gridChild[2]] = parentColor
      end if
    end if
    sprite(colStartCell).blend = 100
    colStartCell = colStartCell - 1
  end repeat
  end if
end
```

The code in Listing 1.22 is a small subroutine that randomly chooses a new color and populates that information for a sprite at the top of a column. Because each token inherits its properties from the one above it in the table, there are naturally tokens in the top rows that have none above them. Because these top row tokens have no parent from whom they inherit properties, they are assigned at random using the subMatch handler.

LISTING 1.22   Code for subMatch Subroutine

```
on subMatch(a)
  sprite(a).member = member(random(6))
  sprite(a).pColor = symbol(sprite(a).member.name)
  grid = indexToGrid(a)
  gTable[grid[1]][grid[2]] = sprite(a).pColor
end
```

The last handler is mAnimateFall (Listing 1.23). This code moves each of the falling tokens down slowly. Once the token reaches the appropriate point, it is moved back to the start position so that it may be switched with the properties of its parent.

LISTING 1.23   Code for the Token Falling Animation

```
on mAnimateFall(cell, column)
-- the actual fall subroutine that moves the onscreen sprite
-- down the screen.
  fallCells = []
  strt = ((column-1)*10)+1
  stop = (column)*10
  repeat with a = strt to stop
    if a < cell then
      fallCells.add(a)
    end if
  end repeat
  repeat with x = 1 to 60
    repeat with b = 1 to count(fallCells)
      sprite(fallCells[b]).locV = sprite(fallCells[b]).locV
      + 1
      repeat with q = 1 to 10
        updateStage()
      end repeat
    end repeat
  end repeat
  repeat with c = 1 to count(fallCells)
    sprite(fallCells[c]).locV =
    (sprite(fallCells[c]).pStartPos[2])
  end repeat
end
```

SUMMARY

To successfully design and develop games for the casual games market, it is important that you create software that is accessible to a mass audience and that excites a diverse population of players. Like hard-core games, casual games must include rules and puzzles that reward players effectively. People like to be challenged. It is fun to solve problems and experience rewards for solving those problems.

Making your games successful means hooking your audience on an easy-to-learn, addictive game that includes plenty of feedback and well-integrated help systems to guide the player through the experience. It should tease the player with the promise of bigger and better rewards. You'll also need to emulate industry standards and navigation conventions.

2 Developing a Casual Game

In This Chapter

- Developing an Idea
- Writing a Treatment
- Film Conventions
- Storyboarding the Flow
- Identifying the Interactions
- Critical Juncture: To Code or Not To Code
- Professional Practice: Margaret Wallace on Games and Stories

Audience demographics are a part of game design and development strategies regardless of the type of game, but demographics play a particularly central role in casual games. They are audience-conscious from inception to delivery, and often games appear to evolve from the known qualities of casual game audiences.

The fact that women love image-seeking games, evidenced by the enormous popularity of the *Mystery Case Files* Series, must have contributed to Big Fish's decision to create *Hidden Expedition Titanic* (Figure 2.1). In addition to a love of image-find puzzles, this demographic no doubt finds anything related to the *Titanic* romantic and alluring. Analyzing and understanding your audience should be at the core of your efforts to develop a game. This awareness informs every decision that you make about the game, from ideas to gameplay mechanics.

In this chapter you will learn how to:

- Develop an idea for a game
- Conceive and evaluate stories
- Write a treatment for a game
- Create a flow diagram to represent the structure of a game
- Identify and design player interactions
- Decide whether to focus on programming or other elements

The last section of this chapter introduces Margaret Wallace, the cofounder and CEO of Skunk Studios, makers of the hit games *Q-*

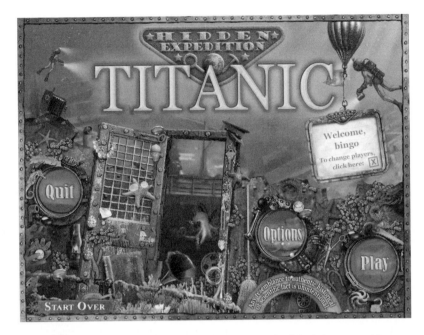

FIGURE 2.1   *Hidden Expedition Titanic* targets the ideal demographic.

Beez and *Gutterball 2*. Skunk's games have a singularly charming and innovative look and feel. Wallace, along with other members of her company, left Shockwave.com to found the studio. She also worked on the *Virtual Petz*™ series for Mindscape, *Dogz*™ and *Catz*™.

DEVELOPING AN IDEA

Getting that big idea is never simple. Often developers struggle to find a winning concept or move ahead too quickly on an idea that seems great but turns out to be much less fun and less addictive than they had initially imagined. The first criterion for any game must be that it is fun to play. This is what makes games addictive and leads to big audiences and eventual sales. Ideas come from lots of places, and they generally come at the worst possible time. One good tactic to retain these ideas is to keep a notebook full of ideas and simply add to them whenever you have one. Assuming that no such journal of germinal ideas exists, and you are now faced with a need for one, you can look for inspiration all around you. Look to literature, art, nature, and other games, and you'll find yourself thinking about the things you experience in different ways.

> Game developers and designers often refer to the preproduction design documents as the "bible" for a given project. This is usually either a file on a common server or a physical three-ring binder, with pages swapped in and out as changes are made.

Once you have some germinal ideas, you can begin to develop them into the preproduction planning materials for a game. Try not to think of these materials as fixed in stone. Preproduction planning materials for games, perhaps more than any other art form, tend to be very flexible. While you don't want to blow with the wind, failing to achieve anything like your game's original vision, you do want to remain flexible. Creating a game requires building a custom work of art and engineering. Some of the features you imagined may be ineffective or even impossible to implement, so you sometimes have to revise your plans to improve your game or make the game functional.

The three major steps to follow when developing your game are creating the story or narrative, identifying the interactions (both of the player with the interface and of the objects in the game with one another), and planning how you will integrate the story and interactions into your finished game.

NARRATIVE

During the narrative development, a *treatment* is often produced. *Character sketches and rough drawings* of interfaces and game levels are common documents developed during this stage.

> A *treatment* is a design document following in the traditions of film. It is a short summary of the major aspects of the game that can be used to quickly explain to anyone from investor to intern the exact nature of the game.

One constant dilemma for game designers and developers is determining how much narrative, if any, to include in a game. People have different opinions about the role of narrative in video games. This is an even more substantial concern in the casual games arena. Some game players suggest that the narrative is absolutely essential to the game; others regard virtually all attempts at narrative as a nuisance and simply click past anything that looks like it might be irrelevant.

While very few casual games use substantial narratives, one successful series of games, *Tradewinds Legends,* makes extensive use of narrative text to bring the player into the imaginary world of the game (Figure 2.2). It is interesting to note that this game is similar to other casual games in the sense that it requires little computer skill to play and encourages the player to focus on strategy without generating unnecessary stress.

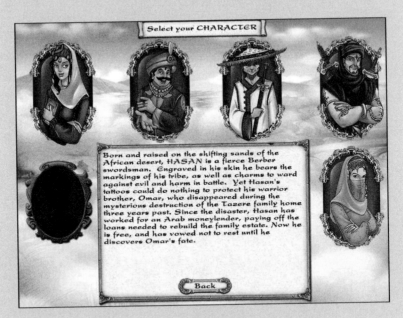

FIGURE 2.2   In Sandlot's *Tradewinds Legends* narrative plays a dominant role. All *Tradewind Legends, Westward,* and *Glyph* properties are trademarks, registered trademarks, or copyrights owned exclusively by Sandlot Games Corporation. All Rights Reserved.

One good way to begin to understand the role of narrative in games is to look at games that have little or no apparent narrative and then consider the way we think about them. A game people often point to when arguing that no narrative whatsoever is required for a fun and addictive game experience is *Tetris*. It is interesting to note, however, that even while creating the game, the developers described its functions with basic narrative conventions. They describe game play as manipulating Tetramino as they fall into the cup. "Tetramino fall into the cup" is a narrative. All of *Tetris* can be described as a sort of narrative: *Spin Tetramino as they fall into a cup in order to make solid horizontal rows of squares. Avoid overfilling the cup by making as many solid, self-clearing rows as possible. Earn points for clearing rows and successfully keeping Tetramino within the cup.*

While this isn't a story about a boy and his dog surviving the depression, it is a story. It relies on narrative conventions or constructs to communicate the ideas. These rules are expressed by visually representing the cup and illustrating the falling Tetramino. The environment of the game tells its story. It doesn't matter if the story is a bit abstract. It only matters that the story informs the player about the rules of play.

> Many of the puzzle games that dominate the casual games landscape today use a very similar model of objects filling a cup too rapidly, which must be eliminated through some interaction in order to win the game.

Another fine example is *Asteroids*. In this classic arcade game players guide a spaceship through an asteroid belt, using weapons to destroy the apparently endless barrage of asteroids. The game interface is simple, a triangle amid complex polygons. The story is immediately apparent to the player. They don't need to know about pilots flying the ship. The story is therefore limited to those concepts needed to understand the game.

In the casual games industry similar examples abound. Consider a game like *Super Collapse* (Figure 2.3). At first pass, this game, like *Tetris*, appears to have no narrative whatsoever. Collapse is quite a bit like *Tetris*. *Identify sets of three or more adjoining blocks in a cup in order to avoid overfilling the cup. Earn points for clearing sets and successfully removing blocks from the cup.*

FIGURE 2.3   *Super Collapse* also uses the clear-the-cup paradigm. Developed by RealNetworks.

This is a story in which the player is the central character and the player's journey provides the backbone of the story. The player wants to identify sets of three or more adjoining blocks in the cup to avoid overfilling the cup (losing the game), but more blocks keep emerging from the base of the cup, so the player works to find matches faster, but the blocks start coming faster, so the player works faster and tries to work smarter. Eventually the player either overcomes the struggle or fails.

One way to describe a narrative plot is through a simple sentence like this: _____ wants _____, but _____, so _____. The first blank is a character or group, the second blank is a goal or objective, and the next one is an obstacle. The last blank is an attempt to overcome the obstacle. To develop a complex plot, simply repeat the last two elements, obstacle and attempted solution, over and over.

All games have inherent narratives, but what about the *back-stories* or *legends* that are pervasive in many games? Some games provide a substantial amount of background information to players to *set* the game within an imagined world. For the most part, this is just the result of frustrated novelists working in the wrong field. While a game is not a film, games do inherit a lot of their basic relationships with narratives from the conventions of popular film. One of the most important of these is that characters and events in films are never passive, never purely exposition.

Telling a story, as you might in a novel, about the ancient war that gave rise to the current state of affairs in your game world is a convention commonly called *back-story*. Hollywood learned long ago that this approach to storytelling can sometimes prove less engaging. Generally exposition that is necessary to understand a film is now integrated into the film itself. This is an approach that has rapidly become the standard in games as well (Figure 2.4).

The basic idea is to reveal the story throughout the game when the background helps guide the player to a more enjoyable or successful experience. Players choose to play a game because they want to play, not read or watch videos. While they do appreciate a sense of story within the game, they often resent story elements that do not help them play the game. The solution is to integrate the story ideas into the game, rather than creating elements that simply report the exposition.

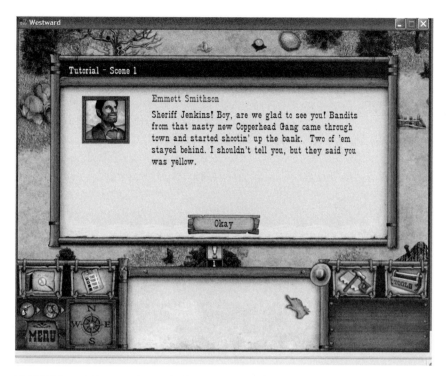

FIGURE 2.4 *Westward* reveals the story to guide interaction. All *Tradewind Legends,* *Westward,* and *Glyph* properties are trademarks, registered trademarks, or copyrights owned exclusively by Sandlot Games Corporation. All Rights Reserved.

By preparing a summary of the game's narrative and the way the game expresses that narrative, developers are able to generate a media list, which becomes the basis for creating assets such as art, sound effects, and videos that will be used in the game.

INTERACTIONS

Interaction matrices and *state diagrams* are the most common documents produced during this phase of preproduction. These documents allow the developer to visualize interactions more thoroughly. The manner in which the game is played and the rules of gameplay often take the form of interactions. By examining the specific interactions, both of the player to the game and of the game elements to one another, developers create a list of things that must be programmed in the game.

Game developers use state diagrams and interaction matrices to map out these interactions and break them down into easy-to-understand steps so that they may be created. A state diagram is a graphical representation of a complex system of events that have multiple possible outcomes. An interaction matrix is a visual representation (usually a chart) that helps developers identify and define all of the interaction results that occur in a game. Later in this chapter, the creation of state diagrams and interaction matrices are discussed in detail.

An interaction is anything that happens, or could happen, because:

- The player provided some input, such as a key press or mouse movement.
- The player failed to do something, maybe because he or she walked away from the game.
- An in-game element, such as an on-screen character, encountered some other game element, such as a hero bumping into an enemy or a ball bumping into a wall.
- An interface element, such as a scoreboard or map, was updated or changed.
- An in-game element, such as the environment or character appearance, was updated or changed.
- An in-game element, such as an enemy or power-up, was added to the world.

Interactions are different for every game, but they all tend to fall under these basic categories. Often the result of an interaction between two things is that one of the things changes states. A state is a narrative convention used to describe the condition or nature of an element. It's easiest to visualize these if we are talking about graphical elements with easily viewable properties. For example, in Skunk Studios' *QBeez* the animated blocks cry if they are left on the board after the time is up (Figure 2.5). The normal state of a QBee is content, but their state is changed to crying when an end-round event occurs.

FIGURE 2.5   *QBeez* cry when they are left behind at the end of a round. © Skunk Studios, Inc.® All Rights Reserved.

Plan the Integration of Interaction and Narrative

The storyboard or flow design, level maps or diagrams, the project schedule, and the technical specification are common documents used during this final preproduction (planning) phase. During this final stage of preproduction, designers and developers figure out how the narrative aspects and interaction elements will be integrated in the final game. They plan the features, estimate the schedule, and figure out what elements must be in place before other (dependent) elements can be produced. There are a variety of ways to do this. The technical specification is the primary document used to describe the functions that will be created for the game. The technical specification will include functions that respond to and generate all of the games events if a button is pressed or a sprite is destroyed.

A storyboard-like document diagrams the order of events and possible events from the point when the game is launched to the time gameplay begins. This includes screens that introduce the game concepts and then provide the player with options for beginning the game. Images of the in-game play screens are also included, along with customization and help screens.

Level maps or diagrams are used to illustrate the appearance of the game environment during various levels of gameplay. These are sometimes used to plan the specific elements, tokens, power-ups, and enemies that appear during a given level. The interaction matrix is used to determine the exact functions that must be created for the game, and the technical specification is basically an elaboration of those functions. It explains how the game will be programmed and what sorts of functions must be created. Project schedules are then created to help the developers and designers figure out which elements need to be created and in what order.

WRITING A TREATMENT

The treatment is often the central document generated during the pre-production planning phase. The concept of a treatment comes to the games industry from the film industry, which traditionally asks writers to create a treatment describing a proposed film. The treatment can take several forms and is often used to convince people that the proposed project is worth the investment of time, energy, and money.

In this section you'll learn the basic elements of a treatment, conventions for writing treatments, strategies for getting them finished, and how to use the treatment to convince others that a game idea is worth considering.

Game treatments do not adhere to a single established standard, but some basic concepts are included in virtually every treatment. There are also some fundamental conventions and guidelines that can be followed to get more out of a treatment. In the end, a treatment is really only useful if it helps plan the production of the game. The following are the most useful elements in treatments along with a definition of each.

TITLE

The name you plan to use to market and distribute the game is the title. You may also give some information about the title. A foreign language title might be better understood with some translation. You may also choose to use a subtitle or say something about the anticipated impact of the title in the proposed market.

AUTHOR

The author of a game is the person who created the initial idea or concept and then developed the plan for the game's features and gameplay mechanics. There are sometimes many authors for a game. Some studios work as a team to create the overall game plan, but most of the time one or two people are largely responsible for the bulk of the creative work on the initial plan for the game. You may keep this as simple as the name of the author or authors, or you may include some brief description of the author's experience in the games industry.

STUDIO

Sometimes this document is used to propose a game idea to a publishing or producing studio. In that case, this area would not be included. More frequently this document is produced by a studio in preparation for the production of a new title. When the document is produced within a studio, the name of the producing studio should be included here, along with a brief history of the studio.

GENRE

Casual game genres are fairly tightly restricted. A casual game is probably a puzzle, card, strategy (especially Mahjong), action/arcade, or word game. If your game doesn't fit one of these game genres, it may not be a casual game. Identify the genre of your game here. You may also have a game that crosses over more than one genre.

AUDIENCE

The intended audience for a casual game is predetermined: a broad-based audience dominated by women between the ages of 25 and 50. These are people who are fairly inexperienced at playing computer games but who enjoy the them when they don't present unwarranted technical challenges. If the proposed audience doesn't include this broad array of people, then you will have a serious problem getting your game distributed within the casual games industry.

RELATED PRODUCTS

Treatments usually include a description or analysis of similar products already present in the market. This serves two purposes. First, it gives potential producers a basis for comparing the proposed work to other finished games they might have seen, and it helps them estimate whether or not the potential market for such a game is already oversaturated. Too much competition from very similar games could make the game harder to sell, and too little activity in the area could indicate that people aren't generally attracted to things like the proposed game.

Often developers produce rough working sketches to better communicate the ideas in a proposed game. In *Podz* the early sketches were integrated into early game prototypes to help the artist better understand how the 3D and 2D worlds of the game interface would be seamlessly blended (Figure 2.6).

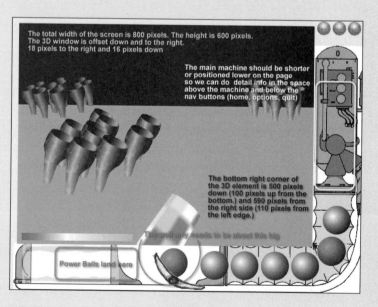

FIGURE 2.6 An early sketch of *Podz* with notes on planned sizes.

CONCEPT

Before you write a treatment, a general concept document is often produced. This document usually contains a description of the proposed game in very general terms. The concept statement in your treatment should summarize that concept document in one or two succinct sentences. The point is to express the nature or gist of the game in as succinct a form as possible. The simplest way to explain the game quickly (when you've cornered that power-producer in an elevator) is a concept statement.

WALK-THROUGH

The walk-through presents the player's experiences during gameplay in active, present-tense form. Writing in this format is explained more fully in the next section, "Film Conventions." The important thing about the walk-through is that the reader gets a vivid image of the game. This is often several pages long and can include alternate threads explaining gameplay experiences that result from different choices a player may make.

GAMEPLAY

The rules and mechanics of gameplay are described in this section of the treatment. Generally the rules are expressed in fairly simple form, and they sometimes include references to the specific keys or input devices that trigger various events under various circumstances. Often the rules of play expressed here become the rules of play that are given to players when they need help understanding how to play the finished game. This section may also include a detailed description of physics or artificial intelligence in the game. In a puzzle it might describe exactly how selection and manipulation of elements on-screen are handled. In a card game it may explain exactly how cards are shuffled or randomized, as well as how the player deals the cards or asks for more.

ENVIRONMENT

Most games have some sort of setting or space in which they occur. This section describes the environment or game space. The description should paint a visual image of the environment just as the walk-through paints a picture of the experience. It helps to keep the description as active as possible.

Some games don't really have environments. They have interfaces, but the interface does not necessarily depict a specific environment. It exists only to serve the needs of the game's rules. It is especially difficult to give a game a unique personality and style if there is no environment. This relates to the concept of narrative in games. It is often easier for a player to relate the game to things with which they are familiar by identifying a common narrative based on a known environment and characters.

Most notably, this section includes a list of all the environments that are planned for the game and a description of the appearance of each. This is then used to help generate the resource list, so that developers, artists, and designers know what environments need to be created for the game.

CHARACTERS

Casual games feature characters less often than hard-core games do. Characters in casual games are often present to add personality and provide a marketing tool (Figure 2.7). This may be because the most prevalent games in the market are puzzle and card games, which gen-

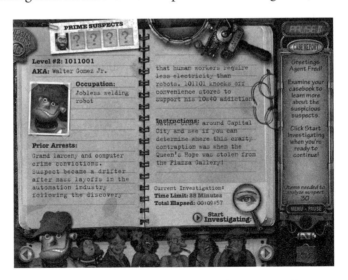

FIGURE 2.7 *MCF Prime Suspects* uses characters and environments. © Big Fish Games. All Rights Reserved.

erally don't focus on conventional stories, but on strategies for manipulating game tokens. Even a game that doesn't use conventional characters essentially substitutes the player for the main character in the game's narrative. Most developers find that a game character can be a tremendous asset when it comes to marketing a game, and it can also create an easily recognizable brand that can be exploited in the form of sequels and related merchandise (Figure 2.8).

FIGURE 2.8   Flow from *Diner Dash* is overwhelmed by her office job.

In this section of the treatment the game's characters, both good and bad, are described. Developing characters for a casual game can be problematic. The demographic is broad and it requires careful consideration to design characters that will be appealing to the widest possible group of potential audience members. Notably, characters that appeal too obviously to kids or that seem too harsh and hostile do not work well in the casual games market. Some successful casual game characters include the QBeez from the game of the same name, Flo the waitress from *Diner Dash,* and Lex the Bookworm in *Bookworm.*

This section of the treatment includes a detailed list, with descriptions of each character that appears in the game, including any special states of those characters that must be animated or reproduced visually. This information can then be transferred to a media list from which the artists, animators, and designers can determine exactly what media need to be created to represent all of the characters in the game. If a character cries, for example, art will need to be created showing the character crying. This could be a single still image that replaces the normal image of the character, or it could be a series of images that form an animation of that character crying.

TOKENS

The tokens for a game are usually items that are acquired or gathered and/or items that are manipulated (Figure 2.9). These are usually called sprites, which are on-screen animated images that represent some object (sometimes a character) in the game. In a puzzle game these would be the puzzle pieces, and in a card game, the cards. In *Mah Jong Adventures* these are the tiles (Figure 2.10), while in a customer service simulation such as *Diner Dash* these would be the

FIGURE 2.9 In *QBeez* tokens become the characters. © Skunk Studios, Inc.®

drinks and food that are served or the money that is collected. Like the environment and the characters, these images and media are added to the resource list that designers and developers use to create a work list and eventually a schedule for producing the game.

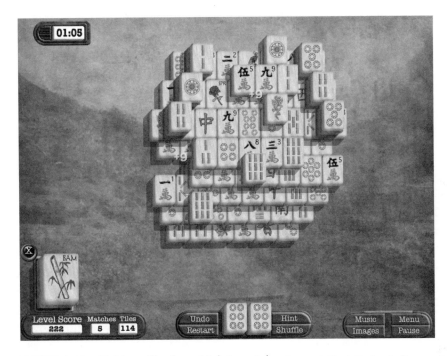

FIGURE 2.10   Mahjong tiles from *Mah Jong Adventures*. © Skunk Studios, Inc.®
All Rights Reserved.

INTERFACE/CHROME

The entire game is tied together by the interface. This is the visual display elements that are used throughout the game. The interface includes things like the start screen from which the game is launched, options screens, and help screens. The visual appearance of this interface is often called the chrome. The treatment should include rough sketches, drawings, and sometimes finished examples of the game's interface.

This can also include general guidelines or principles for creating interface elements for the game. It is important that the game has one look and feel throughout so that it all fits together. Conventions for finding help, navigating screens, and quitting the game should all be uniformly implemented so that the player is never confused about how to access the tools needed to play the game.

The interface is also broken down into a list of required assets, and these are added to the list of assets (media) required for the game. The overall asset list is then used to determine what needs to be done, and as the game is created, individuals are assigned tasks from the asset requirements on the list.

RULES

A game, at its heart, is a challenge to perform a task, given the limitations of certain rules. We enjoy this sort of challenge when the task is difficult, but not too difficult, and when we feel amply rewarded for success. Every game then has rules by which it can be played. Without the rules, the game would not be adequately challenging, and players would quickly become bored.

Unfortunately we also love finding ways to cheat at games. The truth is that people will try everything they can think of to cheat at your games. Because of this, it is critical that developers clearly identify all of the rules of a proposed game and then strictly enforce those rules so that the game can only be played in accordance with these rules.

This section of the treatment states each rule of the game. It may also describe features or functions that must be included in the game to enforce those rules. Evidence of this strategy was provided in the match-three exercise in Chapter 1. Subroutines had to be created that checked to make certain players did not try to swap a token for a noncontiguous token. Tokens are only allowed to move one slot up, down, left, or right. In addition, the `switchback()` routine had to be created to undo if a user attempted to move a token that failed to make a match. In both cases these are functions that had to be created just to prevent people from breaking the rules. An example of rules for a game could be provided by our match-three game.

Typical Match-Three Game Rules

1. Player selects a token and then any adjoining token (up, down, left, or right) to swap that token.
2. The swap must result in a matched set of three or more.
3. Failed matches will be reset.

Of course, our example of the match-three puzzle stops at this point and doesn't deal with the more advanced issues that you would likely find in a fully developed match-three game. Time limits, level-ups, points for matches, power-ups, and complications would also be added to the set of rules defined in a typical treatment.

LEGAL

This section describes anything related to ownership or legal rights to distribute or sell all or any part of the proposed game. Are any of the assets planned for use the property of some other party? Is the engine or the music not fully your own? Is the proposed title subject to trademark restrictions that have been separately negotiated, and if so, what are the terms of such a negotiation? You should include any legal concerns related to intellectual property here.

As you can see, the treatment will rapidly become an enormous document. It makes sense to make it the backbone of your planning and preparation for the game, but it is also generally used as a fundamental document for selling the game idea to potential partners. Some people recommend using the treatment as a "leave-behind" document for potential producers or partners after pitching the game. We discourage that practice, as it leaves you completely vulnerable to loss of your intellectual property through theft or "near-cloning." Just as many of the conventions of games' pre-production come from film, the standard practice in film is to leave a document behind that is a concise executive summary of the proposed project but that lacks all the detail of a final treatment.

FILM CONVENTIONS

Many conventions within the film industry translate smoothly and logically into the games industry. Films are often described using short, simple, single-sentence concept statements called log lines. You might, for example, say that *Bookworm* is *Collapse* meets *Scrabble* with a smart sassy attitude. In just one sentence a potential investor gets a strong sense of what the game is like and understands what things might be appealing about it.

Screenwriters often create documents that are used to pitch (sell) a potential project to producers during a face-to-face meeting. These are sometimes done with poster boards, storyboards, or summary documents. Game designers sometimes use the same methods to pitch their games to potential producers, using images, music, and even early playable demos to convince a producer that a game is worth investing in. Usually game developers will start at this point with a concept document that describes the game in general terms. This gives an overview of the game that is essentially a summary and is not significantly technical.

Screenwriters are often asked to produce treatments, which are 10-plus–page documents that describe the proposed film both from a creative and a marketing perspective. This practice has been widely adopted by the games industry, probably in part because of its usefulness as a crossover document, but also because it is virtually impossible to script a game. This is in many ways the most thorough planning document that can be created for a game. In addition to borrowing the conventions of film preproduction documents, game developers can also benefit enormously by learning from the writing strategies that screenwriters have developed over the past century.

WRITING STRATEGIES

The most significant writing strategy borrowed from the film industry is the fundamental approach to describing films in an active, present-tense voice. While many written forms describe stories and experiences as if they had happened in the past, film treatments and scripts generally describe events as though they were happening right now, on the screen in front of the reader. It is a visually compelling approach to writing, which, when done well, paints a vivid image in the readers' minds. Just as using language to paint an image of the events unfolding inspires filmmakers to imagine the eventual production, this style evokes strong images of the gameplay experience in the minds of game developers.

To write treatment events in this manner, you will have to be careful to choose active verbs and clear and interesting adjectives and make certain you describe the things that happen on the screen, in the game, from the viewpoint of an actively engaged player. For example, you would not state in a treatment, "Superguy found several tokens and then used them to track down and kill Badman." This sentence is written in past tense and does not paint a vivid image. It expresses things that happened in the past, not what is actively occurring in the game right now. Instead of the past-tense, dull version, you would say, "Superguy struts confidently over the hill. His cobalt eyes keenly scan the landscape. His pupils flare, his prey in sight, he pounces toward the . . . ."

It is important to note that there are two big differences between these styles. First, the proper style describes things that are happening right now on the screen. It uses verbs like *struts* and *pounces* to describe events actively in the present tense. Second, it paints much more vivid pictures by describing in some detail how those active events occur and what they look like. The phrase "cobalt eyes keenly scan" could be stated as "he looks around," but it wouldn't paint a very vivid picture of either the character or the intensity and seriousness of the action.

PITCHING THE GAME

You need to keep several things in mind when pitching a game: present yourself as a professional, avoid clichés, and be prepared. You are essentially interviewing for a job. Clean up and dress well. You should always dress at least one level of formality above the appearance you find at the company. This doesn't mean a tuxedo, or even a suit coat and tie. In most such places a nice clean outfit should be perfectly fine, as your potential colleagues will likely be dressed very informally. It is equally important that you speak like a professional. Remember your manners and don't be overly informal with your interviewers. Avoid profanity and try to fit your conversational style to the style of the highest-ranked person in the room. Address your new colleagues by name and come prepared with questions for them.

Prepare by knowing everything you can about their company so that you have a sense of whether they are the partners that you seek. Make your documents look as professional as possible. Everything should be typed, and you should have multiple copies prepared with clear, logical illustrations. You should be thoroughly prepared to describe every aspect of the game in detail and have an executive summary of the game to leave behind.

You may also want to have potential variations prepared to show the publisher that you are flexible and that you are full of ideas like this so that they might be inclined to call on you later if they have an idea but don't have anyone to develop a more detailed treatment. Finally, avoid obvious clichés such as clones of heavily replicated games. There should be something absolutely unique about the game you propose.

STORYBOARDING THE FLOW

The next major document developed during this phase of preproduction is a *storyboard,* which illustrates the various screens players will see as they launch the game and access features such as help and options. Putting together this plan for player interaction can help developers anticipate the player's needs and make sense of the game dynamics (Figure 2.11).

This is often a storyboard-like document that shows images of the game interface for each functional screen. The image can be labeled to show how the interaction will be handled for every item that requires player input. For example, an options page might include explanations of how the sound is adjusted and which icons trigger which effects (Figure 2.12).

1: Butterflies flutter across title and land.
2: Home, options and quit are visible, only quit is enabled.
3: Insight logo appears after two second delay.
4: Page advances automatically after a few seconds.

FIGURE 2.11 This start screen uses numbered notes to explain the board.

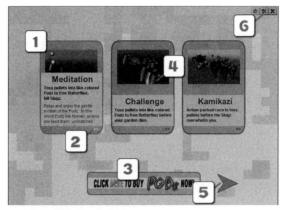

1: Selected mode is outlined in red.
2: Expansion arrows reveal more info about modes.
3: Upsell button.
4: Images of each play mode preview the mode.
5: Arrow launches selected game.
6: Home, options and quit are visible, home is disabled.

FIGURE 2.12   This early flow diagram for *Podz* illustrates basic mode selection.

Often these are working documents and are subject to change. Think of them as a sort of living whiteboard where designers and developers exchange notes with artists about the nature of the planned interaction and the overall look and feel of the project (Figure 2.13).

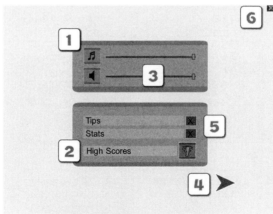

1: Audio Channel adjustments for music and effects.
2: Link to High Score tables.
3: Audio adjusts via horizontal sliders (0-255).
4: Play Button launches or returns to a game.
5: User can toggle off tips and stats.
6: Only the close option is available via this screen.

FIGURE 2.13   Interface design for the options screen.

ANTICIPATING THE USER'S NEEDS

With the flow storyboard or diagram and the individual interaction charts for each screen, you can analyze the player's experience and potentially diagnose problems before they occur (Figure 2.14). A good example can be seen in the interaction chart for the top-score

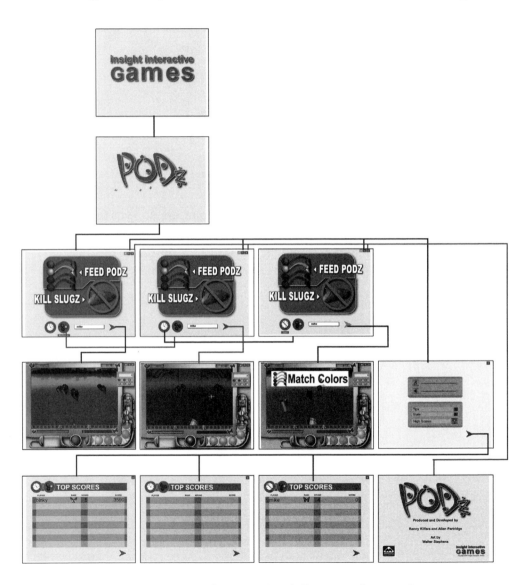

FIGURE 2.14 The flow chart for final version of *Podz* illustrates all connections.

page(s) in *Podz*. One of the problems with multiple modes of game play is that it becomes difficult to represent high scores, because a player may have played more than one game mode, leading to different scores and experiences. While doing the screen for *Podz*, it quickly became apparent that the same buttons that were used to select modes at the start of the game could be used to select high-score modes in the high-score table.

By visualizing the screen, developers are able to carefully consider ahead of time what sorts of choices players might want to make while playing the game. Players might like to compare their high scores in one mode with their high scores in another mode, or they might want to see how they rank compared to other players (Figure 2.15). Each of these things can be visualized in this sort of study. Used in tandem with the flow diagram, it becomes apparent what sort of functions need to be programmed to make the game work the way everyone imagined.

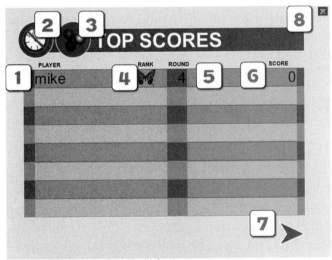

1: Player name listed by highest score.
2: Timer button toggles to reveal different modes.
3: Multicolor button toggles to reveal different modes.
4: Displays highest butterfly rank image earned.
5: Displays highest round completed successfully.
6: Displays highest score earned.
7: To return to game or start a new game.
8: Only Quit is available from default buttons via this screen.

FIGURE 2.15 Buttons 2 and 3 allow users to see multimode high scores.

MAKING SENSE OF THE DYNAMICS

The flow diagram and interaction diagrams also help developers make sense of all the possible states or situations that could exist while a player is working with the software. Especially when a game is played in several modes, and by users with various profiles, it is difficult to know what should be displayed on any given screen at any given time.

These diagrams help developers anticipate potential problems and plan their program to work well under any circumstances. Basically the more choices that are offered to players on any given screen, the more possible outcomes could occur as a result of a visit to that screen. For these reason, it is common to limit the options available via a given path so that players do not unwittingly walk down a path that the developer didn't consider ahead of time.

Anything the developer didn't plan for, but is nonetheless possible, can, and usually does, break the game. There is nothing that makes people doubt the value of a game faster than seeing an error that alerts them some part of the program is broken. By planning these interactions out carefully, you can save valuable development time and avoid lots of problems during beta testing.

IDENTIFYING THE INTERACTIONS

The next major step is generating an interaction matrix to describe the interactions that each on-screen object will have with every other on-screen object and those that the player may have with any on-screen element (Figure 2.16). This table of potential interactions is called an interaction matrix, and it is a tremendous link to moving from imagining a game to actually producing one.

A spreadsheet application such as Microsoft Excel® is a good place to start creating an interaction matrix. The matrix is essentially a table filled with cells that describe the interactions between objects listed in the column and row headings. Each cell describes the event that occurs to both tokens when they intersect, collide, or otherwise interact.

INTERACTORS	Red Pod	Blue Pod	Ylow Pod	Red Ball	Blue Ball	Ylow Ball	Green Slug	Ylow Slug	Orng Slug	Red Slug	Glass Ball	Red Cluster	Blue Cluster	Yellow Cluster	Red Spiral	Blue Spiral	Yellow Spiral	Red Rapid	Blue Rapid	Yellow Rapid	Butterfly Bomb	quake Bomb	Ground
Red Pod				1,2	1,3	1,3	1,3	1,3	1,3	1,3	1,2	1,2	1,3	1,3	1,2	1,3	1,3	1,3	1,2	1,3	16,18	17,18	
Blue Pod			1,3	1,3	1,3	1,3	1,3	1,3	1,3	1,3	1,2	1,3	1,2	1,3	1,3	1,2	1,3	1,3	1,2	1,3	16,18	17,18	
Yellow Pod				1,3	1,3	1,2	1,3	1,3	1,3	1,3	1,2	1,3	1,3	1,2	1,3	1,3	1,2	1,3	1,3	1,2	16,18	17,18	
Red Ball	1,2	1,3	1,3				1,5	1,7	1,9	1,11													1
Blue Ball	1,3	1,2	1,3				1,5	1,7	1,9	1,11													1
Yellow Ball	1,3	1,3	1,2				1,5	1,7	1,9	1,11													1
Green Slug	3,4	3,4	3,4	1,5	1,5	1,5	4,5	12,6	13,8	14,10	1,5	1,5	1,5	1,5	1,5	1,5	1,5	1,5	1,5	1,5	16,5	17,5	
Yellow Slug	3,6	3,6	3,6	1,7	1,7	1,7	12,6	12,6	13,8	14,10	1,7	1,7	1,7	1,7	1,7	1,7	1,7	1,7	1,7	1,7	16,7	17,7	
Orange Slug	3,8	3,8	3,8	1,9	1,9	1,9	13,8	13,8	13,8	14,10	1,9	1,9	1,9	1,9	1,9	1,9	1,9	1,9	1,9	1,9	16,9	17,9	
Red Slug	3,10	3,10	3,10	1,11	1,11	1,11	14,10	14,10	14,10	14,10	1,11	1,11	1,11	1,11	1,11	1,11	1,11	1,11	1,11	1,11	16,11	17,11	
Glass Ball	1,2	1,2	1,2				1,5	1,7	1,9	1,11													15
Red Cluster	1,2	1,3	1,3				1,5	1,7	1,9	1,11													1
Blue Cluster	1,3	1,2	1,3				1,5	1,7	1,9	1,11													1
Yellow Cluster	1,3	1,3	1,2				1,5	1,7	1,9	1,11													1
Red Spiral	1,2	1,3	1,3				1,5	1,7	1,9	1,11													1
Blue Spiral	1,3	1,2	1,3				1,5	1,7	1,9	1,11													1
Yellow Spiral	1,3	1,3	1,2				1,5	1,7	1,9	1,11													1
Red Rapidfire	1,2	1,3	1,3				1,5	1,7	1,9	1,11													1
Blue Rapidfire	1,3	1,2	1,3				1,5	1,7	1,9	1,11													1
Yellow Rapidfire	1,3	1,3	1,2				1,5	1,7	1,9	1,11													1
Butterfly Bomb	16,18	16,18	16,18				16,5	16,7	16,9	16,11													16
Earthquake	17,18	17,18	17,18				17,5	17,7	17,9	17,11													17
Ground				1	1	1					15	1	1	1	1	1	1	1	1	1	16	17	1

Legend:

#	Outcome
1	Destroy Pellet
2	+1 Health Pod
3	-1 Health Pod
4	+1 Health Gslug
5	-1 Health Gslug
6	+2 Health Yslug
7	-1 Health Yslug
8	+3 Health Oslug
9	-1 Health Oslug
10	+4 Health Rslug
11	-1 Health Rslug
12	-2 Health
13	-3 Health
14	-4 Health
15	Shatter
16	Explode Butterflies
17	Explode Smoke
18	+All Health Podz

FIGURE 2.16   Part of the interaction matrix for *Podz*.

An interaction matrix is symmetrical on the diagonal; sometimes these are only completed for half of the matrix. Often the outcome of an interaction is referenced by an index number that can be detailed in a legend that appears below or to the side of the matrix.

In 2005 Reflexive Arcade was honored by the Independent Games Festival (IGF) with the Seumas McNally Grand Prize for a Web/Downloadable game. The game is a visual stunner that has since been ported to the X-Box. It is a fascinating crossover between mainstream game and online experience and features a cool little character named Wik (Figure 2.17).   →

The character Wik evolved over time. Initially the character stood upright and wore clothing, but as the design evolved, the character began to become less humanoid and more tree frog–like (Figure 2.18). Developments like this can help a team evolve a clearer and clearer sense of the game's chrome and of the game's concept. The mechanics and game play strategies tend to inspire the conceptual and aesthetic vision, just as the vision tends to inspire the mechanics.

FIGURE 2.17 Early character study from Reflexive Arcade's *Wik: Fable of Souls.*

FIGURE 2.18 A later sketch of Wik explores his more primitive nature.
© Reflexive Entertainment. All Rights Reserved.

It is important to understand that these illustrations can serve as focal points for the all-important communication of the vision among the entire team. Every facet of the game is open to discussion, and sometimes the sketches become scratchpads for expressing those ideas. As the design for Wik evolved, the creature's name was decided (Figure 2.19).

Once developers at Reflexive agreed on the character's basic look, a 3D model was created and the first render of the strange little tongue swinger was created (Figure 2.20). The render test depicts the now familiar character perched comfortably upside-down on a branch.

FIGURE 2.19   Wik gets a name.

FIGURE 2.20   The initial 3D render test for
Wik.

In his final incarnation (Figure 2.21) Wik is found in a similar perch, surrounded by the lush forest landscape featured in the game. Part mischief, part forest creature, part person, and part frog, Wik is one of the most intriguing characters found in any of today's casual games.

→

FIGURE 2.21 The final version of the little tongue swinger. © Reflexive Entertainment. All Rights Reserved.

WHAT HAPPENS WHEN?

The basic function of an interaction matrix is to analyze and plan exactly what happens when any event occurs in the game. The matrix makes it easier to ensure that developers consider every possible interaction when they plan to produce and program the game. An easy way to think about these events is to ask what happens when for each set of tokens. For example, What happens when the butterfly bomb hits any pod? The pod's health is increased by the maximum health value, causing the pod to instantly morph into a butterfly. The butterfly bomb explodes into a particle burst of baby butterflies, which flutter outward and fade.

Ultimately this effect is easily explained, but much more complex to implement. It will eventually require a 3D particle system with animated baby butterflies, a removal of the initial butterfly bomb image, a detection of the collision, a removal of the pod, a call to the score system, and the generation of a butterfly (the morphed version of the pod.) The butterfly bomb technically has this effect on all of the podz with which its particle system collides, which is a fairly large group in most cases, so this individual example is not the norm. Usually a whole group of podz experience this level-up on collision with a butterfly bomb.

Because these events are more complex than can be explained in a single line or two on the interaction matrix, developers often create state diagrams to better define how changes will occur during the event.

CONVERTING THE INTERACTION MATRIX TO TECHNICAL SPECIFICATIONS

Once the interactions are clearly identified, these events can be converted into a technical specification. You can correlate the events from the matrix and state diagrams to specific functions that must be programmed and design the architecture for the programming of your game that will support the kinds of interactions that need to occur. Move through each event defined in the interaction matrix and ask yourself what has to happen behind the scenes for this to work on the screen in the way that you imagined.

Does the event affect the score? Does the event cause something on the screen to change appearance? Does the event cause a sound to play or stop? Does the event affect any artificial intelligence in the game? Will the game need to remember or report about the event later? Do you want to track or monitor the event so that you can respond to the player's overall experience? Is the result of the event always the same or is it sometimes influenced by past events, conditions or states of the game or other matters? Do you want to offer the player help when this event occurs the first time or under other special circumstances?

Any answer to the previous questions may indicate that you need to write some code to make the things you want to happen actually happen on the screen. Even if you don't have a clue how to program those things, you can write down descriptions of what they are in a clear logical fashion, and that is exactly what is needed to prepare the technical specification. This should include detailed descriptions of all the things that actually are happening (not the narrative constructs, but the actual visible, audible, and data-alteration things that occur).

CRITICAL JUNCTURE: TO CODE OR NOT TO CODE

Once you've figured out what sort of things happen behind the scenes, you can decide how to approach the actual creation of the game. Because of engines like Director and Flash, you can build an enormous amount of some casual games with very little programming. For example, a find-the-image or match game can be created with very little programming. Conversely, a game like *Podz* requires tens of thousands of lines of code. In part, the amount of programming you plan to do will relate to the amount of programming experience you and your team bring to the project. Some games present more complex programming problems than others.

This does not mean, however, that you are going to be able to make a game without any programming. Even simple games require some programming, and virtually all casual games include special functions such as saving and loading profiles and displaying high-score tables that will require some code. In the chapters that follow, you'll see some examples of programming-heavy games and some that are fairly simple to program.

PROJECT SCHEDULING

Scheduling the project is, frankly, a nightmare. To do it effectively in most cases requires a full-time project administrator, and this is a luxury that many, perhaps even most, game companies simply cannot afford. Nonetheless, scheduling your project effectively, especially as the size of your team grows, can give you a serious advantage when trying to maximize resources.

The major problem with scheduling the development of a game is that it is (1) difficult to estimate the amount of time it will take to create each media element or element of code and (2) tough to anticipate exactly where bottlenecks will occur because one person is waiting on work from another to begin an assigned task. The first problem, estimating the time required, will get better with practice and is going to vary somewhat anyway. Generally casual game development teams are small, so they tend to perform functions across a fairly broad range of things. This naturally lends to limiting bottlenecks and anticipating one another's needs.

In our studio we have generally preferred to work intensively with developers in easy shouting distance, especially when the game is well under way. We find that the bottlenecks come when the art required is either beyond our own limits or requires the time and energy of a dedicated artist. In most cases, game development can easily continue with placeholder art filling in until the final images are delivered. The schedule is generally composed of project assignments and milestones.

PROFESSIONAL PRACTICE: MARGARET WALLACE ON GAMES AND STORIES

Margaret Wallace is the cofounder and CEO of Skunk Studios, makers of the hit games *QBeez* and *Gutterball 3D*. Skunk's games have a singularly charming and innovative look and feel. Wallace, along with other members of her company, left Shockwave.com to found the studio. She also worked on the *Virtual Petz* series for Mindscape *Dogz* and *Catz*.

Partridge: *Skunk Studios' games like* QBeez *and* Sveerz *feature some of the most innovative and enchanting narrative integration in the industry. How would you compare story/narrative in casual games to story/narrative in conventional or hard-core games?*

Wallace: With casual games, you don't have untold hours to let a story unfold. Typically, casual game players need to be given some narrative context as soon as possible to understand the main themes of the game in order to establish a sense of purpose. This doesn't mean you can't let a story develop over time—quite the contrary—but casual game developers need to work hard to grab a player's attention out the gate with narratives that make sense and are easily digested. Any in-game narrative begins with the title—so pick a game title that is evocative of your narrative, your game mechanic or, ideally, both.

Also, narratives which emphasize a lot of violence will generally not perform well with your typical casual games audiences. This aversion for violent themes is in marked contrast to the core and hard-core gaming spaces, which do not shy away from your occasional carnage and bloodshed. At least until this point in casual games, this has been the case.

→

Games with a heavy sci-fi slant tend to also not perform very well as casual games, but rules are always meant to be broken. It really all comes down to implementation. However, we have often joked at Skunk Studios about those "dungeons in space" games, i.e., casual games with a heavy sci-fi narrative which tend to perform poorly.

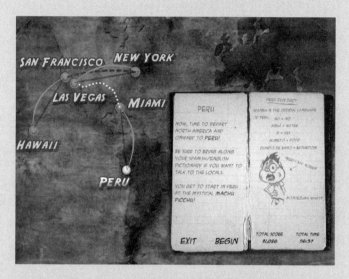

FIGURE 2.22   Wallace's mastery of narrative is evident in all of Skunk's games. © Skunk Studios, Inc.® All Rights Reserved.

Partridge: *Could you share some strategies for generating germinal ideas for games?*

Wallace: Play lots of games and take your cue from your everyday experiences living in a pop-culture–infused world. Blend great game mechanics with relevant themes. Be open to the world around you—what people are doing, reading, talking about. Know your audience.

Partridge: *What processes, or documents, e.g., concept, treatment, executive summary, do you recommend for preproduction game planning?*

→

Wallace: Iterative prototyping is probably most key in successful game development. Use concept documents, project management and collaboration tools, features lists. Every development team is different, and you have to find the tools and methods that effectively allow the team to work together but also independently.

Partridge: *The casual games industry has yet to introduce characters with the lasting power and cultural impact that we've seen in film and hard-core games. Do you think that this is a limitation of the casual game, or is there room for richer narrative in casual games?*

Wallace: I'm not sure I agree that the casual games industry has yet to introduce characters with lasting cultural impact. Think of the character Flo from the *Diner Dash* franchise, for example. This character is widely known and has broken ground in terms of being a memorable character with some cultural clout.

Even as far back as 2001, Skunk Studios was nominated for a Best Character award at the Game Developer Choice Awards for the title character in its first game, called *Tamale Loco*. On some level, this shows a casual game character has broken some cultural ground.

Partridge: *While I'm sure the question is fast becoming cliché, women are seriously under-represented in the games industry. Do you have any advice for women interested in games and finding it difficult to survive in the male-dominated industry?*

Wallace: For anyone to do well in the game industry, you have to have a thick skin and go for whatever you want. If you are waiting for someone to notice you or your abilities, you'll be waiting a long time. If there is some aspect of the games industry you feel passionate about and you are good at what you do, then don't let people try to discourage you or put you in roles that you're not happy about.

SUMMARY

The first step in developing any game is developing the germinal idea and concept. The concept is often drafted into an initial statement or high concept document to explain the basic idea of the game to others. Once the concept has demonstrated some merit, a treatment can be created. The treatment begins to assess the viability of the proposed game from both a developmental and a marketing standpoint. This document explores much more detail than the initial concept document and can contain images of proposed screens, details on their layout and design, as well as information about how the game will flow from one player choice to the next.

The developer will also generate an interaction matrix and state diagrams that can be used to identify and analyze all of the events in the game. This analysis leads to the technical specification, which further breaks down the logical events in the game and proposes an overall architecture for the code, as well as an analysis of what functions must be developed to turn the game idea into a practical software application. Finally, a production schedule is created, with careful consideration given to overlapping deadlines and situations that create dependencies.

All of these processes and documents are ultimately aimed at the same job—taking a very complex project and breaking it down into small, easy-to-define parts. It is important that, above all, you remember that the process is evolutionary, not dictatorial or absolute. Games usually evolve and change as they are being developed, so it is important to constantly communicate any of these changes with all the members of the production team. It is also important not to become overly attached to any piece of media or basic concept. The game can evolve significantly, and you are usually not well served by needlessly holding on to some concept or image that simply no longer works with the game.

3 Minimal Programming Approach

In This Chapter

- Casual Games that Require Little Programming
- Project 1: Create a Mouse-Triggered Event
- Developing a Point and Click Casual Game in Flash
- Case Study: Aunt Abbie's Best in Show
- Project 2: Simple Navigation with Minimal Programming

Some casual games require little programming to create. Generally these are games that simply respond to user mouse events and have fairly simple gameplay mechanics. Most programmers would argue that programming is often a much more productive way to accomplish your goals, potentially saving you time and resources even in a situation where little programming is required. Nonetheless, there are times when it is simply best to take advantage of the resources inherent in one of the third-party engines.

An engine is a core multimedia or software code base that can be adopted, saving the developer from starting from scratch. All engines come with advantages and disadvantages, most notably that in the case of commercial engines, the developer typically has no real control over the limitations and issues that may exist in the engine itself. Engines joined to development environments such as Director or Flash are generally easier to use but less amenable to customization. Engines such as Torque and the PopCap Framework are easily customizable but usually require more of the developer.

The advantage of adopting an engine is that there is no need to write code to handle the basic functions of multimedia, such as displaying text, monitoring system memory, or playing back video.

In this chapter we'll examine casual games that require little programming. Image-find, simple puzzle, basic navigation, and narrative games are discussed. One common multimedia engine used when little programming is required is Adobe Flash. We'll examine the benefits and deficits of Flash, make some comparisons to Adobe Director, and then discuss strategies for developing a casual game in Adobe Flash.

Finally, we'll walk through the development of a game using Adobe Flash.

In this chapter you will learn how to:

- Identify games that require little programming
- Work with Adobe Flash to understand how multimedia engines support casual game development
- Design games that require minimal programming
- Compare and evaluate potential third-party engines
- Develop a minimal programming game with Adobe Flash

CASUAL GAMES THAT REQUIRE LITTLE PROGRAMMING

Several genres of casual games that exist today require very little, or very basic, programming to function as expected and make entertaining games for their audience. These fall into three categories: image-find games, basic navigation games, and narrative, or text-heavy, games.

The common theme behind these games is that the player's simple action of mouse clicking over appropriate or inappropriate sprites will result in positive or negative outcomes. These mechanics are fairly simple. They are like *Whac-A-Mole* games because fundamentally the idea is that you aim the mouse at a location on the screen, like the hammer in *Whac A Mole,* and then you click to actively make a selection or perform a function (Figure 3.1).

Ultimately, mouse selection of targets is a fairly common theme in many casual games. In the match-three game we essentially use the

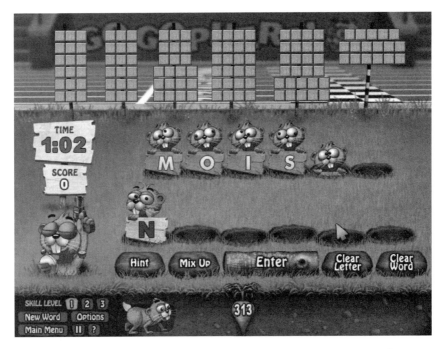

FIGURE 3.1 *Word Whomp* uses the *Whac-A-Mole* paradigm to present letters.
Pogo™ Images © 2007 Electronic Arts Inc. *Pogo, Pogo to Go,* and *Word Whomp* are trademarks or registered trademarks of Electronic Arts Inc. in the U.S. and/or other countries. All Rights Reserved. Used with permission.

mouse to choose targets that either form groups of three or more or must be manipulated to find groups of three or more in a set. In a hidden-image game, you use the mouse to pick or identify the requested image on the screen. In a basic navigation game you use the mouse to choose which object or room you want to explore next, and in a narrative game you use the mouse to choose which objects to explore or to select elements that you want to interact with further.

IMAGE-FIND GAMES

One of the most popular genres of casual games, *image-find games,* are finding their way from the counters of questionable bars into the homes of millions of avid fans. This group of games includes a variety of implementations. In some cases the player is asked to compare two images and identify elements that are different in one of the pictures. In other cases the player is asked to identify things that are wrong with the image. The most popular series recently have focused on finding difficult-to-spot objects within a complex image when given only the name of the object. The *Mystery Case Files* series and *Titanic* both make use of this basic convention, bringing a surprising level of delight to players as they uncover the hidden objects and in so doing, accomplish some secondary objective dictated by the narrative.

The first thing to note about these titles is that they require an enormous amount of media. The basic image of a scene must be covered with dozens, perhaps hundreds, of images, with transparent backgrounds that lay seamlessly over image of the environment. At their heart, however, these are not complex programming problems.

While it does appear that the current wave of image-finding games has included some randomization into the games' requests for images to find, there is really nothing too difficult about creating a list of things that appear on the screen and then removing items from that list (and adding some points) when the item is clicked on the screen. No physics is required, and there are no complex object hierarchies to program. The basic functions of the game are limited to the following:

- Check for mouse clicks on sprites.
- If a clicked sprite was in the request list, remove it from the request list and add points.
- Show a hint about the location of a hidden image when requested.
- Time the round and return the player to the beginning of the game if the time runs out.

As things go, this is not a rough prospect for a programmer. Don't be deceived, though, because every casual game will require some substantial programming just to handle the routine elements such as player profiles and bringing the finished product to market as a solid commercial title.

SIMPLE PUZZLE GAMES

Many basic puzzle games require no more complex interaction than a simple table-top jigsaw puzzle in order to play them. These range from the jigsaw puzzle game, which asks players to reassemble an image from a series of divided segments, to any number of other puzzles that ask players to select an onscreen token and move it, or otherwise adjust it, to achieve some ultimate objective.

In Chapter 1 we examined the most common and successful type of puzzle game, the match-three variation. While our example required some code, some of which may have seemed a little complex, it didn't take much at all to create the game's central mechanics. By contrast, a typical 3D game can easily use tens of thousands of lines of code and requires substantially more math and other fundamental programming skill to create.

Very generally, these puzzles need a way to detect mouse clicks and sometimes movements to convert those clicks into visible animation or *state changes* in the onscreen sprites. For example, if you click on a token in *Collapse*, it will disappear if it is among a cluster of more than two other tokens of the same color. The most important elements of gameplay, the clicking and disappearing, are very simple to code. They would look something like Listing 3.1.

LISTING 3.1   Pseudo-Code for Mouse Event Response

```
function mouseUp() {
  matches = checkNeighbor(activeSprite.pColor);
  if matches > 2 {
    sprite(activeSprite).visible = TRUE;
  };
}
```

The basic assumption at work here is that your software will function based on some kind of event model. An event model allows your software to respond to things that happen and create custom commands for which it has programmed responses. Think of your software as a really literal person. This guy won't do anything unless he has a very specific set of instructions for how to do that thing. If he doesn't know how to handle some chore or task, he'll just ignore it. The software you create will essentially behave this way. If you tell the software what to do when the mouse is released, then it will run the commands inside that mouseUp() event handler. Conversely, if it doesn't have any instructions for what to do when the player presses a key down on the keyboard, it will simply ignore any signal from the system that keys are pressed down.

In the pseudocode in Listing 3.1 the software is given a mouseUp() event handler. When the mouse button is released, the software will run the commands found under the mouse handler. One of them in this case would be a custom handler (one that you also wrote) that is charged with determining whether the color selected matches more than two neighbors. The other command sets a system property, the visibility of the sprite that was clicked.

A common convention in games is to call an instance of a media resource that is visible on the screen a *sprite*. Media resources, things like pictures, movies, animation clips, and shapes, are generally kept in their original form in some sort of repository. This can take the form of an external resource folder, an archived collection, or an internal binary library or cast. To create the image on screen, a copy is made. This copy or *instance* is called a sprite. In most cases additional properties may be assigned to the instance of the resource, and some inherent functions are available, such as determining whether or not a given sprite was the one clicked.

Determining what the player did with the mouse is a very important part of most games. Various languages provide different ways to learn these things. In Adobe Director, for example, you can catch mouseUp, mouseDown, mouseUpOutside, mouseEnter, mouseLeave, mouseWithin, and many other events. Each event informs the game of a different type of player interaction. MouseUp, for example, is triggered when the player releases the left mouse button. A mouseDown event is sent when the player presses the left mouse button down. By separating each event it is possible to create interface experiences that look and feel very sensible to people.

You can also find out more information about the mouse state and position by polling mouse properties such as `clickLoc`, `clickOn`, `doubleClick`, and a host of others. `clickLoc`, for example, stores the position of the last player click on the screen. The point here is that the mouse is a critical part of the overall computer interaction experience, and developers have created some very specific ways of understanding exactly what's happening with the mouse at any given time.

Events happen and a notice is sent to the software that the event occurred. If the software has an event handler (a bit of code that listens for that event to trigger it), then the handler will run. Properties are local variables unique to a single instance of an object. The mouse itself is often implemented as an object. Its position on the screen can then be reported as the x (horizontal) and y (vertical) positions of the mouse.

Monitoring and reacting to mouse events in Adobe Flash can be especially easy, as the objects can often be buttons that are scripted to perform some function when the button experiences a mouse-down event. Flash uses the `buttonObj.onPress` to receive mouse-down events from the system. This could become a foundation for a system that detects mouse clicks and compares objects to a list of requested objects. Try Exercise 3.1 to understand more clearly.

PROJECT 1:   CREATE A MOUSE-TRIGGERED EVENT

 In this activity you will create a new Adobe Flash document, make a button out of a shape and then assign a script to monitor the instance of that shape sprite for a mouse-down event. When a mouse-down event is detected by the shape sprite button, it will trigger a message in the trace window.

STEP ONE: OPEN FLASH AND CREATE A NEW DOCUMENT

1. Open Adobe Flash. If you don't have a copy of Adobe Flash, you can download and install a free demo from the Adobe Web site.
2. Choose File: New Flash Document to create a new Flash project.

STEP TWO: MAKE A BUTTON

1. Use the Rectangle Tool to draw a rectangle on the screen (Figure 3.2).

FIGURE 3.2   Use the Rectangle Tool to draw a box on the stage.

2. Double-click in the center of your rectangle to select both the fill and the outline (stroke).
3. Press the F8 button on your keyboard to open the Convert to Symbol dialog box (Figure 3.3).
4. Choose the button option and name your button anything you like.
5. When you finish, press the OK button.

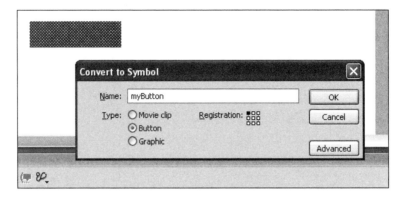

FIGURE 3.3 Convert the shape of the rectangle to a button.

STEP THREE: NAME THE BUTTON INSTANCE AND ADD A SCRIPT TO THE FRAME.

1. Select the button instance on the screen. Be careful not to double-click, as that would put you in symbol editing mode rather than in the scene view.
2. In the Property inspector (use the Window: Properties menu option if it isn't already open) change the instance name of your button to something memorable. Ours is named buttonA (Figure 3.4).
3. Open the Action Editor (Figure 3.5).

FIGURE 3.4 Change the instance name of the button.

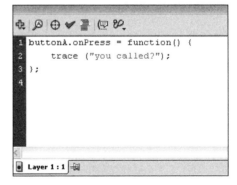

FIGURE 3.5 ActionScript Editor for buttonA.

4. Type the script in Listing 3.2 in the buttonA script of the Action Editor. (Note, the editor displays scripts that are associated with lots of different things. Be certain that you are working on the script associated with this instance of the button script.)

LISTING 3.2   ActionScript for Button Press

```
on (release) {
    trace ("you called?");
};
```

5. Press the Control button and the Enter key to test your movie. Click on the rectangle to see the message appear in the trace dialog.

You can easily extend this idea to cover the basic functionality of an image-find game. The instance names could be compared to a list of names printed as the *missing* items. If the instance clicked is found in the list of missing items, then the item would be made invisible and points would be added to the player's score.

BASIC NAVIGATION OR NARRATIVE GAMES

Navigation games use similar mechanisms to detect mouse action and turn it into navigation. Players point at objects on the screen to view them or move to another game environment (go to another room or world.) In a multimedia development environment like Adobe Flash or Director this often equates to simple frame-based navigation or nonlinear movement through a time line. Both Flash and Director feature this sort of time line. Developers can place different images on the time line at different frame positions and then use markers or labels to jump from one screen to another.

Even if there is no time line in the development language or environment, the basic notion behind this sort of navigation is simply that you move from one image on the screen to a new image on the screen. These images can easily be thought of as screen states, and any game engine may be easily directed to change the basic state of the screen.

DEVELOPING A POINT AND CLICK CASUAL GAME IN FLASH

There is a good deal of debate among developers about the merits and limitations of Adobe Flash. In any examination of any product for your business, it is important to get as much up-to-date information as you can about the proposed product. When Flash was first released, it was a bit like a super-charged gif editor. These were animated image-generating applications developed during the early days of the Web to add visual interest to the small images that dotted the Web landscape. Flash was a substantial innovation in the field because it cleverly combined vector-based graphics with Internet savvy. There was a need for better-looking graphics, smaller file sizes, and easily generated animation, and Flash met that need very well.

The earliest version of Flash was cute and could live up to its name, but it was not a robust programming environment. One of the problems with virtually all developments that center around the Internet and connectivity issues is that they are largely impotent compared to other means of production. Early versions of Flash were not able to do much beyond animation in a Web browser, they were slow and kludgy, the interface was bizarre and complex, and they had significant problems performing consistently across a wide variety of machines.

Ultimately, Flash was the perfect application for its era. It was sold for a low price and offered millions of people an opportunity to create Web applications with exciting interactivity and cool graphics. Most important, Macromedia continued to develop the product and wisely considered all of the implications of database integration, media streaming, and much stronger programming capabilities, making Flash a juggernaut in the field of online development options. Today Flash still has strengths and weaknesses. It is, however, improving. Prior to Flash 8, it was not very good with bitmap images, and it had terribly slow animation speeds. The most recent version boasts substantially improved performance in both regards, and the ActionScript programming language has become mature and fairly potent. The most serious of Flash's remaining limitations is that it is difficult if not impossible to extend the basic capabilities of Flash at runtime.

> Run-time is when the application is running as stand-alone software on the client's computer. Plug-ins play in a browser window. Author-time is when the application is running as an editable document or movie inside the development environment.

FLASH ADVANTAGES

The payoff for developing a casual game in Flash is that in the online market it will have virtually universal ubiquity. It will play back on any browser and on any computer running almost any operating system. It will even play back on cell phones, PDAs, and some game consoles (given the right circumstances). Java may have coined the phrase "author once, play anywhere," but Flash made it happen.

Flash is vector based, which means objects and images in Flash that adhere to its vector definitions will scale perfectly, whether larger or smaller. Graphics will remain cleaner, images will remain sharper, and you don't even need to change the screen resolution to play back your game. If you are willing to leave the bitmap behind, Flash can give you some of the cleanest graphics on the market today.

Flash supports database integration and streaming media as well as anything else you will find. It easily loads and unloads, parses, and makes use of XML and HTML files.

FLASH LIMITATIONS

While there are many advantages to working with Flash, the most prominent is that it isn't really designed as a game development tool. Flash movies are easily hacked and therefore difficult to secure. It is also difficult to get hooks into system-level commands and settings. For example, suppose you want to make your game full screen. This is a simple matter of setting a publish parameter in Director or programming a basic configuration in SDL, but in Flash the operation can be considerably more difficult. Many developers even routinely use Director to publish Flash-based applications just to work around these limitations. (Flash files can be played back by Director applications.)

Flash also suffers from poor performance in some cases. This has gotten significantly better with the newest releases, but playback at high resolutions is still not as strong as it can be using the other engines. There are specific problems with Flash movies playing back at high resolutions that lead to sometimes buggy and often slow speeds. Because standard practice is to wrap Flash-built games in additional engines to provide system access, they often have playback problems and even crash during playback on older systems. Adding layers of abstraction in this sense can multiply the problems of identifying bugs and performance problems. Needless to say, games that crash do not inspire people to pay for them.

PACKAGING FLASH ENGINES FOR PRIME TIME

Several aspects involved in finishing a game and preparing it for mass consumption must be considered as you evaluate your options for multimedia engines or libraries. Your game should be clearly branded as your game, with custom icons consistent with the theme of your game and clear identification in the executable properties that associate your company as the publisher. The game should be either contained in a self-extracting executable or packaged independently for your distributor's installer.

While you can create executables (independent, self–contained, self-powered software that will run on a computer, even if it doesn't have the application that was used to author the product) with Flash, these executables will be too limited to be useful as legitimate commercial games. At the very least, your game needs to be able to:

- Write text files with game state and user preference information to the system
- Read text files added dynamically to the system

$\rightarrow$

- Playback independently
- Change the user's screen resolution
- Reset the user's screen resolution
- Pause when another window or application pops in front of it

These elements are the bare minimum when it comes to system control and access of the client system by a commercial game and as it now stands, Flash executables don't offer that kind of control. Applications that extend Flash's ability to control the system are called wrappers. A variety of wrappers are on the market.

It is difficult to get Flash to behave in some of these ways, but it isn't impossible. A significant number of general engines have been developed to meet the needs that are left by Flash's inadequacies, and Flash has continued to improve with every release. A year ago conventional wisdom was that ultimately the best solution for a company was to either avoid using Flash or build a Flash player that had been trimmed down to include only the functionality needed by that company's games. A careful examination of the applications in Table 3.1 suggests that the landscape has changed. Each of these options are powerful with solid additional functionality, and together they display a surprising level of control, usability, and customization.

An off-the-shelf Flash player that adds broader read/write access and encapsulates the files in a less accessible form could be too large to be a practical solution for casual game developers. Some players are being targeted toward game developers, but even they have to have a somewhat general approach, which will lead to a bigger download. The cost of developing your own playback engine will be substantial and ultimately is probably too high for most small developers. You could just ignore the security issues and inability to go natively full screen, but this will make your game less marketable and decrease the odds that a portal will pick it up.

TABLE 3.1 Comparison of Major Flash Wrappers Available

	Security Added	File Access	Screen Resolution Reset	Launch External Files	Support PC/Mac	Extensible	Menu Disable	File Size Added
Jugglor™ 3rd Eye Solutions™	Yes	With JSystem	320x200 320x240 512x384 640x480 800x600 1024x768 1280x1024 1600x1200	With JStart	Windows 95, 98, NT, ME, 2000, XP	Write Cutom dll files with C++, VB, or Delphi	Yes	290K Variable because JTools can be added and removed
Northcode SWFStudio v3	Blowfish encryption	Can write to executable	Polls system available with desktop object set to any available resolution	Uses a shell launch object	Windows 95, 98, Me, NT, 2000 and XP	Plugins, Northcode authors	Yes–pop-up commands	3.4 MB *Includes licensed Flash player
MDMZink Multimedia Ltd.	Blowfish encryption	Mdm file system built in	System setResolution and getDisplay modes enable setting to any available resolution	Uses mdm process to launch with parameters	Windows 98SE/ME/ 2000/XP Max OSX.2	Custom dll supported via mdm script	Yes	2.35 MB Includes Flash player

At least one of the major developers, Oberon Media, has produced titles in Flash using an internally constructed Flash wrapper to deal with the system access issues. There are, after all, significant advantages to using Flash. It handles animation well, uses a familiar scripting language, and can handle a broad array of media types natively. The companion CD-ROM includes a demo of the Jugglor Flash Wrapper for you to explore. Jugglor features automated ActiveX® downloading for the few people who don't already have a Flash player installed and skips the player to get an incredibly small player. This is not a serious option with Director, but not a bad way

ON THE CD

to save two or three megabytes of file size when you consider the fact that Flash ubiquity is generally cited at well over 90%.

CASE STUDY: *AUNT ABBIE'S BEST IN SHOW*

Follow along now as we walk one step at a time through the development of an actual casual game. Insight Interactive Games will produce and publish the title. The initial work is described here from the idea through each of the initial stages of development. The basic thrust of this puzzle game comes from our understanding of the demographic characteristics of a typical casual game consumer.

IDEA

The most popular genre of casual games purchased as online downloadable software is the puzzle genre. *Best in Show* will definitely be a puzzle game. The qualities of a typical buyer tell us that she loves animals and pets. We strongly suspect that she is watching dog shows on cable television and will find the opportunity to manipulate (dress, pamper, treat, and train) a virtual dog that may be similar to a dog she is fond of entertaining and fun.

The title *Best in Show* provides an *instant recognition opportunity*. The phrase is too widely used to be *word-marked*. That means it may be used as a title without fear of trademark infringement because other entities may own logos or "looks" in association with the phrase, but the phrase itself belongs to the public because of its common use within conversation.

While this presents a disadvantage in that we can't own the title, it presents an opportunity that far outweighs the deficit. The phrase will instantly communicate a sophisticated love of animals and dogs as central to the game. Our consumer will know that the dog show experience is familiar and enjoyable for her. It is an as-yet untapped area in casual games, so we feel confident that if we can get it out quickly, it has a good chance of being widely distributed and downloaded.

To answer the need for ownership and to create a friendly accessible face with which the player can communicate, we'll create a character that will appeal to our core consumer and that can easily reflect her ideas, as well as guide her through the game's features and challenges. This will be a professional woman who looks and acts like a role model.

In order to meet the needs of the marketing systems that dominate the distribution portals, we will include at least three different game looks, or primary interfaces. This way, the traditional three screenshots will each have a unique but simple and appealing look and feel. The character will become the primary brand identity and will be attached to the logo/name in every appearance. A dog or dogs will also be tied to the identity.

CONCEPT

This match-three-or-more puzzle game features dog-themed power ups (tricks) and interactive shopping for both gameplay upgrades and nifty customizations. Designed to appeal to women 35 and older and people who love dogs, the game will have a conventional empty-the-cup gameplay mechanic, with unique dog-themed elements based on the standard repertoire of dog tricks.

Roll over, for example, a typical power-up, will be available to the player once she has trained her dog to perform the trick. He tires easily, so she may only ask him to perform a trick n times in any given round. When she calls the rollover trick, the dog chips of one color all roll, side over side, into grouped sets and, of course, pop out of the puzzle, clearing a large chunk of the board.

The player will have the opportunity to spend the points earned, represented as cash, on a variety of in-game power-ups and customizations. She will do this at the store. The store will display the available items for purchase as icons on a shelf and will include a pop-out detail display of additional text-based information about each item and its uses.

If the player chooses a customization, she will be able to view her dog in a pop-out window. This window will show the dog and then show the dog with the customization. As the player wins rounds, she will acquire ribbons from the various shows that she's won. As she wins sets (groups of 10) ribbons, she will be awarded dogs at the milestones. A progress map will include miniature dots to represent the ribbons and images of the first several dogs that may be earned. Dogs at the higher levels will be either silhouettes or shadows with question marks to encourage anticipation about what sort of prizes might await. These locks will be absolute in demo mode and will only open up completely after the player has upgraded the game.

There will also be locks on certain shopping items that are triggered by high scores and are disabled in the demo version of the game.

TREATMENT

Title: *Abbie's Best in Show*

Author: Allen Partridge. Contributions by Michael Link and Mary Partridge.

Studio: Insight Interactive Games. Creators of *Word Whacky* and *Podz*. Distribution experience with Oberon Media and Reflexive Arcade.

Genre: Puzzle

Audience: The target demographic for the game is women, 35+, with a definite sense that the appeal will remain extremely broad both because of widespread popularity of this type of puzzle and the widespread love people have for pets (especially dogs.)

Related Products/Description: Match-three meets simulated shopping meets dog show in this exciting puzzle game for every audience. The addictive qualities of a match-three puzzle are seamlessly infused with a bit of shopping simulation under the theme of dog shows to create an extremely marketable match-three variant that will have women and families alike howling for more.

Platform: Produced in Adobe Flash and Director, this game will be compatible with Windows 98+, Mac OS9+, and even Unix/Linux computers with a Flash plugin. Our initial target is PCs, but we may migrate the game to PDAs and cell phones, given the ease of transition to the additional platforms.

Walk-Through: The experience begins. Insight Interactive Games fades in, and after the usual musical sting, an adorable mid-sized dog barks a greeting. The main logo

→

morphs into a puppy with a text subtitle, "Gone To the Dogs." A distributor logo fades in and out. *Best in Show* titles slide in, and our heroine appears in a particle burst of puppy paws and sparkles. She introduces each launch option verbally as they slide onto the main title launch screen. Because this is our first play experience, a pop-up window asks for our name and we type it into the dialog. The name gathering bubble doesn't disappear; it shrinks and hinges itself to the side of the interface, clearly visible for later. It now reads, "Welcome to the show, *Player*." This is followed by, "If you are not *Player*, click here."

We select Play from the list of available options and immediately the launch screen fades and the puzzle cup screen appears. We encounter a simple but very attractive screen where our heroine is still our guide on the side. She immediately explains via text bubble that we must move one pup chip to make a match set of three or more. She even asks us to move one at a time in order to fully grasp the concept. Her help bubbles include an option to disable help, but for now we indulge her assistance.

Following our heroine's instructions, we switch the two dog tokens and create a match of three. The three matching dog tokens sparkle and then swell while sliding to the side of the screen. They drop neatly into a rack of faded dog tokens covered by numbers that change from 0/3 to 1/3 after the tiles land in the rack. The faded dog token grows 1/3 more opaque. A $5 cash token appears and flies toward the bank/points display. Approving crowd noises remind us that we've done well, and we are left to ponder our next move. Still a bit confused, and several seconds pass with no choice being made on our part. Particles begin to sparkle near a token that could be moved to make a match, and the dog on the suspect token barks as its token swells and shrinks in synch with the hint.

If we waited another 20 seconds our heroine would pop up yet another help tip to explain that this was a hint and that you could switch the tokens like this to make a match.

$\rightarrow$

We are not quite that confused, however, having understood the general concept the first time. We switch the hinted token into its proper position and then begin the search for another. This time we find a really good one. When switched, it creates a match set of four. The particles twinkle, tokens fade, and the cash icon indicates that $10 will be added to the bank. A dog biscuit falls into one of the replaced empty positions. The biscuit is colored to match the background of one of the dog chips. Our hostess pops up a text bubble explaining that we should match the colored biscuit with the dog tokens of the same color.

When we finally score that match with the dog biscuit, all the dogs of that color are removed from the board and we are awarded $100 in addition to the prize money for the match. Once we've made three matches of each variety of dog token, the round is complete. A timer that reads "Time to next show" has been ticking down the entire time. Thank goodness we finished before time ran out. If we hadn't, we would have forfeited our profits and been forced to restart the round.

The cup-filling play screen fades in a blur of enthusiastic cheers and puppy feet particles, and the progress map appears. A pop-up window reveals our ribbon for the round along with statistics about the session. We click to close the window, and the ribbon flies off the pop up and plants itself on the progress map in the first spot. If we want to return to that round at any point in the future, we only need to click on the ribbon and we'll be returned to the round.

The game remembers our high score for each round, so we can return to improve our record in any round at any time. A button on the progress map allows us to move on and play the next round as well. We start the game already owning one dog. After every nine rounds, we play a bonus round for which we will be awarded a new dog. Grey images of the first several dogs will appear on the launch screen followed by mystery icons to let the player feel the desire to

$\rightarrow$

obtain the more advanced dogs. Dog owners may shop for power-ups (in the form of training dogs to do tricks that aid game play) or for dog treats (give dogs more endurance to perform more tricks) or for dog clothing. These are customizations that are purely for the amusement of the player and don't contribute to the game play experience.

Gameplay and Rules

1. Player selects a token and then any adjoining token (up, down, left, or right) to swap that token.
2. The swap must result in a matched set of three or more.
3. Failed matches will be reset.
4. Successful matches yield points.
5. Match three = 5$, four = 10$ and five = 25$.
6. Match five earns a power-up.
7. Money earned may be spent on power-ups and customization.
8. Rounds are repeatable.
9. High score per player per round is tracked.
10. Cumulative high score per player (all round high scores) is also tracked.

Environment: The primary game environment is a clearly devised interface, consisting only of dog-show–themed decoration and specific game tokens and player tools. The secondary game environment is a pet shop, with shelves of products represented as tokens.

The remaining game environment is a virtual showroom, where players may view their dogs. Only one dog may be viewed at a time. Dogs are minimally animated and can model custom outfits in this window. The player may choose to change which dog is in the viewer by selecting a different dog from the menu. Players are also given the opportunity to name their dogs or accept the default names.

$\rightarrow$

Characters: Each of the dogs in the game has a unique personality, but the central character in the game is Abbie. She hosts the game and provides guidance and instruction to players as they uncover the many treasures. She will handle the sales of merchandise and is a constant companion through the player's experience. Abbie is a middle-aged woman, slim, and statuesque. She is a dog show judge and owns a family pet store. She's bubbly and sometimes silly and, above all, enthusiastic about this game.

Tokens: The primary tokens in the game are the chips in the cup that must be matched in order to make sets. There are initially six of these tokens. More appear as new breeds of dogs become available. Each token features the image of a dog and has a solid-color background. The tokens may be thought of as colored tokens, except for the images of dogs. In one potential complication, the colors of the backgrounds may change, and the player might be asked to match the dogs, ignoring color, or may be asked to match color, ignoring dog breed. Perhaps extra points could be earned for creating match sets of both color and breed.

Chrome: The game has a slightly sophisticated look. Colors are a bit subdued but very appealing. It is designed to appeal to women but not put off men and children. It feels a bit high brow, like a dog show, but also feels common, largely because of the dogs. A concept image (Figure 3.6) shows the color palette and an early version of Abbie.

FIGURE 3.6   A design sketch for *Abbie's Best in Show*.

Legal: All of the images and sounds in the game are the property of Insight Interactive Games. No third-party materials (other than those for which permission has been acquired) are included in the game.

STORYBOARD/FLOW DIAGRAM

The flow diagram demonstrates the basic player controls and gives a sense of the total media required for the game (Figure 3.7). It forms a kind of button map for usability and can help coordinate exactly what information needs to be stored in what fashion.

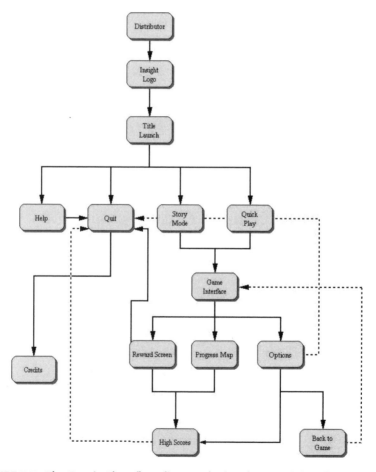

FIGURE 3.7 The *Best in Show* flow diagram depicts the game's interface structure.

INTERACTION MATRIX

There isn't much need for an interaction matrix in this case, as the puzzle pieces interact in a manner that is sort of atypical. Rather than evaluating the interaction of nonmatched pairs, you generally evaluate the interaction of matched pairs. There are some interactions between power-ups and like-colored treats, but this also is a fairly basic logical function.

HANDLING MINIMAL INTERACTIONS WITH MINIMAL PROGRAMMING

Once the game is designed and it is clear that interactions will be minimal, the task of creating the game may begin. If we had chosen to create a navigation game, there might be no need for programming anything more complex than dragging prebuilt scripts onto the time line. In the case of this match-three game, the programming will be slightly more complex, but still not very in-depth. In Chapter 1 we covered the basic code involved in creating the matching game itself. The rest of the proposed game involves navigation from one point to another in the time line. The initial screen displays the company logo, and then we see the game's title screen. Then buttons are pressed to move us to the match-three area of the game. In the next activity we'll walk through the basic steps involved in creating and programming the movement from one area of the time line to another area of the time line in Flash.

PROJECT 2:   **SIMPLE NAVIGATION WITH MINIMAL PROGRAMMING**

The basic navigation in *Best in Show* is simple. Just play through opening screens and then provide a choice of several options on the launch screen. In this activity, we'll mock-up the basic navigation for the game using placeholders for the art.

STEP ONE: MOCK-UP SOME PLACEHOLDER IMAGES

We know what the opening sequence of the game is like, because it was described to us in the treatment. With that information in hand, you can start by creating a placeholder for the company logo. There is a copy of the finished version of this exercise on the companion CD-ROM in the Tutorial\ch03media folder. The file is named bestInShowNavigation.fla.

ON THE CD

1. Use the Text tool in Flash to put your company name on the screen.
2. When you finish typing, press F8 to convert the text to a symbol.
3. Choose the Graphic radio button.
4. To create a shadow, copy your text and create a new layer. Paste the copy into the new layer (Figure 3.8). In Flash you can simply drag the layer to a new position in the time line.

NOTE

It is important to note that in Adobe Flash, layers are stacked in the time line just as they are on the stage. This means things in the top layer of the time line will also be on the top layer of the stage. Your shadow should fall below your title, so you will want to place it in a layer that is beneath your initial layer on the time line. This is the opposite of Adobe Director, which places items in the time line (called a score in Director) in reverse order. In Director, items at the top of the time line appear on the bottom of the stack on screen.

FIGURE 3.8 Place a darkened copy of the name on a second layer.

5. Select the instance of the title symbol that is in the bottom layer.
6. Note that the Property inspector now shows options to manipulate the display properties of this instance of the symbol.

This is a perfect example of the joys of creating multiple instances of sprites from the same resource file or original media. The symbol in the library remains constant. It does not need to change appearance, but the bottom instance on the screen would be more useful to us as a shadow. Therefore, we alter the properties of this display instance only and use both instances of the same resource differently in the project.

7. Adjust the color property for this instance of the symbol to set the tint at about 50% (Figure 3.9).

FIGURE 3.9 Set the tint color property to approximately 50%.

Step Two: Set Up the Time Line for the Opening Fade

With the basic images in place, we are ready to fade the image in and back out again. In this step you will add keyframes to the time line. The keyframes determine what the screen will look like at that moment in time. The computer will interpolate or slowly transition between one look (or state) and another set by these key frames.

> The concept of *keyframes* comes from *cell animation*. Cell animation is the early process of 2D animation that involved painting illustrations of characters on clear plastic cells that were filmed against still backgrounds. In this process animators would draw the character at significant, or key positions, and then skilled copyists would draw the same characters in all of the positions in between. These copyists were often called inbetweeners or tweeners. The process of rendering the interim states between the critical animation moments became known as *tweening,* and the bit between keyframes is today called a *tween.* Computers have long since taken the place of the original copyists.

1. Create a new keyframe in your Flash time line for each of the layers that contain an instance of your company name. Select frame 30, right-click the mouse, and choose Insert Keyframe (Figure 3.10). Select frame 70, right-click the mouse, and choose Insert Keyframe. Doing this twice will make the words stay for a little while.
2. Move the playback head (the red rectangle on the top of the score) to the first frame of your Flash time line. Be sure you are working with the instance at the first frame, not on one of the later ones.
3. Select the front instance of the title.
4. Note that the color properties appear in the Property inspector for this symbol. Change the color to alpha and the value to 0%. The sprite will disappear.

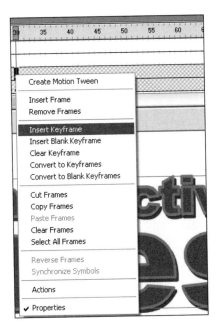

FIGURE 3.10 Create new keyframes on frame 30 of the back and front layers.

The concept of color on computer screens is a bit different than it is in the pigments we see and work with in the natural world. The color scheme for most objects on the computer is divided into four basic color components: red, green, blue, and alpha. This is often called an rgba color palette. The basic colors may seem strange, but they are just the base colors in light. We are used to red, blue, and yellow as base colors in pigment. The last one, alpha, is a value reserved for visible levels of opacity. Many things on a computer screen are carefully layered. The edges of those layers are often not simple shapes, but gradual blends of varying levels of transparency.

5. Repeat steps 3 and 4 for the back (shadow) instance (Figure 3.11).

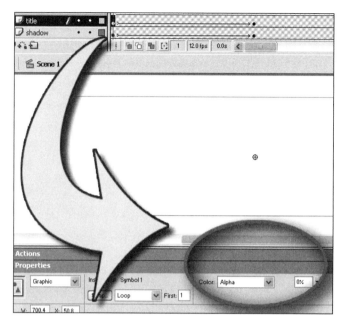

FIGURE 3.11 Set alpha to zero for both instances of the title in the initial keyframe.

6. In Flash interpolation is not automatic. You need to specifically tell a sprite to tween between one keyframe and the next. You can do this by right-clicking in the open space between the first two keyframes of a layer and choosing Create Motion Tween. Do this to create motion tweens for both the front and back layers.

7. If you scrub the time line, you will now see the company logo blend in from nothing to fully visible.

The phrase "scrub the time line" is used to describe the process of moving the playback head (the little red rectangle at the top of the time line) back and forth across the frames in order to observe the result. The term comes from early video, where editors would turn a knob on an editing deck slowly backward and forward to check for small dropouts in the signal on the videotape.

8. Next create another keyframe in frame 120 of each layer. Right-click and choose Insert Keyframe in both the front and back layers.
9. To fade the logo out, we'll set the alpha of each instance to 0% at this point on the time line as well.
10. Right-click the middle of each layer sprite between the frame 70 and frame 120 keyframes and choose Create Motion Tween.

You may notice that a black arrow appears on the sprite layer when you insert a motion tween. In some cases this operation will fail, and the arrow will appear with a dotted line rather than a solid black shaft. Only certain types of data can have motion tweens applied. If you find that you're staring at dotted motion tweens, try converting your on-screen objects to symbols first, then apply the motion tween. You can remove a motion tween using the right-click (context) menu.

When you scrub the time line now you should see the company name appear from nothing and then fade out. Our next task is to add a little sound to accent the company slate.

STEP THREE: ADD A SOUND TO THE TIME LINE

In this step we will import a sound file and then add it to the stage at the beginning of the timeline.

1. Choose File: Import to Library from the drop-down menu at the top of the Flash interface.
2. From the dialog that appears, choose a sound file (any *.wav file will do).
3. The sound asset will appear in your Flash Library. You can view the library by pressing the F11 key (Figure 3.12).
4. Add a new layer to the time line. This will be used for the sound.
5. Click on the first cell of the new layer and then drag the sound from the library onto the stage. You will see the sound appear in the layer on the time line (Figure 3.13).
6. Press Ctrl-Enter to test the Flash movie and preview your work thus far.

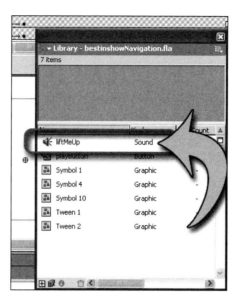

FIGURE 3.12 The sound appears in the Flash Library.

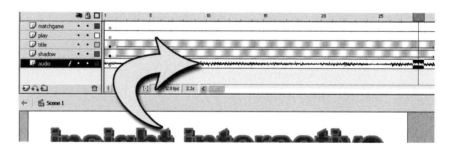

FIGURE 3.13 The waveform appears in the layer when you drop the sound on the stage.

STEP FOUR: TRANSITION TO THE GAME TITLE SCREEN

During this step you will create an animated transition from the main game title screen to the launch page. In step 5 you will use the basic script we provided earlier in the chapter to navigate from the launch page to another page.

1. Click on frame 121 (the first frame after your sprite ends) in the first layer.
2. Right-click and choose Insert Blank Keyframe to create a new empty keyframe.
3. Click on frame 210 in the first layer.
4. Right-click and choose Insert Frame to extend the sprite across the entire range of frames (note that this layer is still blank, so it will appear white, rather than blue).
5. Click on the initial keyframe and create a text block that contains the title of your game.
6. Select the text element and press the F8 key to convert it to a symbol (graphic).
7. Select frame 160 and then right-click. Choose Insert Keyframe from the list of options.
8. Move the playback head back to frame 121 and reselect the text symbol.
9. In the Property inspector change the color property to alpha and drop the level to 0%. This will cause the text to fade in.
10. Select the layer sprite on the time line between frames 121 and 160 and right-click. Choose Create Motion Tween.
11. Select frame 210 of the first layer and then right-click. Choose Insert Keyframe from the Context menu.
12. Select the text symbol on the screen. Resize the onscreen instance and move it to the upper right corner of the stage. *Note that you must not double-click the symbol. You want to work with the instance on the stage, not edit the symbol itself.*
13. Now select the layer in the time line between frames 160 and 210. Right-click and choose Create Motion Tween to make the final motion tween.

Tweens are used to interpolate between various states for various objects. Motion tweens will work for many different types of on-screen changes. Earlier we used motion tween to fade an object in. Here it is used to change the position and size of the object.

When you finish, press Ctrl-Enter to test your project in Flash. You should find that your company logo fades in and then out again. Then your game title fades in, shrinks, and moves off to one side.

STEP FIVE: TRANSITION TO THE LAUNCH SCREEN

In this step we will create a new layer, add an instance of a button to that layer, and then add a script to the button so that pressing the button will take the player to a new position in the time line. We will name a position in the time line and then add a couple of basic stop() scripts to halt the playback in a given position.

1. Press the Create Layer button in the time line window to create a new layer. Select frame 211 in the new layer and right-click. Choose Insert Blank Keyframe from the context menu.
2. Move to frame 275 in the same layer and right-click. Choose Insert Frame from the context menu.
3. Select the keyframe in frame 211 and then draw a small rectangle on the stage.
4. Double-click the rectangle and press the F8 key to open the convert to symbol dialog box.
5. Choose the Button option and then convert the shape.
6. In the Action Editor (under the script for the button) type the script in Listing 3.3.

LISTING 3.3   Code for the Play Button

```
on (release){
  goToAndPlay("matchThree");
}
```

7. In the title layer, select frame 211 and right-click. Choose Insert Keyframe from the context menu.
8. Move to frame 275 in the title layer and insert another keyframe. Right-click and select Insert Keyframe. This will copy the title onto this area of the time line.
9. Add one more layer. This layer will hold the match-game placeholder. Select frame 276 in the match-game layer and

right-click. Choose Insert Blank Keyframe from the context menu.

10. In the Property inspector name the frame matchThree. We'll use this label later to jump directly to this section of the time line.

11. Use the text tool to type "match game" on the stage.

12. Select the stage and open the Actions Editor. [The drop-down menu at the top of the Action Editor should read "Actions for Frame 276 (Labeled matchThree) of Layer . . ."].

13. In the editing window of the Actions Editor type the stop(); command.

14. We also need the playback head to stop at frame 275. You can arrange this by selecting the keyframe in the Play button channel at frame 275. Then choose the "Actions for Frame 275 . . ." script and type the same stop(); command in the script editor.

15. Press Ctrl-Enter to test your finished work. When you are done, save the movie and quit the application. ✄

SUMMARY

The decision to base an application on a Flash engine with minimal programming is generally rooted in a desire to tap the vast power of the Flash development environment, but it can turn out badly because of the limitations of the Flash engine. If you are beginning to consider developing a game in this arena because you believe that it will be easy, slow down and think carefully.

There are a couple of dominating misconceptions in life that people accept without question. The first is the misconception that they cannot draw or have no artistic ability. The second is that they cannot program a computer or have no mathematical or logical aptitude. Both of these assumptions are silly, and they defy thousands of years worth of evidence that all people possess fundamental creative and logical aptitudes. Without them, you wouldn't be able to write or comprehend written material. You wouldn't be able to count your change at a store without logic, nor would you be able to make reasoned decisions about everyday things.

Just figuring out who to pick up from what location first on a routine family roundup or picking a color to paint your kitchen are logical and creative acts. People think they aren't artistic, because they haven't *practiced* seeing things and manipulating visual artifacts and they aren't familiar with the language used by artists to describe visual phenomena. People think they cannot program a computer because they haven't *practiced* programming and are unfamiliar with the language used by programmers to describe logical things.

Barring brain damage, you are capable of separating effective images from ineffective ones, and you are capable of working through the logical problems involved in creating a typical casual game. You just need practice to move from capable to competent. How much practice you need depends on how much you've practiced working with images and logic in the past and how easily these concepts come to you. Substantial practice will eventually trump even significant talent and natural ability, but if you are in a hurry and lack the natural blessings, working with talented people can be an amazing time-saver.

In the end, deciding to develop with minimal programming may seem like a wise move if you doubt your ability to generate large volumes of code, but you will probably find that you need considerably more code than you initially imagined and that there are significant obstacles to producing a Flash-powered commercial application.

4 Code Till You Drop

In This Chapter

■ Developing a Heavily Coded Game in Director
■ Project 1: Using MagicRes to Reset the Screen Resolution
■ Fundamental Programming Concepts
■ Project 2: Add Game Subroutines and Content
■ Designing an Architecture
■ Project 3: A Simple Approach to Save and Load

Take a deep breath, remain calm, and above all do not panic. You can get a free demo of Adobe Director from the Adobe Web site to work with the examples in this chapter. In this chapter you'll walk through all of the major steps necessary to produce and finish your casual game. You'll learn about Adobe Director and the power it can add to the development process, as well as its limitations. Packaging and finishing techniques such as creating custom icons and generating your own setup installers are described and demonstrated, as well as fundamental game architecture approaches.

Screen resolution resetting is demonstrated. You'll see an example of these practices used in commercial casual games. Interaction hierarchy and game logic are demonstrated, and you'll get advice on optimization and common programming pitfalls. You'll learn code-based approaches to saving and loading user statistics and preferences and practice creating code that performs these basic functions.

In this chapter you will learn:

■ How to implement your casual game with Adobe Director
■ Packaging and finishing techniques
■ Advantages and disadvantages of third-party engines
■ How to make custom icons, set up installers, and manipulate the client system
■ Architecture traditions and implementations for games
■ Using objects to optimize code
■ How to avoid common programming mistakes

DEVELOPING A HEAVILY CODED GAME IN DIRECTOR

Adobe Director (formerly Macromedia Director) is the longest-lived, most powerful multimedia engine available to casual game developers today. The engine is a core player, capable of playing back media of virtually any type on either Windows or Macintosh operating systems. The major advantage of using the Director engine is that common functions such as displaying text and managing memory are handled automatically, and the amount of programming required to perform basic functions is greatly reduced.

A good developer with experience programming in both C++ and Director's language, *Lingo*, will be able to produce the same application using Director's engine about five to ten times faster than if they used C++ and libraries. What makes Director infinitely more powerful than Flash or virtually any other multimedia engine is that Director is *runtime extensible*. That means that if there is a media type that Director doesn't already understand natively, or a function that a developer would like to add, the developer can simply build the extra functionality into a dynamic link library-like module called an xtra that can be added to Director.

The limitation of engines like Director is that developers are limited by the release schedule and repair priorities of the engine developer. If Adobe were to refuse to update the core engine or change the current licensing policy (which requires no additional fees for use of the engine in commercial applications), then developers would suffer an enormous hardship.

In this section the use of Director to publish and finish a casual game is described. This is a common choice for casual game developers, for the reasons mentioned above, and it is a good way to learn the basic principles quickly, because you won't get so bogged down in the details of memory management and data types that you can't see the forest for the trees.

| PROJECT 1: | USING MAGICRES TO RESET THE SCREEN RESOLUTION |

Once you have installed Director, you'll need to add a copy of the Meliora magicRes xtra in the configuration xtras folder before you launch the application. You'll find a copy of the Meliora magicRes xtra on the companion CD-ROM in the Demos folder. To add an xtra to Director, browse to the directory on your computer where you installed the application (Figure 4.1). Save the MT xtras folder in the xtras folder.

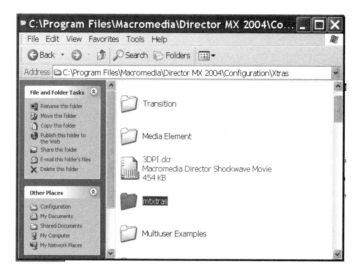

FIGURE 4.1   Save the Magic Res xtra to your xtras folder.

Once you have added the xtra to the configuration: xtras directory, open Adobe Director and create a new blank file. From the Modify menu, choose Modify: Movie: Xtras and choose the Add button (Figure 4.2).

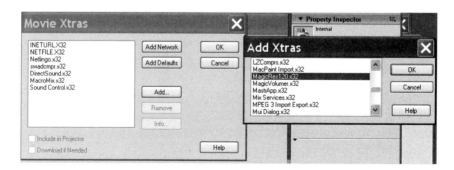

FIGURE 4.2   Add the magicRes xtra to your available xtras.

The magicRes xtra is used to reset the client computer (the one that hosts your game) screen resolution to a different size. The first thing your application will need to do is change the screen resolution of the host computer to the size of your game. Most games today are designed at 800 pixels wide and 600 pixels high. It is customary to change the screen resolution to fit your game's screen size.

To change the screen resolution using the magicRes xtra, you will want to add the following code to your Director project, in a movie script.

1. Open a script window and make certain the script type is set to the movie type in the Property inspector (Figure 4.3).
2. Add the `startMovie()` and `stopMovie()` event handlers to the script. (Make certain the script type is set to movie, as seen in the Property inspector to the right in Figure 4.3.)

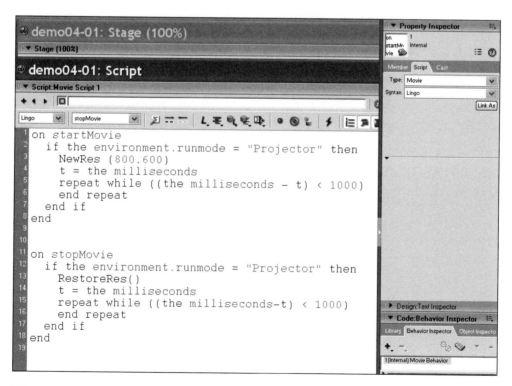

FIGURE 4.3   Open a script editor (movie).

3. Type the script into the window as shown in the illustration. (Note that hogging the processor in a closed loop for one second is not really good programming practice. This is done in this way to ensure that nothing is on the screen as the application loads.) This script will only be executed if the engine is in the executable version (running as self-contained software) indicated by the environment.runmode property. The runmode will be "Author" when you are working in the authoring environment, so you will need to make some standalone software in order to test your screen reset.

4. To create the standalone software, choose: File: Publish Settings (Figure 4.4). Make certain you create an *.exe executable for a PC and check the box at the bottom to preview. Then press the Publish button. Watch closely because the application will quickly launch, resize the screen, reset the screen resolution, and then close. (The application doesn't do anything other than reset the screen resolution and close.)

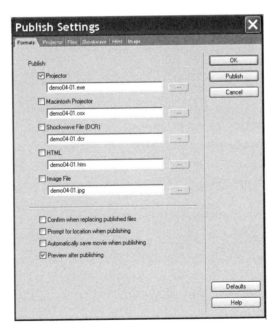

FIGURE 4.4   Create an executable and preview the results.

If you have any trouble, you can open the sample application, demo04-01.dir, in a copy of Director to see the sample and code. Note that the magicRes xtra is for PCs, so if you are using a Macintosh, you won't be able to use this method. ✄

FUNDAMENTAL PROGRAMMING CONCEPTS

It isn't really difficult to program a game, but it does require a significant amount of time and perseverance. It doesn't really matter whether you are working with a code library, third-party engine, or development environment; some fundamental concepts will help guide you to success. Even if you don't plan to program yourself, you'll understand the work of programmers a good deal better if you can master these basic foundations of programming: *assignment, sequence, events, lists,* and *objects.* There are a lot of other concepts, but these tend to be the hardest for people to understand.

VARIABLE ASSIGNMENT

In assignment, you let a container, called a variable, represent some other thing, such as a number. Whenever a game implementation is discussed, the strategies and methods of programming are generally of considerable interest to developers. Unfortunately, it is also common for readers to find programming examples one of the most difficult things to comprehend and translate into action that they can adopt in their own work. To help readers who have had little or no prior experience with computer programming, some examples of these basic, universal programming concepts are included.

What is the value of x in Table 4.1? How about y? Most programmers would easily say that both x and y equal 2. People with no programming experience are often very puzzled by this question. They might even say, "Where's the question?" That problem demonstrates one absolutely essential skill for game programmers: variable assignment. In variable assignment a value (such as a number, a word, or maybe even a digital image of a cow) is assigned to a container, or reference, called a variable.

TABLE 4.1   Variable Assignment

x = 1
y = 2
x = y

Container is a good word for a variable because it's easy to imagine how a container called "color" could hold something, #blue, for example. It's also easy to understand that the container could hold #green or #yellow or #red.

In the variable assignment exercise the container called x is assigned (that's what equals [=] does) to hold the number 1. Then the container called y is assigned to hold the number 2. Finally, on line 3 of the exercise the container named x is assigned to . . . what value? Well, whatever value is currently held inside the container named y. In this case the value is 2.

> Just like different languages use different words to say hello or thank you, different computer languages use different operators to assign values to variables. Many have very specific rules about what kind of information (such as a number or an image) can be assigned to a given variable.

Understanding this variable assignment makes understanding programming in most computer languages much easier. Look at the first line of the exercise again in several computer programming languages (Table 4.2).

Experienced programmers should note that this discussion of assignment is deliberately simplified for the beginner.

NOTE

Basically each of the examples in Table 4.2 is the same. They all assign the number 1 to the variable named x. You probably noticed semicolons at the end of some examples. Some languages need a special character to end a line of code. The semicolon is usually used for this. Some of the examples add a word before the variable name. This process, called *declaration* is used to create a *new* variable in some languages. In JavaScript and Flash ActionScript this declaration word is *var*, short for variable. In C++ many declaration words exist. There is one for each *type* of data that goes into the container. Think of it as flour, sugar, and coffee jars. You wouldn't put sugar in the coffee jar, would you? In some languages you only put one type of data in a particular variable. In others, such as Lingo for Adobe Director, you can put any kind of data into your variables.

TABLE 4.2   Variable Assignment in Several Common Languages

Lingo for Adobe Director (Shockwave)	x = 1
ActionScript for Adobe Flash	var x:Number = 1;
C++	int x = 1;

SEQUENCE

Another fundamental and universal concept that often trips up beginners is the *sequence*, or order, in which the computer performs each task. Now in the first example each line is executed in order from top to bottom. This method is called consecutive. Some scripts (groups of commands for the computer) are executed as soon as your game starts, one command after the other, using this *consecutive sequence*. They are usually things that only need to happen once, such as checking for a license or resizing the screen. The script in Figure 4.3 uses variable assignment and consecutive sequence in just this way to resize the screen when the software starts.

The problem with this consecutive approach is that most of the time you will want to be able to perform a task for your game more than once. Imagine, for example, that you reset the player's volume when you start the game. You want the player to have easy volume control. You might even want your software to remember what the player's volume preferences were, so setting the volume becomes more than a one-time command. It's a complex task (requiring several lines of programming to do things such as set and get player preferences) that will likely happen many times and at unpredictable intervals.

For this challenge, a consecutive sequence would be bad. You want to isolate the commands that make the volume adjustment from the rest of the start-up sequence. That way you could execute that function while starting up your game as well as any other time the player wants to change the volume. In the next example the code for the match-three puzzle game is added to the basic screen-resetting application. Code for routine and repeating functions is divided up into smaller blocks of frequently called functions and handlers.

EVENTS

Just as the name implies, *events* are things that happen. In games the computer must be given very specific instructions about how to respond if an event occurs. Computers will only perform the requested operations if the exact event occurs and if the programmer has created a subset or grouping of code that is assigned to be performed when the event occurs. This cluster of *commands* (things the computer should do) is called an *event handler,* because it handles the computer's response to a given event.

> The term *handler* is short for *event handler.* An event handler responds to a call from the system or from other code that some event (generally triggered by user interaction) has occurred. This can include things like a key press or mouse click as well as things like system time-related events. The term *function* is generally used to refer to code that performs some service or calculation. Functions usually return a value or a result. For example, there is a subroutine in the match-three demo program that returns a grid value for a cell called indexToGrid().

This sort of decoupling, or separating, of subroutines in programming can be done a few different ways (subroutines are sometimes called *methods, handlers,* or *functions*). You can create a block of code.

This block of code can be given a name (which becomes its container, just like the variables). The block of code may then be activated by calling the name in another procedure. Most games, however, are *event-driven* and rely on user interaction to trigger these blocks of code.

In Problem 2 you will create several of these subroutines within an Adobe Director Movie script. This is a public (or open to anything) script that serves as a central library of subroutines.

PROJECT 2:   ADD GAME SUBROUTINES AND CONTENT

ON THE CD

1. Open the demonstration application demo04-02complete. dir located in the ch04media folder in the tutorials directory using Adobe Director. Rewind and press Play to observe the basic functions of the game in its current state. This is the complete and functional version of this exercise that you may use to compare your results.
2. Open the demonstration application demo04-02incomplete.dir using Adobe Director.
3. Open the Script Editor, Window: Script (Figure 4.5). Set the Script Type to Movie.

There are four subsets of code in this script. The first is triggered by a time-out object, which is a way of creating an event that will occur at some regular or predictable interval (such as once a minute or every 5 seconds). The second chunk of code looks for matches in the table, based on potential moves. In other words, it simulates the movement of one cell in any legal direction and then reports the existence of viable matches for various purposes. Most notably, it is used to create the auto-hinting feature, so that a player who cannot see an available move can be given a hint about the position of such a move. This function is called by the time-out event, generated by the time-out object from the first handler.

The two remaining chunks of code are subcommands called by the potential match-finding handler. They are broken out on their own, because they contain logic that is called repeatedly, and it saves space not to type the same commands over and over many times.

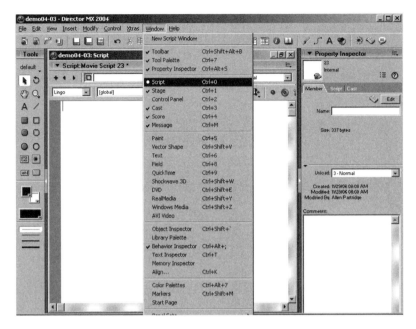

FIGURE 4.5   Open the Script Editor.

1. Type the first handler into the script editor exactly as it appears in Listing 4.1.

LISTING 4.1   The Time-Out Constructor

```
global gTable, gCols, gRows

on potentialMatch()
  timeout("inactive").forget()
  subPMatch(1)
end
```

The global declarations at the top of the handler are simply there to simplify access to the table of cell types. In some languages code can be triggered sequentially without falling inside a specific handler. In Adobe Director's *Lingo* all code except global and property variable declaration must fall within a specific handler. In Director those handlers all start with the word *on* and end with the word *end*, so a prototypical handler would look like the pseudocode in Listing 4.2.

LISTING 4.2   Pseudocode for a Handler

```
on eventOrCustomCommandName()
      command()
end
```

The command in Listing 4.1 is called by a time-out event. The event is set to trigger after 30 seconds of user inaction, specifically if there is no mouse event for 30 seconds. That translates to the player not finding a valid match for 30 seconds, so it means a hint will be triggered every time the player fails to find a match in 30 seconds. The code in this handler first destroys the time-out object. If it didn't, the time-out would fire again 30 seconds later. Then the handler simply triggers the next handler, which checks potential matches if a single tile is slid into a new position.

1. Type the code in Listings 4.3, 4.4, and 4.5 into the script window exactly as it is written. Note that the handler is split up into three parts to provide explanations of the code as you work.

LISTING 4.3   Code for Checking the Potential Matches

```
on subPMatch(flag)
  matchList = []
  repeat with a = 1 to (gCols * gRows)
    -- for each cell
    grid = indexToGrid(a)
    if grid[2] > 1 then
      if grid[1] > 1 then -- not in the left row
        tTable = gTable.duplicate()
        tType = tTable[grid[1]][grid[2]]
        tTypeSwitch = tTable[(grid[1]-1)][grid[2]]
        tTable[grid[1]][grid[2]] = tTypeSwitch
        tTable[(grid[1]-1)][grid[2]] = tType
        match = evaluateMatches (grid, tTable)
        b = gridToIndex([(grid[1]-1), grid[2]])
        if flag then
          if match then
```

```
          matchList.add([a,b])
      end if
  else
     if match then RETURN 1
  end if
end if
```

The first chunk of code in Listing 4.3 is called by the time-out event to generate hints and by another handler to make certain the table has a potential match. If there were no potential match combinations, the game would be broken. The call to check for potential matches for a broken table is more optimized, so it sends an argument to the handler that forces some optimization.

The first command in the handler creates a new list called `matchlist`. In Director a list is created by assigning the variable name to a set of straight braces like these: `[]`. Items in the list are separated by commas. Things may be added to the list using the `add()` command.

The next command tells the system to repeat the following commands a given number of times. In some languages a repeat loop is called a *for-loop*. The command tells the system to repeat a set of commands but also gives a variable or *iter* (short for iteration, meaning a number that is counting up or down, usually by one). In this case the variable *a* will represent numbers 1 – *n*, where *n* = the total number of cells in the table. It may seem odd that we don't just say 81 cells or some other number, but one of the features of the game is that the table can grow larger or smaller based on the difficulty. This way the number of cells remains dynamic.

The next command, `grid = indexToGrid(a)`, is a function that returns the `[x,y]` position of the cell and stores it in the variable named grid. The `[x,y]` value is a list, so we can request a value from the list by using the syntax `listname[indexNumber]`. This is the same as saying, "Hey, give me the *n*th item in that list please." So in practical terms the conditional statement `if grid[2] > 1` is the same as saying, "If the current cell in the table is not in the top most column." To simulate the movement of tiles, we will go through each cell and figure out what would happen if we moved it left, right, up, or down. Unfortunately, some cells can't move in some directions. This is the case with the cells in the left-most column, the right-most column, the top two rows, and the bottom row.

The next command, `tTable = gTable.duplicate()`, makes a copy of the table list. The difference between a reference or pointer to something and a copy or duplicate of something often confuses new programmers. When you assign a variable to another variable that contains a list, you are creating a pointer or reference to the first list, not making a copy of the initial list. That means that if you changed a list value using either reference, you'd get the same change in the one list that now has two variables pointing to it. They are both pointing to the same list, not each pointing to their own unique copy of the list.

To copy a list, you must specifically duplicate that list with the `duplicate()` command. In this case we don't want to mess up the actual table of values; we want to tinker with a simulated table that shows us what would happen if certain moves were made.

The four commands that follow make the switch between the cell and the one to the left in the duplicate table. After that, the command `match = evaluateMatches (grid, tTable)` calls the primary subroutine to evaluate the potential match.

Finally, the conditional statements either return the value 1, indicating the presence of a match in the optimized form, or the match itself is added to a list of matches. The list is generated so that the hints will not always appear in the same area of the table but will be randomly selected from all available matches on the board.

In Listing 4.4 the other conditions are evaluated: match to the right, match above, or match below. This code could be further optimized by stripping checks on cells that are found in matches already identified. In other words, this code gets all matches, even if a match is a reverse duplicate of a previous match. For example [5,6] and [6,5] would both be counted and calculated as matches in this implementation.

LISTING 4.4   The Potential Match Subroutine Continued

```
if grid[2] > 2 then -- not in the top(2) row
  tTable = gTable.duplicate()
  tType = tTable[grid[1]][grid[2]]
  tTypeSwitch = tTable[grid[1]][(grid[2]-1)]
  tTable[grid[1]][grid[2]] = tTypeSwitch
```

```
          tTable[grid[1]][(grid[2]-1)] = tType
          match = evaluateMatches (grid, tTable)
          b = gridToIndex([grid[1], (grid[2]-1)])
          if flag then
            if match then
              matchList.add([a,b])
            end if
          else
            if match then RETURN 1
          end if

      end if
      if grid[1] < gCols then -- not in the right row
        tTable = gTable.duplicate()
        tType = tTable[grid[1]][grid[2]]
        tTypeSwitch = tTable[grid[1]+1][grid[2]]
        tTable[grid[1]][grid[2]] = tTypeSwitch
        tTable[(grid[1]+1)][grid[2]] = tType
        match = evaluateMatches (grid, tTable)
        b = gridToIndex([(grid[1]+1), grid[2]])
        if flag then
          if match then
            matchList.add([a,b])
          end if
        else
          if match then RETURN 1
        end if

      end if
      if grid[2] < gRows then -- not in the bottom row
        tTable = gTable.duplicate()
        tType = tTable[grid[1]][grid[2]]
        tTypeSwitch = tTable[grid[1]][(grid[2]+1)]
        tTable[grid[1]][grid[2]] = tTypeSwitch
        tTable[grid[1]][(grid[2]+1)] = tType
        match = evaluateMatches (grid, tTable)
        b = gridToIndex([grid[1], (grid[2]+1)])
        if flag then
          if match then
            matchList.add([a,b])
```

```
         end if
      else
         if match then RETURN 1
      end if

   end if
 end if
end repeat
```

If the optimized algorithm was used, the successful match will already have been returned to the calling handler. This section of code is used for the hinting function to place the hinting sprite on the screen in the correct location and orientation to indicate the position and direction of a potential match (Listing 4.5).

A potential match is selected at random: `tIndex = random(tCt)` and `tMatch = matchlist[tIndex]`. The random function will return a random number between 1 and the total number of available matches. Then the actual match, a list of two numbers, is retrieved from the list.

The list is sorted so that the math will always return a positive value. Sorting a list puts the values in numerical order. The next conditional statement determines whether the match is horizontal or vertical. If the value of the subtraction is 1, the cells are vertically aligned, because the sprites are arranged in vertical rows. The value of horizontal matches would be equal to `gRows`. If the match is horizontal, the highlight sprite is horizontal, but if the match is vertical, the sprite is rotated 90 degrees. Finally, the sprite is positioned over the two cells that would make a match to hint at the match for the frustrated player.

LISTING 4.5   The Last Section of the Potential Match Subroutine

```
tCt = count(matchlist)
 if tCt > 0 then
   if NOT voidP(flag) then
     tIndex = random(tCt)
     tMatch = matchlist[tIndex]
     tMatch.sort()
     if tMatch[2] - tMatch[1] > 1 then
```

```
   -- horizontal match
   sprite(157).rotation = 0
   sprite(157).locV = sprite(tMatch[1]).locV
   split = sprite(tMatch[2]).locH -
   sprite(tMatch[1]).locH
   sprite(157).locH = sprite(tMatch[1]).locH +
   (split/2)
else
   sprite(157).rotation = 90
   sprite(157).locH = sprite(tMatch[1]).loch
   split = sprite(tMatch[2]).locV -
   sprite(tMatch[1]).locV
   sprite(157).locV = sprite(tMatch[1]).locV +
   (split/2)
  end if
 else
   RETURN tCt
 end if


else
  RETURN 0
 end if
end
```

The final two subsets of code have been left in the movie for your convenience. It doesn't matter that they are in a different script cast member, because they are globally available.

When you finish typing these scripts, save, rewind, and press Play. Your movie should now perform exactly as it did before.

LISTS

One thing that often surprises game developers is that virtually every game is ultimately a product of list manipulation. This is especially true with casual games. Every one of those tables or grids is generally the result of manipulating data in a table. In Adobe Director there are two different kinds of lists. *Linear Lists* are sequential lists of data that are separated by commas and contained by straight braces, such as `[1,2,3,4]`. *Property lists* are lists that contain both names and values in pairs separated by colons. A property list might look like `[#this:1, #that:2, #theOther:3]`. Both types of lists are very useful and can be used to rapidly access and store complex sets of information that help keep track of the current state of the game or even player preferences. The `gTable` in the demo match-three puzzle is a property list. It contains all of the type information for the tiles and is accessed frequently to determine the state of the game board.

It can be especially difficult at first to visualize how all of the code in these table manipulations works if you don't have a solid image of the table, the columns, the rows, and the cell indices. In Figure 4.6 these elements are presented visually to help you understand how the table is laid out.

	Col1	Col2	Col3	Col4	Col5	Col6	Col7	Col8
Rw1	1	9	17	25	33	41	49	57
Rw2	2	10	18	26	34	42	50	58
Rw3	3	11	19	27	35	43	51	59
Rw4	4	12	20	28	36	44	52	60
Rw5	5	13	21	29	37	45	53	61
Rw6	6	14	22	30	38	46	54	62
Rw7	7	15	23	31	39	47	55	63
Rw8	8	16	24	32	40	48	56	64

FIGURE 4.6 A graphical guide to the token table layout.

→

It is important to keep in mind that the table is dynamic. The number of cells, rows, and columns are all susceptible to change based on how many rows and columns are called during a given round.

OBJECTS

Objects can be wonderful friends or miserable enemies, but their concepts aren't that hard to master. They are essentially a collection of code chunks that have been assigned to a variable name. One advantage of objects is that they can contain properties or variables that are local or specific to the object that was created. The other major advantage is that you can create more than one of them with different values and functions.

The time-out that is created in the demo movie is an example of this. A new time-out object is created with an interval property of 30 seconds. You could create any number of these time-outs, each with their own interval and other properties.

While the time-out is based on a built-in set of code, you can also create objects that are based on scripts that you wrote yourself. You may have noticed that the demo movie script contains many global variables. While these are a handy way to pass and store variables, they are not clearly contained, so the practice is generally frowned upon. A better implementation (though more confusing and therefore not appropriate for these examples) would be to make the script type a parent script and use it as a template from which an object could be generated. The variables could then be localized properties, and they would be less exposed (and therefore less susceptible to problems).

PACKAGING A DIRECTOR ENGINE FOR PRIME TIME

One of the problems with using a third-party development environment to create your application is that you don't want your application to be easily identified as the product of the third-party company. When you create a published executable using either Flash or Director, the executable inherits the icon and properties from Director or Flash. Professional games have their own icons and usually have information about the company that manufactured them. You may also need to create a custom installation for your application. Several excellent applications can ease your development of these packaging and finishing aspects of your game. You'll need a good icon editor, a solid setup generator, and Versiown from Goldshell.

Creating a Custom Icon

The icon will be the primary link to your game for many players once they've downloaded the game. You want it to be attractive and to strongly suggest the game. There will not be much room for letters or characters, and the graphic will have to be extremely simple. It is incredibly difficult to create an effective icon, but it is considerably easier if you start with a good application for editing icons. One such application is the Icon Cool Editor (Figure 4.7).

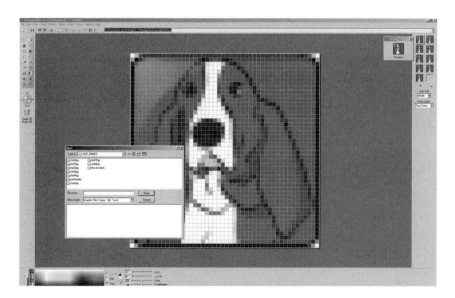

FIGURE 4.7   Editing with Icon Cool.

In this case, we simply imported one of the dog tokens from the game into the icon editor and set it up as a multiformat icon for various color formats. Note that there are two issues at play, first that the computer system could display the icon in one of several different color depths, and second that the icon could be displayed as one of several basic icons. Put that together and you actually need nine icons in various sizes (48 × 48, 32 × 32, and 16 × 16 pixels) and various color depths (True Color and 256- and 16-color varieties for each size).

To attach the icon and change the properties of the executable, Goldshell makes a little widget called Versiown. This software allows you to change the icons and change the properties of the executable so that your own company information will appear if the player examines the executable file (Figure 4.8).

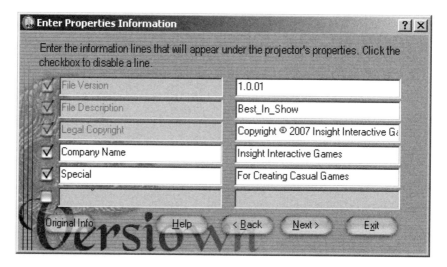

FIGURE 4.8 Attaching the icon and resetting properties with Versiown.

The last stage of self-packaging will often not be required from portals and distributors because they will have their own setup utilities. Nonetheless, you will probably want to package the file yourself at some point, and users of casual games will definitely want the setup process to be as easy as possible.

One of the best setup-generating utilities available is also free. Inno Setup, available online, is the result of wonderful free software development. It is incredibly easy to use, easy to customize, and devastates the competition with its price point—nothing. Packaging a setup with Inno is fairly effortless with the built-in wizard (Figure

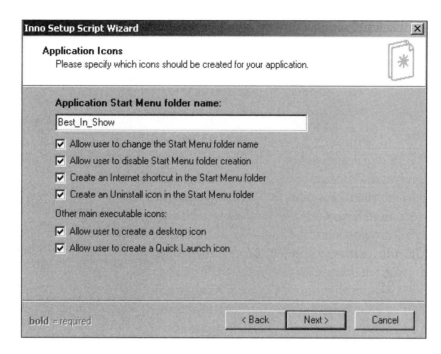

FIGURE 4.9 Creating a setup installer with Inno Setup Wizards.

4.9). You can also create your own script to control virtually every aspect of the setup process.

Inno Setup includes a basic wizard that will guide you through the creation of your main script on launch. All you need to do is fill in the fields after you launch the application, making certain to point to your own application and choose your own preferences. It is very well documented, so it is easy to add custom language to the compiler to make your setup exactly the way you like.

Once you finish making a setup installer, you can preview it (Figure 4.10). You'll find a sample installation file for the match-three game, along with the Inno script that was used to create it in the Chapter 4 media folder. Another advantage of setup installer files is that they reduce the file size substantially by compressing them. The installation file for the match-three game is only 3.05 MB, while the actual application is 5.5 MB. That reduction is huge when you consider the tens of thousands, even hundreds of thousands of downloads casual games invoke. Bandwidth translates into money, so saving bandwidth will save a substantial amount of money.

ON THE CD

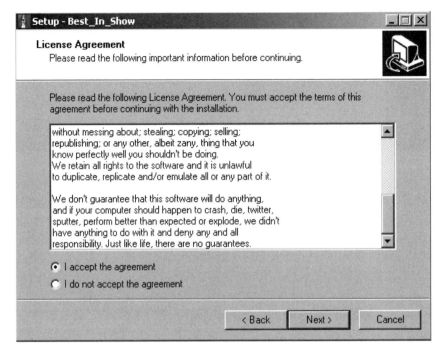

FIGURE 4.10 Previewing your installation.

In the early days of casual games, few developers recommended games larger than 5 or 6 MB. There was substantial concern that the barrier to download was simply too large. Today it isn't unusual to see games clocking in around 12–15 MB, and some games are even being produced in the 30 MB range. At the same time, more and more distributors are moving to adopt a pay-for-bandwidth model that can reduce a developer's profits.

DESIGNING AN ARCHITECTURE

One of the best ways to understand the architecture of most games is to examine the historic examples of games and the manner in which they have often been developed. Every game is unique, so there is no right way to design the architecture of your code. That said, there are some common practices that may be followed, which have been demonstrated as effective in all sorts of software for many years.

One very good approach to game architecture is to separate the primary elements of the game from one another to maintain control over as much of the on-screen image and sound as possible. If you decouple the game logic from the commands to draw images on the screen, for example, you can enable cool tricks such as drawing special effects when nothing else is happening on the screen and adapting the speed of the game to play about the same regardless of how bad the performance is on the computer hosting the game.

The basic elements of the game can then be thought of as core objects, each reporting back to a central control object that makes certain functions don't interfere with one another, and that allows for maximum control over any individual aspect of the game. Using this model a developer may define the core objects; create rules (hierarchy) for which actions and interactions get preference; plan to deal with the various states of the game such as pause, play, and round rewards; and design the basic game logic and insulate it from the other aspects of the game and in so doing avoid several common programming pitfalls.

DEFINING CORE OBJECTS

The common core objects in most games include a *sound control* object, a *logic* object, a *drawing* object, and a *save/load* object. Each of these objects reports to a backbone, or *main* object or script that controls the order of access and monitors the state of the game. Many casual games don't use complex enough sound to warrant a sophisticated sound control object. This would be needed if you expected to have frequent calls for many sounds that should play simultaneously or if you need to build fundamental sound control because of limitations of your development environment. The sound control object commonly monitors the use of sound channels and assigns various requested sounds to use various channels in order to ensure that certain sounds are given priority and the available channels are assigned first to the most critical sound effects. One recent casual game that took full advantage of sound with a rich soundscape and sound-based interface experience was Skunk Studios' *Sveerz*.

This charming game encourages players to create matched sets based on musical tones.

The logic object is central to virtually any game. This is where all of the data and scripts that are used to determine the positions and states of various game elements and tokens are stored. In the demo04-02.dir example, much of the game logic is contained in globally available scripts. In the example demo04-04.dir, however, the logic has been ported to a parent script and is initialized as an object.

The language is a little different. For example, `indexToGrid()` is now `gLogic.indexToGrid()`, but the implementation is cleaner and the number of globals in the project has dropped from dozens to just one (Figures 4.11, 4.12). This could be taken even further by decoupling the scripts from the time line altogether and using properties of the object to allow looping iterations that would continue while still accommodating player input, such as mouse events. In the current implementation, a good player may find the inability to act while tokens are falling frustrating. If the falling was handled without repeat loops (which inhibit our ability to detect things such as mouse events), you could facilitate the player's requests immediately rather than waiting for the blocks to fall.

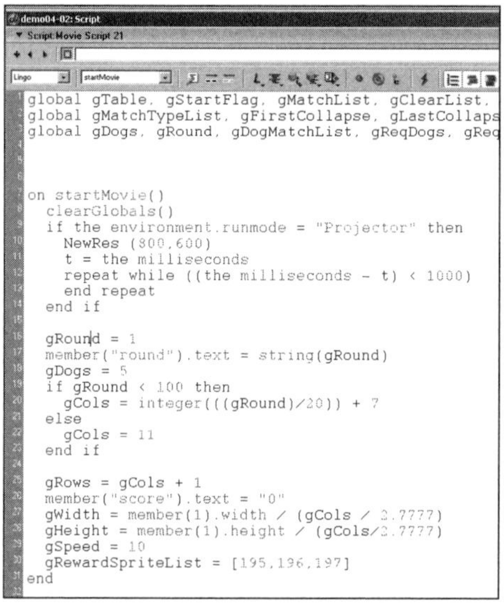


```
global gTable, gStartFlag, gMatchList, gClearList,
global gMatchTypeList, gFirstCollapse, gLastCollaps
global gDogs, gRound, gDogMatchList, gReqDogs, gReq



on startMovie()
  clearGlobals()
  if the environment.runmode = "Projector" then
    NewRes (800,600)
    t = the milliseconds
    repeat while ((the milliseconds - t) < 1000)
    end repeat
  end if

  gRound = 1
  member("round").text = string(gRound)
  gDogs = 5
  if gRound < 100 then
    gCols = integer(((gRound)/20)) + 7
  else
    gCols = 11
  end if

  gRows = gCols + 1
  member("score").text = "0"
  gWidth = member(1).width / (gCols / 2.7777)
  gHeight = member(1).height / (gCols/2.7777)
  gSpeed = 10
  gRewardSpriteList = [195,196,197]
end
```

FIGURE 4.11 The original version uses global variables.

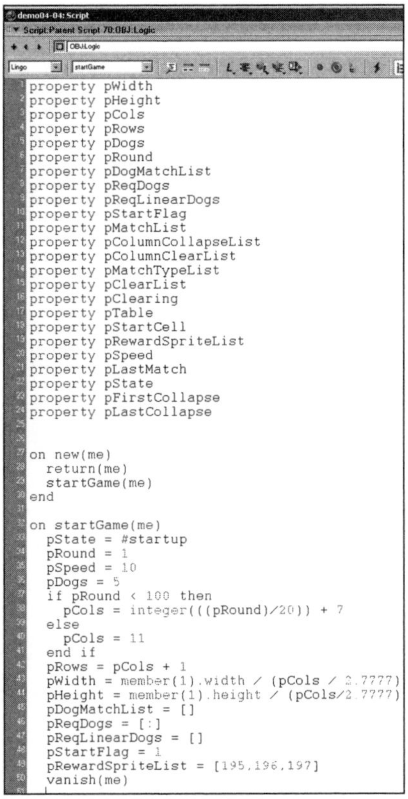

```
property pWidth
property pHeight
property pCols
property pRows
property pDogs
property pRound
property pDogMatchList
property pReqDogs
property pReqLinearDogs
property pStartFlag
property pMatchList
property pColumnCollapseList
property pColumnClearList
property pMatchTypeList
property pClearList
property pClearing
property pTable
property pStartCell
property pRewardSpriteList
property pSpeed
property pLastMatch
property pState
property pFirstCollapse
property pLastCollapse

on new(me)
  return(me)
  startGame(me)
end

on startGame(me)
  pState = #startup
  pRound = 1
  pSpeed = 10
  pDogs = 5
  if pRound < 100 then
    pCols = integer(((pRound)/20)) + 7
  else
    pCols = 11
  end if
  pRows = pCols + 1
  pWidth = member(1).width / (pCols / 2.7777)
  pHeight = member(1).height / (pCols/2.7777)
  pDogMatchList = []
  pReqDogs = [:]
  pReqLinearDogs = []
  pStartFlag = 1
  pRewardSpriteList = [195,196,197]
  vanish(me)
```

FIGURE 4.12 The revised script uses properties to insulate the values.

Another limitation of the current implementation is that the speed at which blocks fall is directly determined by the speed of the computer. On a slow computer the blocks will fall slowly, and on a more modern machine they will fall so quickly some of the animation may be invisible. Perhaps even more important, in five years, they'll fall so quickly the experience will be completely invisible to human eyes. Ideally, the draw rate would be choked (limited to a given frame rate).

DEFINING PRECEDENCE AND HIERARCHY

Once you've established an object-based system, you also introduce inherent problems with asynchronous behaviors. If each object were completely independent, using its own time systems to update states and properties, the chances of creating conflicts and improper sequences would increase dramatically. Sometimes resource issues are also at play. A slower computer can't easily perform animated effects that look cool and accent the game but aren't necessary to play the game. If precedence is defined, and the drawing mechanism has been isolated from other elements within the code, the system can choose whether it has enough time and resources to perform less important graphics operations such as decorative animation.

In *Podz* this sort of optimization was absolutely necessary. Because the game was 3D, many players did not have computers that were up to the task of displaying the animations while continuing to shoot pellets at very rapid rates. We felt strongly that shooting was far more important than detail in the animations, so we wrote the screen-drawing and animation handlers to self-monitor the performance speeds of the host computer and reduce or increase the detail of the animations (more images per effect and more interpolations between each rotation or change in position). The effect is surprising, because the game looks and feels smoother on newer machines, but the animation, while less attractive on slower machines, doesn't slow down significantly on slower machines. In Listing 4.6 the code checks to see how significant the average lag (or performance delay) during an animated frame of the game is and then adjusts the way that frames are drawn based on performance speeds.

LISTING 4.6   A Performance-Enhancing Algorithm

```
if pLagCheck < 50 then
  pLagList.add((the milliseconds - pLastLagTime))
  pLastLagTime = the milliseconds
  pLagCheck = pLagCheck + 1
  if pLagCheck = 50 then
    repeat with a = 1 to 50
      pLag = pLag + pLagList[a]
    end repeat
    pLagList = []
    if pLag > 0 then
```

```
        pLag = pLag / 50.00000
        case TRUE of
          (pLag < 23): - better than 60 fps
            pDrawRate = 1
          (pLag > 22 AND pLag < 33 ):-- between 30 to 60 fps
            pDrawRate = 1
          (pLag > 32 AND pLag < 40): -- between 25 to 29 fps
            pDrawRate = 2
          (pLag > 39 AND pLag < 50): -- between 20 to 24 fps
            pDrawRate = 2
          (pLag > 49 AND pLag < 60): -- between 16 to 19 fps
            pDrawRate = 3
          (pLag > 59 AND pLag < 70):-- between  14 to 15 fps
            pDrawRate = 3
          (pLag > 69): -- fewer than 14 fps
            pDrawRate = 4
        end case
      end if
    end if
  end if
```

The code in Listing 4.6 checks the lag time on the client computer every 50 cycles. The time intervals will be different on different computers and will be more effective if the time intervals are averaged to compensate for irregularities caused by intense processes. The code in Listing 4.6 stores the lag times in a list and then calculates the average lag. The case statement then sets the drawRate, which will determine the number of cycles that will be drawn on the host computer. This makes it possible to get virtually the same animation speed on computers playing the game back at speeds as low as nine frames per second compared to machines playing back the animation at 60 or more frames per second.

The animation will not look as clean because the details are omitted at the higher draw rates (higher rates are slower in this model). For example, in *Podz* 12 animated cells are used to draw the opening and closing of a *Podz* mouth. At full speed, all 12 cells are displayed, but at the slowest speed only a few images are used. Similar optimizations are used throughout the draw object to make the animation perform much faster on slower computers.

Avoiding Pitfalls and Bogus Calls

One of the most common problems with programming is that developers often fail to follow the basic conventions of the profession regarding code commenting and naming conventions. The problem is that we often come back to code we have written months even years earlier and spend significant amounts of time analyzing the code to determine how it works. Inconsistent naming conventions, poor commenting, insufficient planning, and lack of error checking are the most common causes of delays and frustrations in programming.

When all else fails, and a bit of code simply will not function as you think it should, the best advice is to comment every line of your code, verifying as you work that each line does what you think it does. In demo04-05.dir (found in Tutorials\ch04media) the code has all been updated and commented extensively. This should have the added benefit of making each handler much easier for you to understand, even if it wasn't detailed here. The main points of this sort of conformity are *use comments extensively*, identify your variables based on their *types*, use *descriptive variable names*, and *check for errors* when passing arguments.

A good set of comments will include information such as who wrote the code and when, along with contact information. It will include a version history and then at least descriptions of each handler and in many cases each line of code within that handler. It will generally include descriptions of all variables and what they contain, along with some explanation of the general sequence of the code or description of the architecture to form a quick visual map of the code.

Generally, global variables are assigned types using the letter *g* to precede the variable name. For example, a variable named *logic* would be renamed *gLogic* to denote its *scope* as a global variable. A property variable would be preceded by the letter *p*, as in *pLogic*. Temporary or local variables are often preceded by the letter *t*, and methods or handlers are often preceded by the letter *m*. This can help easily identify and classify variables, making it easier to debug an application.

The scope of a variable is the range within which it retains its value. A local or temporary variable is only available inside the handler that created it. When the handler reaches its end, the variable is lost. A property variable is viable as long as the object that hosts it is instanced (exists). It is restricted to the object, however, so you will have to ask the object to give you the value of the property. That's why you say things like `sprite(n).width` to get the width of a sprite and why the sample code uses the form `gLogic.pWidth` to get the width property assigned to all tokens.

Error checking can range from simply verifying that a method has received the correct type of argument in each position to careful analysis of logical moves in the game or manipulations of other elements. It varies depending on the specifics of the code segment, but the best rule of thumb is that if there is anything that is likely to go wrong, it's a good idea to add some error handling to make your application more robust. After a while you learn that some things are considerably more likely to happen than others. Accessing remote files is likely to create problems on some systems, so you should do substantial error checking when you attempt to access files on a host computer. Consider the code in Listing 4.7, which uses an xtra object (a bit of C++ code hooked into Director) to perform file input and output operations (FileIO).

LISTING 4.7   Saving with FileIO in Director

```
on promptSave(tList) --REQUIRES A DATALIST
    if voidP(tList) then
      ALERT ("ERROR 000: File save failed on ARGUMENT.")
      RETURN 0
    else
      if tList.ilk <> #proplist then
        ALERT ("ERROR 001: File save failed on ILK.")
        RETURN 0
      else
      end if
    end if
```

```
gSaveDialog = new(xtra "fileIO")
  tRes = tList[1]
tList = tList.string
err = gSaveDialog.status()
if err <> 0 then
  ALERT ("ERROR 002: File save failed on INITIALIZE.")
  RETURN 0
else
  -- MOVING ON CREATE
  gSaveDialog.createFile(tRes)
  err = gSaveDialog.status()
  if err = -122 then
    -- the file already exists
    gSaveDialog.openFile(tRes, 0)
    err = gSaveDialog.status()
    if err <> 0 then
      ALERT ("ERROR 005b: File save failed on OPEN.")
      RETURN 0
    end if
    gSaveDialog.delete()
    err = gSaveDialog.status()
    if err <> 0 then
      ALERT ("ERROR 003b: File save failed on DEL.")
      RETURN 0
    end if
    gSaveDialog.createFile(tRes)
    err = gSaveDialog.status()
    if err <> 0 then
      ALERT ("ERROR 004b: File save failed on CREATE.")
      RETURN 0
    else
      -- MOVING ON OPEN
      gSaveDialog.openFile(tRes, 2)
      err = gSaveDialog.status()
      if err <> 0 then
        ALERT ("ERROR 005c: File save failed on OPEN.")
        RETURN 0
      else
        -- MOVING ON WRITE
```

This handler goes on for another 100 lines. The irony is that it only checks to see if the file exists, and if it does, it opens, reads, writes, and closes the file. If it doesn't exist, it creates a file and then follows this sequence. The error checking is responsible for two-thirds of the code. Every process is checked, evaluated, and potentially responded to. Another common method of error checking performs several procedures, each returning a number representing its success. All of the numbers are added together, and if the result is higher than expected, a general error message is generated.

PROJECT 3:   A SIMPLE APPROACH TO SAVE AND LOAD

In this exercise you'll implement a simplified save and load feature for the demo game used in previous exercises. One of the benefits of working with Adobe Director is that a simple, small text file may be added to the host machine regardless of whether the application is running as an independent executable or as a Shockwave application within a browser. This means you can skip the FileIO and simply write player data and preferences to a preferences file using the setPref() and getPref() commands as illustrated in Listing 4.8 and 4.10.

LISTING 4.8   Simple Approach to File Save

```
on saveGame(me)
  tSave = getPref("bis.txt")
  if voidP(tSave) then
    setPref("bis.txt", "[]")
    tSave = [#pRound:pRound, #pScore:pScore]
  else
    tSave = value(tSave)
  end if
  tSave.pRound = pRound
  tSave.pScore  = pScore
  setPref("bis.txt", string(tSave))
end
```

The saveGame() handler in Listing 4.8 is contained within the gLogic object script. The first line of the handler, tSave = getPref ("bis.txt"), stores a copy of the preferences found on the client machine in the variable tSave. It doesn't matter what the file specified in the argument of the getPref() command is, as long as the file name is the same in both the saveGame() and LoadGame() subroutines. You should, however, be a careful about making the file name fairly specific, because others can write files to the client using this method. One approach is to use the name of your company or the game in a long form, to reduce the chances that another game or application will store settings in a file of the same name.

It is also important to note that this method will write the player's preferences to the system using a plain text, easily readable file, so hacking the preferences will be as simple as editing a preferences file. There are two implications here. First, if you have competition regarding the scores or other stored data, you would need a more secure method of storing data, and, second, players could easily corrupt their own preference data by deleting or altering this file. You will want to take steps to ensure that the data in the file is valid and that the file is present to ensure reliable performance regardless of such player interventions.

The conditional statement in Listing 4.8 checks to see if the preferences file was present by evaluating the tSave variable for a VOID result. If the file is not there, the basic data will be created from scratch, whereas the data will be evaluated and updated if the file is present. This handler could be improved by adding an additional error check to evaluate the type of data that was found in the saved preferences file to make sure the file has not been manipulated externally in such a way that the data is no longer in a valid format.

ON THE CD

Open Adobe Director and open the file demo04-06.dir from the companion CD-ROM in the Tutorials\ch04media folder. Open the script for the gLogic object named OBJ:Logic. You'll find the code from Listing 4.8 and 4.10 at the bottom of the script.

1. Add the following logic (Listing 4.9) to the listing on a new line following the command tSave = value(tSave):

LISTING 4.9   Add This after the Words value(tSave)

```
if tSave.ilk <> #propList then
    tSave = [#pRound:pRound, #pScore:pScore]
    setPref("bis.txt", string(tSave))
end if
```

The code in Listing 4.9 checks to ensure that the result of the value conversion on the data in the preference file was a property list. If the result of the conversion is not a property list, the subroutine rewrites a fresh data set to the preferences file. The net result of adding this error check is that even if the data in the preference file is dramatically altered, the system will simply erase the corrupt data and create a clean copy. The benefit is that while players will lose their data, they will not suffer a crash or other interference with the application performance.

2. The same evaluation can now be added to the `loadGame()` handler. Add the code from Listing 4.9 to the code from Listing 4.10 in the `gLogic` object script after the line `tLoad = value(tLoad)`.

LISTING 4.10   Simple Approach to Preference Loading

```
on loadGame(me)
  tLoad = getPref("bis.txt")
  if voidP(tLoad) then
    saveGame(me)
    tLoad = getPref("bis.txt")
  end if
  tLoad = value(tLoad)
  pRound = tLoad.pRound
  pScore = tLoad.pScore
  member("score").text = string(pScore)
end
```

SUMMARY

Sooner or later, most game developers realize that there are dramatic advantages to creating code-heavy games in some cases and dramatic advantages to using a development engine to handle graphics display, memory management, and animation in some cases. The longest-lived multimedia development environment and engine available today is Adobe Director (formerly Macromedia Director).

The engine provided by Adobe Director is a core multimedia player, capable of playing back media of virtually any type (2D, 3D, text, and sounds with no added libraries or additional licenses to buy) on both Windows and Macintosh computer operating systems. Using this sort of development environment can take a lot of the hassle and worry out of the game development process, but it adds some limitations. The engine will only be updated by Adobe when they decide to do so, and there are no guarantees that they will update those elements of the engine that they believe are most beneficial or appealing to their customers. Director remains popular in spite of this limitation because it is possible to extend the functionality of the core engine by adding custom C++ scripts.

Publishing and packaging your finished game means working with a variety of applications to design and attach elements such as custom icons and setup installers and storing and retrieving data about the player's preferences and status in the game. Your job can be made easier through the consistent implementation of code standards and careful preparation and design of code architecture.

5 RAD for Fun and Profit

In This Chapter

- Using RAD Strategies to Serve the Market
- RAD Maxims
- RAD Implementation
- Case Study: Iterative Prototyping with RAD
- Object-Oriented Programming in ActionScript

This chapter includes a brief definition of *rapid application Development*, or *RAD*, and provides some methods to determine when RAD is the right approach for your team for a given project. This section describes the what, when, why, and how of RAD for casual games.

In this chapter you will learn how to:

- Identify games that are good candidates for a RAD approach
- Understand how to use RAD to develop a casual game
- Know when to use RAD strategies
- Identify factors that reduce the advantages of a RAD approach
- Understand how to work with consumers to create the best product

USING RAD STRATEGIES TO SERVE THE MARKET

Three central elements define the RAD strategy: accelerated development schedule, parallel testing and development, and a commitment to iterative development and prototyping (Figure 5.1). Obviously any system that heavily considers the input of the eventual audience and allows for an accelerated (and consequently less expensive) development schedule is a serious contender for casual game developers.

FIGURE 5.1 RAD requires an iterative cycle of design, development, and assessment.

There are actually several different approaches to RAD, and the information in this chapter is a summary of the basic ideas that will help you implement your concepts as you create casual games.

Simply accelerating the development schedule will only result in rushed or down-and-dirty development. It won't improve your chances of success, and it certainly won't be more cost-efficient. RAD works when there is room for some negotiation of the feature set and the economic constraints of the software, when performance is not an overriding feature, and when the team is good at communicating and able to make intelligent and reasonable sacrifices.

INTEGRATING THE AUDIENCE INTO THE DESIGN AND REVIEW PROCESS

It's the acceleration that gives RAD most of its appeal. Critical to the success of RAD, however, is a process of parallel testing and development. This process is often combined with test marketing as joint teams of users and developers meet to iron out the feature set and performance requirements. The team has to consider the potential compromises early on, as secondary features must often be dropped to meet the prescribed schedule. This sort of *time boxing* dictates that delivery is more important than features—and is one of the reasons to avoid RAD in some situations.

The basic idea behind milestones and time-boxing is that internal deadlines can prevent an extensive problem known as *feature-creep*. Feature-creep is the addition of new features or game elements after the planning is done. Game developers are by definition creative people. It is virtually impossible to shut off that creativity while a game is in development, and the inevitable result is that new ideas, sometimes great ones, will come up during development. The problem is that because these ideas haven't been thoroughly vetted during the design and planning process, they can sometimes become huge time-wasters, drawing focus away from the things that must be done to deliver the game on time.

The basic approach requires integrating the consumer into every aspect of the development process. Developers ask the audience upfront what sort of things they will look for in the eventual software and listen carefully to their ideas. Working with potential consumers, the developers design a list of features and then rank them according to priorities and practical limitations.

An important part of the process is understanding that while there are a core set of features that must be included in the eventual game, there are also features on the list that are ranked as lower priorities and are likely to be forfeited to release the game within a reasonable time frame.

Always a Working Prototype

As the features are implemented, the team works to ensure that a functional version of the software is always available for further market testing and the audience is consulted regularly to determine their reaction to various features. The mantra of a RAD project soon becomes, "Test early, test often." The development team tests both the stability and usability of the software and the effect of the software on the target market.

In conventional programming the finished application is tested and evaluated after the bulk of the work is complete. In RAD the creation of a working model, or *prototype*, is part of the initial process. A prototype is a version of the software that includes the basic features but may not have finished art, sounds, and many of the features. The prototype is constantly updated and maintained in a functional version throughout the development of the game. Sometimes prototypes are used to help pitch a game to a publisher to seek funding to complete a project.

In order to work, RAD requires a commitment to *iterative prototyping*. Many developers have long held the belief that you never leave a project that isn't able to at least run, however crippled it may be. The notion of iterative prototyping mandates that working prototypes be delivered at extremely frequent milestones (in some cases daily) so that they can be reevaluated and changes can be pressed into the cycle.

WHEN IS RAD THE RIGHT COURSE OF ACTION?

Several factors can be regarded as clear indicators that a RAD approach is the right strategy for your next casual game project. These include the preexistence of an engine or development environment on which to build your game, a small development team, and control over the features that will be implemented.

- If you already have an engine, RAD is a serious possibility.
- If you have a small development team (three to eight people), RAD is a reasonable direction to take.
- If you have control (or a reasonable sense that the client will compromise) over the feature set, RAD may be the right method.
- If your team is good at communicating with one another, RAD may work for you.

When all of these things are true, you are probably better off trying a RAD approach to the project. While this isn't the case every time, it is certainly the case most of the time with casual game development. Generally you are producing the game for yourself and therefore have complete control over the features that will be implemented, and most casual games are based on some sort of core engine technology developed externally.

WHEN IS RAD THE WRONG APPROACH?

RAD is not always the best solution. Several factors may contribute to a very poor environment for a RAD project methodology:

- You need unusual new features.
- You have a very large team.
- You have no control over the feature set.
- You are developing mission-critical systems.

If you need a lot of new, unexplored, unusual features in your software, this is not the direction to go. New features take time to implement, and they will bottleneck the work flow, at best, and maybe even destroy it completely.

If you have a large team, it is unlikely that you will be able to maintain the level of communication necessary to stay on such tight schedules. RAD teams need to be small and fast, so that they can quickly communicate and respond to changes.

If the feature request/demand list is completely out of your hands, it would be unwise to try RAD development. Limiting yourself to a prebuilt engine or body of code means that you may not be able to implement some unforeseen feature, leaving you and your team a complete failure in the eyes of that finicky and insistent client.

If you are developing mission-critical or performance-driven applications, RAD is not for you. You are unlikely to spend a lot of time optimizing your RAD application, and even if you do, you are limited by the performance speeds of the host engine. Using RAD for a mission-critical system would be irresponsible because you would likely have no control over features built into the prebuilt engine.

RAD MYTHS

Several myths about RAD confuse people about when it is an appropriate approach. People believe that there is a constant ratio between time invested and quality achieved, but this just isn't true. Time invested can often turn into time wasted if the developers, artists, producers, or even managers are not well prepared. Software development is ultimately a creative act in a dynamic medium featuring the input of inherently flawed machines (people). Preparation, self-discipline, and planning can increase your odds of getting positive results quickly.

Many think that aggressive early development will result in early project completion; unfortunately, aggressive early development usually results in huge delays, endless design meetings, and sometimes complete failure. This is the most dangerous and perhaps the most common myth. One-third of project time should be devoted to planning and preparation. If insufficient time is invested in planning, the demands for planning will bog down or overwhelm the project when the needs for development time are the greatest.

No matter how many people believe it, or how good it might sound, flooding a project with money will not necessarily accelerate development, though starving it of money will definitely slow it down. It isn't about how much you spend; it's about how you spend it. Consider spending money to acquire assets, engines, and even designs and scripts. More experienced programmers may cost more, but they are nearly always worth their weight in gold. They can cut weeks off the development cycle with one or two contributions.

RAD MAXIMS

Several maxims of RAD may help you understand why the approach can work. Time, money, and resources—a shortage of any of these will slow development and make your project less efficient. Limited time usually leads to insufficient planning. This is the worst possible response to a tight time frame.

Limited money leads to inexperienced developers, artists, and equipment. All of these reduce efficiency. Limited resources mean investing time and money into reinventing the wheel. If it's available, it's almost always cheaper to buy a resource ready-made than it is to create it in house. The problem with this strategy is that you are rarely able to settle for the media and other resources that are readily available. The amount of reworking necessary to bring the media into alignment with the rest of the game's aesthetic and aural elements may cancel out any benefits you gain by acquiring the media. This tip is probably of more use to small companies and start-ups who are investing less in resources and design.

For every hour spent planning, you'll save two hours revising. Planning your project will always save you time, money, and resources. There is no more important strategy. Advanced planning saves time by identifying the materials and features that are needed. It saves money because you'll know what materials you need, and you can shop around for a provider. It saves resources because you can trim excessive, impractical, or inefficient features and media in the planning stage.

One of the biggest problems with development tools is that the easier they are to use, the less potential they present for control. You'll get better results if you know the limitations of the tools going into the project. Realize that limitations of a development tool can result in bugs in your software. The trade-off is often worth the loss of control. The difference in average development times with Adobe Director, for example, compared to C++ can be staggering, with common reports that projects can be created in Director in 10% or less of the time required using C++, even when an engine or library is available.

In the end, every feature must be questioned. Culling a project down to the most essential features is basically about identifying how much bang you'll get for your buck. The following are a set of filters that you can use to help you estimate whether or not a proposed feature really is cost-effective:

- Is it necessary?
- Is it relevant?
- Is it redundant?
- Is it exciting or innovative?
- Will the feature contribute to the experience?
- Will the feature contribute to sales of the product?
- Does it have enough merit to warrant the cost of development?

KNOW THE ACTUAL COST AND BENEFIT

It is seldom profitable to add features to a salaried or contract game. The only time to consider adding a feature is when you will earn money based on sales. Sure, you didn't think about flame-throwing butterflies during the initial planning stages of your game, but you love the idea and know it might be a tough sell with so many features finalized.

Any proposed feature must go through a set of filters. What's the bang for the buck ratio of the proposed flame-throwing butterfly feature? Marketing looks good; people always smile at the notion of flame-throwing butterflies, and it has a peculiar sort of cross-gender appeal. The potential for gameplay looks good; it improves the fun factor by increasing challenge without frustrating the player. The cost is low, so the cost/benefit ratio is good.

RAD IMPLEMENTATION

The implementation of RAD can basically be summarized in four steps: centralize your architecture, develop everything at once, use object-oriented programming techniques wisely, and, above all, apply some common sense.

Centralizing your application architecture starts with a clear and sensible vision of the underlying design. The trap here is in either over-thinking the problem (creating a seriously over-reaching architecture that is unimaginably more capable than it needs to be) or ignoring the architecture and spending too much time writing multiple procedures and objects with redundant functionality. If you already wrote code that does something, you shouldn't be writing more that does something very similar.

It sounds cliché, but it couldn't be truer. One of the biggest time wasters in development is in nonstandardized naming. Develop a standard naming rule set for your team and stick to it rigorously. Tons of time can be lost working out issues that can be easily attributed to inappropriate or sloppy naming conventions.

OBJECT-ORIENTED PROGRAMMING WHEN THE PAYOFF IS CLEAR

Use object-oriented programming techniques but use procedural techniques as well. The idea is to use an object when it is bound to be reusable in this project or in a future one and when it is fairly universal. Once the code gets specific, procedural programming will likely be faster. Anticipate which is wiser in any given feature.

Consider using custom xtras to create reusable code objects and accelerate performance. Xtras can be developed out of house—there is probably already one that does what you need—and they are generally easy to use and include.

RAD calls for simultaneous evolution rather than sequential production. Each member of your team should be producing and modifying their contributions in response to the constant loop of feedback coming from the test group and other members of the team. It is this feedback system that makes the evolutionary development of the product possible—and the limitations of time and resources that keep it from growing out of control.

This system only works when communication is healthy among members of the team. Everyone needs to be able to focus on the project and direct critical evaluation at the product and not at themselves. If people take the criticism personally, they'll soon be too frustrated to contribute effectively.

Working in as tight a space as possible creates the ideal production environment. When you can ask questions, make requests, and offer opinions without any obstacles (phones, faxes, emails) you get instant feedback, and that contributes to teambuilding.

Once the work is well under way, it is particularly helpful for the artists to be able to adjust their project timetable to meet the immediate needs of the programmers. The rewards we enjoy come each time we accomplish a task, and they are immediately amplified when a cooperative task yields that finished or nearly finished look and feel. Both members of the team (this works with sound as well) are immediately rewarded doubly by seeing that element completed.

SOMETIMES A PROCEDURAL APPROACH MAKES MORE SENSE

When is a procedural programming approach better than an object-oriented programming approach? Object-oriented programming almost always takes longer to implement than a procedural solution, so it is only beneficial if you are reasonably certain the object will be reused either in this application or in future applications. Generally, major elements in games are better off as objects, but there are always special cases, and keeping your eyes open for them can save time.

Another major timesaver is integrated debugging code. Set a globally available debug variable and then switch it on or off to tell your handlers whether or not to report their status. It means a few extra lines of code to have every handler output its error code to a central error routine, but it can be a huge plus when things start to get too dense to visualize easily.

Director's object inspector is amazing. The object inspector is a dialog window that lets you view in real time every object, property, and global variable in the active application. It uses simple tree-view menus to show you the properties of an object and even breaks down lists into subparts. You can even enter or update the values of properties from the window. The object inspector gives a clarity to nested lists that is unprecedented. You rarely have to look beyond the object inspector to find a bug, and it is always the first place to look when the application is behaving badly.

Flash integrates a similar debugger/inspector that is also wonderful. These tools allow you to quickly identify the problems in your code, and their value cannot be overstated. The Flash debugger allows you to watch variables, select various objects, and inspect their properties and step though handlers as they run to verify that the scripts you have written are functioning as you expected them to.

APPLY COMMON SENSE

The last major method for implementing RAD should probably be a method for implementing any development. Productivity, especially for logical and creative work, decreases when people aren't well rested. Encourage your team to take plenty of breaks. Make sure the work environment is as comfortable and ergonomic as possible.

Make certain that everyone gets plenty of sleep. You'll lose more time with tired people than you ever will from sending them home for some sleep. If you have a multitalented team, encourage them to trade tasks occasionally. Let the developers make that sound or bit of art. This has the joint effects of building better mutual understanding, reducing monotony and therefore fatigue, and mining for hidden talents within your organization.

Finally set and stick to reasonable milestones for your project. This time-boxing may require feature reduction, but that's a part of this approach from the starting gate, so your team will be prepared for it.

CASE STUDY: ITERATIVE PROTOTYPING WITH RAD

ON THE CD

Included on the CD-ROM in the Tutorials\ch05media folder are nearly 100 functional versions of a game entitled *Abbie's AlphaBet* that demonstrate the process of iterative prototyping and RAD. The finished prototype was developed by the author in about a week, using one previously created graphic (the image of Abbie from *Best in Show*) and one stock sound file (a stinger that is used for the introduction to Insight Interactive Games' games).

The goal of the project was to create a proof-of-concept prototype that might be used to evaluate the game's entertainment value by testing with an audience that fits the target demographic. You will be able to see the entire process of development (including the not-so-pretty flaws) by examining each of the versions, numbered sequentially. Many are discussed here, and the evolving code is described.

The game is developed in Adobe Flash, using ActionScript, which is an *ECMA*-compliant scripting language very similar to JavaScript. The language is not as reader-friendly as Lingo to inexperienced developers, but it is a very robust language that can be easily adapted and expanded to meet the needs of many projects.

Prior to 1994 ECMA was known as the European Computer Manufacturers Association, but the name was changed to Ecma International (European Association for Standardizing Information and Communication Systems) to more

accurately reflect the international scope of the organization. The group is an industry association dedicated to the
standardization of information and communication technology and consumer electronics. Establishing standards
for various electronic communication and consumer products makes the eventual widespread adoption of the technologies easier.

To follow along with the rapid prototyping of *Abbie's AlphaBet*
you'll need a copy of Adobe Flash. If you don't have a copy, you may
download one from Adobe's Web site which will function as a free
demonstration for 30 days. The first version of the game is actually
just a rip-off of a shell you saw earlier in this book. The match-three
game introduction has been drafted to quickly mock up the titles for
this one. Abbie'sAlphaBet.fla (found in Tutorials\ch05media of the
CD-ROM) is just a copy of that initial title set.

ON THE CD

Because there will be many versions of the game, a better naming
convention should be established to ensure that information (versions) is not lost because of saving over earlier versions.

Versioning is the process of saving multiple versions of a file
in order to be able to trace back if some change has caused
a problem in the file. This is good practice with every file
you work on, not just games. Many times files become corrupt, or you introduce errors that could be most easily fixed
by stepping back a few versions. A good practice in development is to always use the *Save As* feature of your applications rather than the *Save* feature. When you save the file,
create an extension to the file name that is at least three dig-
its. Using this system, myfile.txt would become myfile001.
txt. The reason for the leading zeros is so the files will be
listed in alpha-numeric order on your computer. If you
didn't include the leading zeros, the files wouldn't sort
properly.

Open the file AbbiesAlphaBet_002.fla (found in Tutorials\ ch05media folder on the CD-ROM) in Adobe Flash. The file is similar to the previous version but now contains a graphic (the image of Abbie) and appropriate titles. The file also contains a background of pale gray squares (Figure 5.2). These blocks were drawn using the Rectangle tool (the square box on the toolbar). Create one box and then copy and paste it into many. Finally the boxes were all selected simultaneously, and the F8 key calls the convert-to-symbol dialog. The blocks were converted to a graphic symbol.

FIGURE 5.2 The gray blocks are grouped as a graphic symbol.

Because the gray blocks are a symbol, they may now only be edited or changed by viewing the symbol. When you double-click on a symbol in Flash, the symbol will be opened in front of the other elements on the screen. Note that the navigation display (identified by the arrow in Figure 5.2) will tell you whether you are editing the primary flash movie or the contents of a symbol.

To import a graphic file in Flash, File: Import: Import to Library is used. The graphic file (abs.psd) was imported to the Flash Library. Use the F11 key to call up the library in the side viewing pane (Figure 5.3).

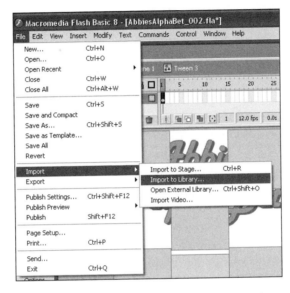

FIGURE 5.3   The library stores symbols and other media that may be reused.

A couple of *hot tips* will speed up your understanding of Flash. These are things that beginners frequently fail to see. The first is to *always pay attention to your time line depth navigation bar.* This is the bar at the top of the time line that lists the current viewing level (Figure 5.2). It is easy to accidentally drill down (by opening shapes inside of symbols within a time line) into movie clips and other symbols without realizing it. Just clicking on something on the stage too many times can put you into an edit mode that might easily seem disorienting. Flash will behave differently depending on the editing mode and depth, so it is critical that you know what you are working on.

$\rightarrow$

The next thing to keep in mind is that *the time line may be expanded to include multiple channels* (called layers), and those channels may be contained in handy folders. This is critical if you are using the drawing tools, as items drawn on the same layer will create compound objects by immediately flattening and combining the vector graphics. *If drawn on separate layers, vector elements will remain separate.*

In version 4 of the game in the Tutorials\ch05media folder of the CD-ROM, a color effect is added to the instance of the boxy background graphic (Tween 3). The onscreen instance of the graphic creates the checkerboard pattern in the background, which is now fading into mint green instead of gray. A tint effect is added in Flash (Figure 5.4) by changing the color filter value in the Property inspector while the on-stage instance of the symbol is selected.

If you have trouble seeing the color filter drop-down options, you may need to reselect the on-stage instance of the symbol. Only symbols will display this property.

FIGURE 5.4 The color filter value setting in the Property inspector.

Version 5 of the game (found in Tutorials\ch05media of the CD-ROM) creates button symbols to be used for navigation (Figure 5.5). Buttons in flash contain their own time lines in order to ease the process of creating mouse-over highlights, mouse-down appearances, and default appearances. The idea behind any button is that it provides the user with visual cues they can use to understand that the object on the screen is a button. Flash does a lot of this work for you by automatically changing the cursor and moving to various parts of the prebuilt button time line based on player interaction.

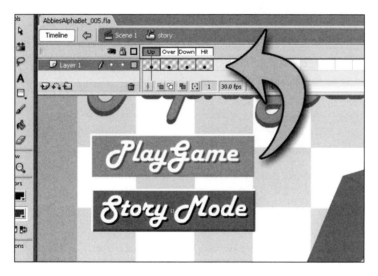

FIGURE 5.5 A button has its own time line.

The time line of each button includes four frames rather than the standard numbered frames of a generic timeline. These are Up, Over, Down, and Hit. Each frame represents a state of the button. The Up state is the neutral state of the button. This is its normal appearance on the screen. The Over state (Figure 5.6) is the highlighted state of a button.

The Down state of a button is usually just a darkened or some other variant of the button that appears to be depressed (physically, not emotionally). Finally the Hit state of the button is not an appearance at all, but a region. Anything that is defined by a shape or other element in this frame will become the area that is used by the system to report a mouse-over or other mouse event.

FIGURE 5.6   The Over state of the button is similar to the Up state, but glowing or brighter.

It is important to keep in mind as you make buttons in Flash that you must create a keyframe for each frame that will have a different appearance. The state of the button in the correlating keyframe is the state that will be displayed during that event.

ON THE CD

In version 6 (Tutorials\ch05media\AbbiesAlphaBet_006.fla) some text fields have been added to the program's launch screen to introduce the word game flavor. To add the text and make it appear to fall behind various elements on the screen, it was necessary to place it on the time line near the bottom (Figure 5.7). Flash time lines are sorted in order from the top of the time line to top of the stack, or z-order. This means things on the bottom of your time line in Flash will fall below things on the top.

This is exactly the opposite in Director.

NOTE

FIGURE 5.7   Letters are added between the buttons and the background.

ON THE CD

In version 7 (Tutorials\ch05media\AbbiesAlphaBet_007.fla) the layer with the text is shortened by one frame, and keyframes are added to facilitate blending the letters in along with the mint green boxes. The keyframes are placed at the beginning and end of the blend, and the whole group of letters is combined into a single symbol (select them all and press F8). The initial keyframe is selected, and the color filter is assigned to set the alpha value to 0%. When the motion tween is assigned to the layer, the letters will blend from invisible (alpha = 0) to visible (alpha = 100 is the default value of the alpha property). Finally the cursor is used to select a frame in the layer between the two keyframes, and a right-mouse-click followed by choosing Create Motion Tween adds the motion tween to animate the blend (Figure 5.8.)

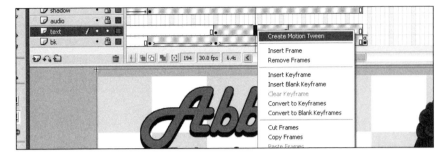

FIGURE 5.8 Create a motion tween to animate the fade from invisible to visible.

Version 8 (Tutorials\ch05media\AbbiesAlphaBet_008.fla) begins to create the crucial text blocks for the game. There will be six letters in the game that can be used to create words of three to six letters. At this point layout becomes even more critical, so the grid is used to align objects on the screen. To access the screen, you may simply choose View: Grid: Show Grid (Figure 5.9).

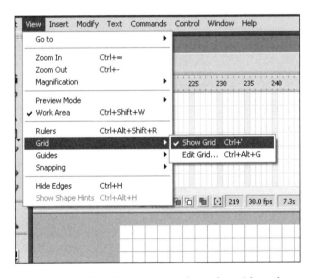

FIGURE 5.9 Use the View menu to show the grid on the screen.

The layout of the gameplay screen continues in version 9 (Tutorials\ch05media\AbbiesAlphaBet_009.fla). To get better alignment we adjusted the grid to use 10 pixel by 10 pixel squares (Figure 5.10).

The grid settings can also allow the objects created to snap to grid positions, encouraging easier alignment.

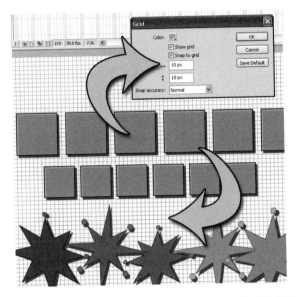

FIGURE 5.10 To adjust the grid size use View: Grid: Edit Grid.

The next step was to create the little stars. They are fairly simple objects built entirely from the default primitive vector tools found in Flash. You can make your own using the following steps:

1. Select the Poly Star tool from the toolbar (Figure 5.11).

Once you've selected the Poly Star tool, the Property inspector will change to show the tool's properties. Among the elements in the Property inspector is a button labeled Options. Press this options button to view the options for the tool (Figure 5.12).

2. Open the Poly Star: Options dialog.
3. Set the style to Star and the sides to 8. Leave the point size at 0.50. Press OK.
4. Click and drag on the screen to create a star (Figure 5.13).

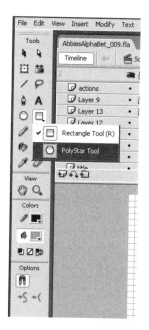

FIGURE 5.11 Select the Poly Star tool.

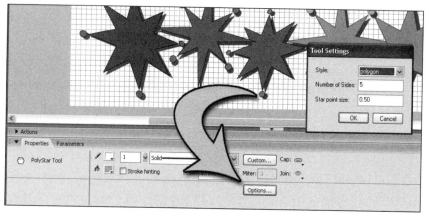

FIGURE 5.12 Open the Poly Star Options dialog.

You've probably noticed that the resulting star is not exactly like the ones in the sample movie. To get a little visual interest, the stars were further modified using a custom transform to skew them and even altering the points of one to make some of the arms shorter than the others.

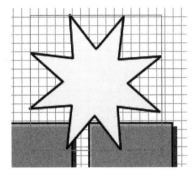

FIGURE 5.13 Click and drag to make a star.

5. Choose the Subselection tool from the Tool menu (Figure 5.14). Note that the Subselection tool is not the same as the Selection tool. It is a white arrow, rather than a black one. It is able to select and edit individual vertices rather than whole objects.

FIGURE 5.14 Select the Subselection tool from the toolbar.

A *vertex* is a point or intersection of lines (like a corner or anchor) in a vector-based drawing object. By editing the *vertices* (the plural of vertex), you will be able to make changes to the shape of an object. Vector objects are drawn using instructions that tell the system to draw lines of a given type (some straight, some curved) between two or more points (vertices).

6. Select the vertex for one of the points and move the point using the arrow keys on your keyboard (Figure 5.15).

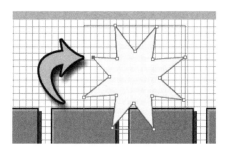

FIGURE 5.15   Select a vertex and move it inward toward the center of the star.

You can continue moving individual points until you are satisfied with the general appearance of the star.

It may help to rotate the star so that the points are oriented straight up and straight down as they are in Figure 5.16.

7. Add simple circles to the long points of the stars. Use the Circle/Oval tool to draw the circle and then snap it to the end of the points. You can use the arrow keys to adjust the position (Figure 5.17). Cut and paste the circle to make exact copies that can be snapped to each point.

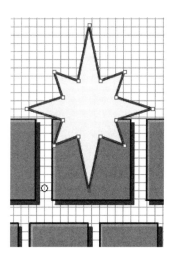

FIGURE 5.16   Keep moving the vertices until you like the results.

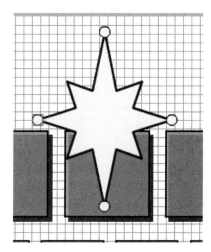

FIGURE 5.17   Use the Circle/Oval tool to draw a small circle.

For the next step, it is important that you select all of the shapes (the circles and the star) and make certain that they are broken apart (Ctrl-B). Once the objects are selected, you will be able to apply the Modify: Transform: Distort tool.

8. Choose Modify: Transform: Distort from the Modify menu. You may then modify the star by changing the positions of the corners (Figure 5.18). This will allow you to create false perspectives for your stars and make them look more interesting.

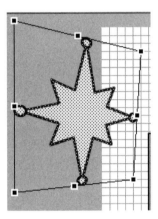

FIGURE 5.18 Use the Distort tool to modify your star for the finished look.

One of the major design issues people face when designing images and interfaces for their games is that the screens can easily and quickly become cluttered and disorganized. A great way to prevent this is to cluster together common ideas on the screen so that people will be able to create a simple organizational map in their minds.

The stars along the bottom are decorative, but they are also meant to help organize the reveal group (the baby words that would have been possible to guess in a given round of the game). The problem is that in version 9 of the game these stars break the space up but don't strongly bind the bottom third of the screen into one zone. To combat this, we added a background element that serves this purpose (Figure 5.19). This additional background element is the purpose of version 10, Tutorials\ch05media\AbbiesAlphaBet_010.fla.

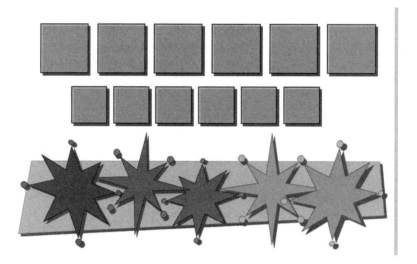

FIGURE 5.19 A background element can tie a group of smaller objects together.

The next step was to add time and score windows. The backgrounds for these elements are made from the same shape that forms the background behind the stars. A tint filter is used to change the color, and a text element has been added above each to label the displays. Text has also been added to each so that we will be able to code the game to display the time remaining in the round and to add value to the score field (Figure 5.20).

By version 16 (located in the Tutorials\ch05media folder on the CD-ROM) of the game, a little bit of script has been added. The scripting is added to the frame script for frame 1 (Listing 5.1).

LISTING 5.1 ActionScript for Frame 1 of AbbiesAlphaBet_016.fla.

```
fscommand("fullscreen", true);
fscommand("showmenu", false);
```

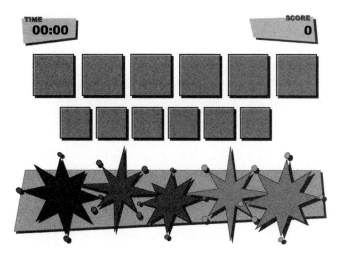

FIGURE 5.20   The score and timer fields are added.

In Flash there is no need to place every command inside a separate handler. These two lines call the fscommand function and change the Flash application to play full screen in an executable. This isn't the same as resetting the screen resolution, but it has the same end effect for the player in that the application will then be viewed full screen. The next command instructs Flash to disable the flash context menu.

In viewing the executable version of this file (AbbiesAlpha-Bet_016.exe), you get the full effect of one of the biggest benefits of using Flash with vector graphics. It doesn't matter how big or small you make the game; the graphics display perfectly. This benefit should not be understated, because it gives the game a finished quality that really instills confidence in potential consumers. You can use the Escape key to reduce the application back down to its default size for a comparison.

To make an executable version of a file in Flash, you need only select File: Publish Settings and then choose the formats in which you wish to publish. Then press the Publish button to publish the application (Figure 5.21).

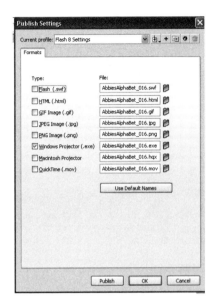

FIGURE 5.21 Use the Publish Settings dialog to create your application.

ON THE CD

You may note that it is possible to create Macintosh executables as well as online Shockwave Flash files and a variety of other files from this dialog. The dialog includes a host of additional settings that may be used to adjust the parameters of the final executable.

As the versions of the game move into the 20s (Tutorials\ch05media\AbbiesAlphaBet_021.fla), programming the game becomes a much more significant part of the project. There will be two major internal scripts in this project. The first a set of definitions on frame 1, and the other is a set of functions on frame 219. If you open version 21 and choose Control: Test Movie, you will see that the betting field has been added and you can now add value to your bet, and the bet will be withdrawn from your account. The clock counts down from 150 to 0 seconds, and this countdown is translated into language that makes sense to your audience, 2 minutes and 30 seconds (Figure 5.22).

Several scripts had to be introduced into the project to facilitate these basic interactions. To understand these scripts, it is important that you begin to think about the scope of the variables and functions that are defined in the ActionScript.

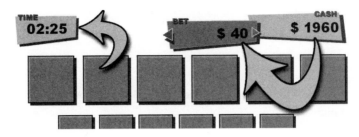

FIGURE 5.22   Betting is now allowed, and the clock reports the time remaining.

Variables declared in the first frame of a time line in Flash are called time line variables, and they are available via `_level0.*` to scripts anywhere within the time line.

In Listing 5.2 two lines of additional code have been added to the application. Each line is a combination of variable declaration and variable assignment. Declaring these variables in this location establishes their scope as available to other scripts using an absolute reference. For example, we could call `_level0.currentBet` from another script, and it would be able to tell us the value of the `currentBet` property defined in Listing 5.2. These two variables will store the current winnings (score) for the game and the current bet.

LISTING 5.2   Version 21 of the Frame 1 Script

```
fscommand("fullscreen", true);
fscommand("showmenu", false);
var currentBet = 0; // this is now available elsewhere
var currentCash = 2000;
```

The amount of the bet is initially assigned at 0, and the player is initially given $2000. These figures will likely change, and it will be easy to change them here.

The Raise and Lower buttons are the little red buttons on either side of the betting display region. The script in Listing 5.3 creates a function and associates it with the mouse-up event for the little red button that is used by the player to raise the bet. The first part of the code creates a reference to the instance of the button that has been named raise. Instances are named using the name box on the Property inspector when the instance is selected on the stage. You can see that this instance is named raise (Figure 5.23).

LISTING 5.3 Version 21 of the Frame 219 Script: onRelease for the Raise Button

```
this.raise.onRelease = function() {
    var tMax = _level0.currentCash;
    var curBet = _level0.currentBet;
    var curBet = curBet+5;
    if (curBet<=tMax) {
        _root.bet.text = "$ "+curBet;
        var tReduc = tMax-curBet;
        _level0.currentBet = curBet;
        _level0.currentCach = tReduc;
        _root.cash.text = "$ "+tReduc;
    }
};
```

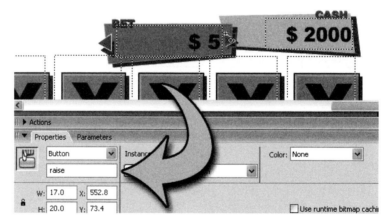

FIGURE 5.23 The instance is named in the Property inspector while selected.

Some variables will be used for this function that don't need to be accessed outside the function. They are declared on the following three lines. Here we introduce a classic error: the programmer will refer to `_level0.currentCach` instead of `_level0.currentCash`, which we set to be available elsewhere earlier. The programmer won't realize the mistake until version 70 or so, because he cleverly programmed around it. You definitely wouldn't want to copy this example, because it doesn't work properly. The lines that follow are a clumsy attempt to calculate the amount that should be in the betting text field. Loosely translated, they say if the current bet is greater than the minimum bet allowed, set the text of the bet field to the newly calculated bet amount.

Then create a variable to hold the new cash amount available to the player and set the main `currentBet` property to the value calculated. Next attempt to update the cash amount, but fail, because you misspell cash. Finally set the value of the available cash to the proper, revised amount.

The Lower button's `onRelease` function is very similar to the Raise button's function (Listing 5.4). It simply calculates the same values in reverse, allowing the player to lower the total amount of the bet.

LISTING 5.4   Version 21 of the Frame 219 Script: `onRelease` for the Lower Button

```
this.lower.onRelease = function() {
    var tMin = 0;
    var curBet = _level0.currentBet;
    var curBet = curBet-5;
    if (curBet>tMin) {
        _root.bet.text = "$ "+curBet;
        var tAdd = _level0.currentCash-curBet;
        _level0.currentBet = curBet;
        _level0.currentCach = tAdd;
        _root.cash.text = "$ "+tAdd;
    }
};
```

The variable declarations and cleanup settings are run when the application first hits frame 219 (Listing 5.5). It starts by setting the base value of the first bet to 0 and the field to display $0. Then it clears all of the x's out of the text members on the screen. There is a movie clip that contains all of the objects that will appear between rounds called popupBonus. The next line sets the popupBonus movie clip to disappear. It will be recalled later when a round ends.

LISTING 5.5 Version 21 of the Frame 219 Script: Initial Setup And Variable Declarations

```
var tBet = 0;
this.bet.text = "$ "+tBet;
this.block1.text = "";
this.block2.text = "";
this.block3.text = "";
this.block4.text = "";
this.block5.text = "";
this.block6.text = "";
this.char1.text = "";
this.char2.text = "";
this.char3.text = "";
this.char4.text = "";
this.char5.text = "";
this.char6.text = "";
popupBonus._visible = 0;
var pTimer = 150;
this.time.text = "2:30";
var intervalId:Number;
var count:Number = 0;
var maxCount:Number = 150;
var duration:Number = 1000;
```

The clock in the game needs several parameters to function. First, the length of the timer must be set. The line pTimer = 150 sets the clock to 150 seconds. Next the initial text of the clock field is set to "2:30." The clock will need several variables, intervalID, count, maxCount, and duration. Each is declared and assigned in the next set of statements. You may have noted, though, that something extra appears in these declarations. It is possible, and generally best practice, to explicitly set the type of data that a variable will hold. In this case each of the clock variables will be used to store a number value, so the data type :Number follows the name declaration.

The executeCallback() handler (Listing 5.6) is called every second because of the time-out object called by setInterval in Listing 5.7. A variable named rTime is created to store the time in seconds. Another named min is created to store the minutes. The minutes are calculated by dividing the total number of seconds by 60. An operation called floor (a function of the Flash Math object) is used to get the value as an integer (a whole number). Next the seconds are calculated by subtracting (60 * min) from the total seconds.

LISTING 5.6   Version 21 of the Frame 219 Script: Timer Callback

```
function executeCallback():Void {
    pTimer = pTimer-1;
    var rTime = (this.maxCount-this.count);
    var min = (rTime/60);
    min = Math.floor(min);
    if (rTime>0) {
        var tText = ("0"+min+":");
        rTime = (rTime-(60*min));
} else {
        tText = "00:";
}
if (rTime<10) {
        // a placeholder zero must be added to the display
        tText = tText+"0";
    }
    this.timer.text = (tText+rTime);
    if (this.count>=this.maxCount) {
        clearInterval(intervalId);
        popupBonus._visible = 1;
        // revealAnswers();
    }
    count++;
}
```

If there are more than 60 seconds, the minutes are added to the text field as minutes. Otherwise the minutes are recorded in the text field as "00:." Finally the seconds are added to the text field. If there are fewer than 10 seconds remaining, a placeholder value 0 is added to the string so that seconds appear as :09 and so on. rather than just :9. When the timer runs out, the popupBonus movie clip is made visible.

The timer is started by the startTimer() function. It is called when the round begins, and its code is in Listing 5.7. It initially checks to make sure that another instance of the timer isn't running. If one is, it clears the instance. Next it creates an instance called intervalID and tells the setInterval function to call the executeCallback function one time every second.

LISTING 5.7 Version 21 of the Frame 219 Script: Start the Timer

```
function startTimer():Void {
    if (intervalId != null) {
        clearInterval(intervalId);
    }
    intervalId = setInterval(this, "executeCallback",
    duration);
}
startTimer();
```

By version 35 (Tutorials\ch05media\AbbiesAlphaBet_035.fla), two external ActionScript classes have been introduced to the project to facilitate the dictionary object. It is possible in Flash to create projects that refer to external classes for the definition of new objects. The class scripts are in your Chapter Five media folder as ins_lw.as and ins_dictionary.as. The code for the dictionary is in Listing 5.8.

LISTING 5.8 The ins_dictionary ActionScript

```
class ins_Dictionary {
        // private instance variables
        private var __dictionaryName:String;
    private var __p3lw:Object;
    private var __p4lw:Object;
    private var __p5lw:Object;
    private var __p6lw:Object;
    // constructor statement
    public function ins_Dictionary(pName:String) {
        this.__dictionaryName = pName;
    }
```

```
    // get/set dictionaryName
    public function get dictionaryName():String {
        return this.__dictionaryName;
    }
    public function set dictionaryName(value:String):Void {
        this.__dictionaryName = value;
    }
    // get/set 3lw (three letter words)
    public function get p3lw():Object {
        return this.__p3lw;
    }
    public function set p3lw(value:Object):Void {
        this.__p3lw = value;
    }
// get/set 4lw
    public function get p4lw():Object {
        return this.__p4lw;
    }
    public function set p4lw(value:Object):Void {
        this.__p4lw = value;
    }
// get/set 5lw
    public function get p5lw():Object {
        return this.__p5lw;
    }
    public function set p5lw(value:Object):Void {
        this.__p5lw = value;
    }
// get/set 6lw
    public function get p6lw():Object {
        return this.__p6lw;
    }
    public function set p6lw(value:Object):Void {
        this.__p6lw = value;
    }

}
```

A class is a sort of template for an object. To understand objects, you only need to look around your immediate environment. Objects are all around us. To understand the concept of object-oriented programming, you must first understand that the initial approach most people take to programming is *procedural*. A procedural approach is one that takes logical steps one after another to cause the program to function in a logical and simple causal fashion. This is often sufficient for programming a game, but there are times when the approach is a bit limiting. Specifically, when a bit of code, a function, or even a group of attributes or properties will be used and reused many times with only slight changes, the program might be done more effectively by calling on an object.

Sometimes an object is useful simply because it is easier to refer to the object and to conceptualize the information, functions, or properties as parts of an object. This was the case with the dictionary. It is just easier to think of the dictionary as a thing that can be called upon to answer questions. In this case the question is generally, "Can I get a list of all of the words with the following qualities?"

The dictionary object is fairly simple one. It contains a constructor (which is the function that is designed to birth new instances of the object) and a series of getters and setters that allow the programmer to get and set the values of various properties of the object. The object script places everything within the class method. This class name must match the name assigned to the ActionScript itself without the *.as extension. The variables are then defined. These variables are declared as private variables in order to limit the scope of the variable to instances of the object.

OBJECT-ORIENTED PROGRAMMING IN ACTIONSCRIPT

Consider, for example, designing a car both *procedurally* and as an *object*. A car needs to accelerate, turn, reverse, honk, and many other things. It has many properties such as paint color, size, and weight. If you wanted to make more than one car, you would need to have a separate script for each instance of a car. Using the procedural programming method, you would need to have new variable names for the second car's paint color, size, and weight (Listing 5.9).

$\rightarrow$

LISTING 5.9   Pseudocode for a Car's Properties

```
car1.weight = 20
car2.color = #red
```

In an object-oriented model, the objects or instances of a script contain the defining elements of the class script, but they each have discrete properties. This means that in object-oriented programming `car1` has its own paint property, and so does each additional car.

No matter what you call it—a movie clip, a parent script, a behavior, a sprite, or an instance—the basic unit of every Adobe Flash and Shockwave game is an object. Because both ActionScript and Lingo support object-oriented programming methodologies and because games often call for many instances of similar objects, creating games that echo these structures is often the most intuitive and sensible approach.

The concept of objects and object-oriented programming exists in dozens of computer languages. The object model is implemented with sometimes slight and sometimes substantial differences in each of these languages. The approach in Adobe Flash's ActionScript is particularly well done, in no small part due to its strong allegiance to ECMA standards.

Adobe Flash uses an entirely object-driven paradigm, and as a result it uses prototypes rather than classes to form the basis of object instances. In Adobe Flash everything is an object. Automatically instanced class scripts (object definitions) in Flash are called prototypes. You can also create objects based on external ActionScript files that are loaded and added as prototypes when the application starts.

An object is a discrete entity. It would be fair to call it a thing, a node, or a widget. In object-oriented programming an object is the product or instance generated by a class. An

→

object can have properties, exhibit behaviors, execute methods, and calculate and return values. Reusability and encapsulation are the two most obvious benefits of object-oriented programming paradigms. You can use a single class script to create an unlimited number of specialized instance objects, and each of those objects is a protected, encapsulated instance. In other words, the instances don't affect or alter the class; they don't affect or alter one another.

There are two fundamental types of object: the composition object and the inheritance object. These are often thought of as the *has a* object and the *is a* object. Composition objects are based on physical things such as a food pantry. The food pantry object is not empty. It *has a* series of shelves inside, and each one contains other objects. The top shelf, for example, *has a* box of crackers on it. To recap, the food pantry *has a* shelf. The shelf *has a* box of crackers on it. The box of crackers *has a* quantity of crackers inside it.

The relationship between multiple objects within the composition object implies spatial containment. The grocery bag contains product boxes and bags of things such as peanuts and peppermints. The boxes and bags contain individual products. The relationship between these objects is similar to the relationship between composition objects. In Adobe Flash a vector graphic has a vertexList, which has a vector, which has an x and a y value. This approach is evident in Flash every time you open the Property inspector. Many of the properties of a selected object are all composition objects.

The other variety of object is called an *inheritance object*. These objects are generally used to model conceptual relationships rather than spatial ones. Lots of things exist only as conceptual or classification concepts and have no physical form. These are the sorts of things that fit well in this type of object structure.

$\rightarrow$

What sort of fruit is a fruit? Can you ask for fruit at breakfast and be certain of the result? Only in the sense that you'll probably be given some sort of fruit, but you have no idea whether to expect strawberries or bananas. Yet there is a substantial difference between strawberries and bananas. A strawberry *is a* fruit. A banana *is a* fruit, as *is a* kiwi. Because of this conceptual (*is a* type) relationship between objects, these objects inherit certain common qualities from their original classification. Fruit are all plants, and all are sweet, and all have seeds (barring genetic manipulation). This group gets their name, *inheritance object*, from this relationship. They are all able to descend from one class because we are able to conceptually link these things together. Their common origin exists in our heads.

To create a simple instance of any object, all you need to do is use a simple command—new. The new command calls a block of code called a constructor. In virtually any language that supports the object-oriented programming paradigm, the constructor creates an instance of the object based on the class template. Basically this statement creates a reference to the object, allocates memory for it, and initializes it. It isn't limited to these functions. It can do whatever you want it to. For now, think of it as the block of code that creates the instance of the object.

This is part of a more extensive discussion of object-oriented programming, including a comparison of the object-oriented programming methodology in Flash and Director available in the article "Shock Me, Flash Me, Just be Sure You Objectify Me: Object Oriented Programming in Flash and Director" (A. Partridge, 2004) in the Adobe Developers Center on the Adobe Web site (*www.adobe.com/devnet/director/articles/oop_dir_flash.html*).

It is also important to note that the properties of the objects within the class script are preceded by two underscores. This is required for each property of the object. These scripts are not complicated, but you must remember that they will create objects that can be referenced for custom functions or to simply act as efficient storage containers for some value (in this case the dictionary will store the three-, four-, five-, and six-letter word objects). The *n*-letter word objects will in turn store alphabetized lists of all the words. You can see this relationship in Figure 5.24.

Name	Value
$version	"WIN 8,0,22,0"
currentBet	0
currentCash	2000
⊟ dictionary	
__dictionaryName	"insDictionary"
⊟ __p3lw	
⊞ __A	
⊞ __B	
⊞ __C	
⊞ __D	
⊞ __E	
⊞ __F	
⊞ __G	
⊞ __H	
⊞ __I	
⊞ __J	
⊞ __K	
⊞ __L	
⊞ __M	
⊞ __N	
⊞ __O	
⊞ __P	
__pSize	3
⊟ __Q	
0	"QAT"
1	"QUA"
2	"QUO"
⊞ __R	
⊞ __S	
⊞ __T	
⊞ __U	
⊞ __V	
⊞ __W	
⊞ __X	
⊞ __Y	
⊞ __Z	
⊞ __p4lw	
⊞ __p5lw	
⊞ __p6lw	
focusEnabled	true
⊞ keyListener	

FIGURE 5.24 The relationship of the dictionary to the lists of different-sized words.

With every game, you will be challenged to reexamine fundamental paradigms and assumptions. This game is no different. One basic assumption with such a game is that dice are rolled randomly to choose six letters. This is probably neither the most efficient nor the most effective way to handle the selection of words for the game. The players will want to be able to solve the puzzle (or at least believe they might have been able to solve the puzzle). To get that feeling, they will need to get words that are reasonably common. The dictionary shouldn't be too overwhelming, or the players won't feel that they are having a positive gameplay experience.

The best way to select a set of letters is to choose a six-letter word at random. This avoids the possibility that no six-letter word can be created from the letters selected, removes the need for special code to adapt to the letter Q, and takes care of the problems created by vowel to consonant relationships.

We further optimized word selection by writing some code to ensure that all of the selected words would yield results of at least 6 and not more than 40 matches. The words were also restricted to those that would not cause overflow in the columns by exceeding 16 3-letter or 16 4-letter words. This could be further optimized by looking through the selected words to sort those that are very common, common, and less common. These typed lists could be used to create easy, medium, and hard versions that would adapt to the bet.

The major problem that remains is to figure out all of the words that might be guessed based on the major word and then create little placeholders for them on the screen so that the player can see how many words they have to guess. This logic is handled by the `rollDice()` function (Listing 5.10).

LISTING 5.10 The `rollDice()` Function: Variable Declarations

```
function rollDice():Void {
    var consArray;
    consArray = Array("A", "B", "C", "X", "Y", "Z");
    // Note that D-W have been removed here to avoid line
        wrapping.
    // You would need to have the entire alphabet in this
        list as it
    // is in the actual code.
    var tCharNum = randRange(0, 25);
    var tCharVal = consArray[tCharNum];
    var tDictionaryList = p6lw;
    var tWordList = tDictionaryList[tCharVal].slice();
```

```
var tWordListLength = tWordList.length-1;
var tWordPos = randRange(0, tWordListLength);
var tMasterWord = tWordList[tWordPos];
var tCharIter = 0;
_level0.roundMasterWord = tMasterWord;
var tLetter = "";
var iter;
var tIter;
var letters = 0;
var let;
var tLetterList;
var tKill3 = 1;
var tRange = 6;
var place;
var pLastWord = "";
var tLet2;
var tKill;
var dupList;
var tword;
var tWorkWord;
var remWord;
var tKill4 = 0;
var tDupString = "";
var getPos;
```

Many variables are involved, because the handler will loop through several cycles. If you think about it logically, the program must:

- Check each letter–word object
- Check each list of alphabetically sorted words within each object
- Check each word in each of those lists
- Eliminate from the potential characters any characters already used
- Check every letter in a potential matching word (at least until it finds an illegal letter and disqualifies the word)
- Valuate the potential word for:
  Duplicate characters
  Illegal characters
  Duplicate words
- Keep a record of legitimate words

Ultimately you also want to do this all very, very quickly. A typical player should have no idea that it took the computer a quarter of a million calculations or so to move them on to the next screen. It should seem instantaneous. The variables in Listing 5.10 are all small contributors to these loops. The basic approach of the design is geared toward minimizing operations. If any disqualifying condition is discovered, the loop moves out and on to the next word. This ensures that only viable candidates will go through all of the procedures used to validate a word. Most words won't make it past a single character check because the last letter of the word will not be included in the list of available letters. You can visualize this method as one that narrows the list of options with every test so that the pile of potential matches is thinned by a substantial percentage with every test, and only the very near misses are expensive in terms of processor time.

This is in some ways the least glamorous aspect of game programming and should not be overlooked. It makes a big difference to people that their gameplay experience is smooth and available completely on demand. People may not even be able to articulate why they didn't like an under-optimized game, but they will not enjoy the sluggish buttons, delays between screens, and other hassles that are sometimes seen when the code has not been carefully optimized. Now that this game is at a solid prototype stage, a great deal of time (far more than the 10 days that were spent on the initial development) will be invested in optimization and the details of the gameplay experience. This sort of tweaking is critical to the success of any game. In RAD these adjustments become integral from the outset, and testers will start letting you know their concerns and the quality of their experience immediately.

The code in the next section of the `rollDice` handler (Listing 5.11) clears out any previous characters in the array that will hold the list of active characters. The splice operation can be used to add or delete elements from an array. In this case the zero in the first argument indicates that the array should begin deleting in the first position and delete six entries. There are only six elements in the array, so this will clean the array for the next setup.

LISTING 5.11 The `rollDice()` Function: Out with the Old, in with the New

```
_level0.ranList.splice(0, 6);
for (tCharIter; tCharIter<6; tCharIter++) {
    _level0.ranList.push(tMasterWord.charAt(tCharIter));
}
_level0.tActiveWords.splice(0, _level0.tActiveWords.length);
```

The array is then built by adding six elements, each a character from the chosen master word. The characters are initially added in order. Left unchanged, this would result in displaying the letters in the master list of available letters on screen in the exact order that they are used in the full-length word. That, of course, would significantly reduce the challenge of the game. Later the list will be rearranged in order to prevent this.

The next section of code (Listing 5.12) jumbles the letters in the master word array that we just built by sorting the list alphabetically. Then the task of displaying the available characters for the player is done. The scope of variables and objects is critical in understanding what any given code in Flash will do. Earlier each of the small blocks was given an instance name in the property inspector. That instance name can now be used to refer to each instance of character text. We will need to change the text to reflect the available letters. Invisible buttons (square shape instances with an alpha value of 0%) were added above each character block so that the player could have a button to click to submit a letter. (Many players will prefer to type, but making both options available is generally the best practice.)

In the code the command `_root.char1.text = _level0.ranList[0];` sets the text of the corresponding character block to the text that was placed into the array in the previous bit of code. This is then repeated for each character. The buttons, called `let1 ... let6`, are then enabled. If the buttons were always enabled (the default), they would be clickable while the player was betting and choosing the Play button. This would cause problems with letters being selected before they were defined. The best practice is to prevent the call altogether. Now that we are going to move to the game area, the buttons must be enabled so that they will function as expected.

LISTING 5.12   The `rollDice()` Function: Show the Letters and Enable the
Buttons

```
_level0.ranList.sort();
_root.char1.text = _level0.ranList[0];
_root.char2.text = _level0.ranList[1];
_root.char3.text = _level0.ranList[2];
_root.char4.text = _level0.ranList[3];
_root.char5.text = _level0.ranList[4];
_root.char6.text = _level0.ranList[5];
this.let1.enabled = 1;
this.let2.enabled = 1;
this.let3.enabled = 1;
this.let4.enabled = 1;
this.let5.enabled = 1;
this.let6.enabled = 1;
```

Now the loops begin. It may help some to get a visual sense of the
manner in which the script approaches the problem. Figure 5.25 depicts
graphically the various loops that are used to parse the viability of each
word and identify the list of words that meet all of the requirements.

The outer loop represents the letter–word length objects in the
dictionary object (Listing 5.13). Each object is used, starting with the
largest (the six-letter word object) followed by each of the smaller
ones. The loop ends when the list requested is 2 (because we don't
care about or have two-letter words). It's important to remember
that these are the objects that in turn hold 26 sorted lists each.

LISTING 5.13   The `rollDice()` Function: The Outer Loop (for Each
Word–Length Object)

```
for (tRange; tRange>2; tRange--) {
    // for each word length
        // do this once for 6-letter words, once for 5, and
           so on
        let = (tRange-1);
```

Now while there are 26 letter lists contained in each of the letter
list objects, we don't need to look at all 26 of them. We know that

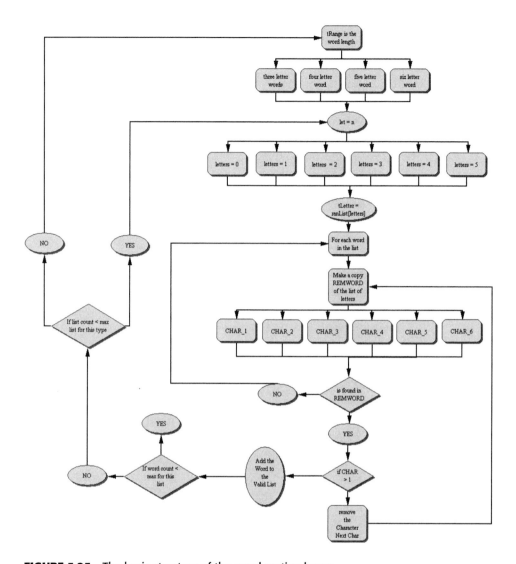

FIGURE 5.25 The basic structure of the word-sorting loops.

there are only six letters used in the word, so only the lists beginning with those letters are needed.

While Listing 5.14 starts the loop that collects the list of words, Listing 5.15 works with each individual word in the given list. A copy of the master word list is created that may be manipulated to ensure that characters from the allowed set are used only once. This is also prepared as a string to facilitate easy searching for character matches in the word.

LISTING 5.14   The `rollDice()` Function: The Second Loop (for Each Available Letter)

```
        // step through each letter in the ranList of letters
        for (letters; letters<6; letters++) {
            // for each letter available
            // get the alpha list object of this char length
// for the corresponding letter for each letter
// available
            tLetter = _level0.ranList[letters];
            // get the pNlw list - 6,5,4,3
            place = ("p"+tRange+"lw");
            // make a duplicate of the list
            tLetterList = _level0[place][tLetter].slice();
            // stores the length of the list of n letter
            // words for the current letter
            iter = tLetterList.length;
            // for each word in the list
```

LISTING 5.15   The `rollDice()` Function: The Third Loop (for Each Word In The List)

```
        for (iter; (iter>0); iter--) {
            //trace(iter+" ITER");
            // counting down from the end for each word
            // make a duplicate of available letters list
            dupList = _level0.ranList.slice();
            //remWord = dupList.toString();
            remWord = "";
            var tRemString = 0;
```

The small loop in Listing 5.16 is used to assemble the `remWord` string. Each character in the list of characters is concatenated to a string to make a string of the letters. This can then be used to perform string searches.

LISTING 5.16 The `rollDice()` Function: A Baby Loop (Assemble `remword`)

```
for (tRemString; tRemString<dupList.length;
    tRemString++) {
    remWord = remWord+dupList[tRemString];
}
```

Each of the letters in the proposed word is examined in the cycle depicted in Listing 5.17. The word is loaded, and then a working copy (one that can be chopped down into smaller bits) is created as tWorkWord. The word is examined one letter at a time, starting with the last letter and working through the length of the word. The `indexOf()` function tests to see if a letter is found in a string, so the letter of the main word is checked against the trial word. If the letter is not found in the trial word, the returned value will be -1. The number is loaded into a variable called tKill. If tKill holds a positive integer, then the loop continues, but if it is a negative number, the loop will be broken and the handler will go on to the next word.

LISTING 5.17 The `rollDice()` Function: The Third Major Loop (for Letters in Current Word)

```
tword = tLetterList[iter-1];
tWorkWord = tword;
for (let; (let>0); let-) {
// check each letter to make sure its
// legal
    tLet2 = tWorkWord.charAt(let);
    //dupList[let];
    //tDupString = dupList.toString()
    tKill = remWord.indexOf(tLet2);
```

Additional conditional tests of the proposed word and character further evaluate whether or not it is a viable candidate for the potential match words. The code in Listing 5.18 is used to adjust the testing elements. The successful match characters need to be removed from the testing strings so that they will not be options during the next loop.

LISTING 5.18   The `rollDice()` Function: Kill Conditions

```
// if not in remword -not a match
if (tKill<0) {
    tKill3 = 1;
    break;
} else {
    tWorkWord = tWorkWord.substring
    //(0, let)+tWorkWord.substring(let+1, tWorkWord.length);
    getPos = 0;
    for (getPos; getPos<dupList.length; getPos++) {
        if (dupList[getPos]==tLet2){
            dupList.splice(getPos, 1);
            remWord = "";
            var tRemString = 0;
            for (tRemString; tRemString<dupList.length;
            tRemString++) {
                remWord = remWord+dupList[tRemString];
            }
            break;
        }
    }
    tKill3 = 0;
}
tKill = null;
}

let = (tRange-1);
// the remword is the bits of the main word
// left (some having been applied)
remWord = "";
var tRemString = 0;
for (tRemString; tRemString<dupList.length; tRemString++) {
    remWord = remWord+dupList[tRemString];
}
```

Finally a check is run on the word to make certain it isn't already among those in the list of potential matches (Listing 5.19). If it is, the handler will throw the word out and the loop will be sent back for the next word. Basically any time you see a break, it's sending the loop back because there was a failure to find a valid word for one reason or another.

LISTING 5.19 The `rollDice()` Function: Conditions on Survivors

```
if (tKill3<1) {
    if (remWord.indexOf(tWorkWord.charAt(tWorkWord.
        length-1))>-1) {
        tIter = 0;
        for (tIter; tIter<_level0.tActiveWords.length;
            tIter++) {
            if ((_level0.tActiveWords[tIter] == tword)) {
                tKill4 = 1;
                break;
            }
        }
    }
```

When a valid word is finally found (Listing 5.20), the verified word is added to the list of active words for the current round. The word is removed from the list of items in the alphabetical list of words. After this, some general resetting is done in anticipation of the move back to the beginning of the loop. The process continues until all of the relevant words have been evaluated.

LISTING 5.20 The `rollDice()` Function: A Verified Word Is Found

```
                        if (tKill4 == 0) {
                        _level0.tActiveWords.push(tword);
                        tLetterList.splice(iter-1,1);
                        }
                    }
                }
            tKill3 = 1;
            tKill4 = 0;
            }
        remWord = "";
        }
    letters = 0;
    }
```

Once all of the words have been found, the handler calls the `layoutMinis()` function in order to create the tiny blocks that will suggest to the player how many words remain unsolved (Listing 5.21). They will provide a position for the reveal of the puzzle's solution and will encourage the player to feel assured that words remain that are yet to be discovered.

LISTING 5.21   The `rollDice()` Function: Call the Baby Blocks

```
        layoutMinis();
        _level0.pDuplicateRoundWords =
        _level0.tActiveWords.slice();
    }
```

The `layoutMinis()` handler uses the `attachMovie` function to dynamically attach the `babyChip` movie clip to the current movie. This is necessary because the elements that will be placed on the screen for a given round will be different depending on how many words can be used to solve the puzzle given the available options. While we know there are two columns of eight three-letter words and two columns of eight four-letter words, we don't really know how many three- to six-letter words will be used for any given master word. The on-screen cues then must be dynamically created based on the results of the `rollDice()` handler.

Fortunately Flash provides an easy method for dynamically loading a movie clip, in this case the small pink box. This `attachMovie` function simply adds the movie to your existing application on top of all the other layers (Figure 5.26). A text field is then added to the movie clip, so that it may display the character that corresponds to that chip.

The task of tracking the movie clips is a bit more involved because they are dynamically generated. This means that when they are created, their instance names must be stored in a list and they can then be recalled by using the list of movie clip names and comparing it to another list that stores the start position of each word.

There are two separate loops, one nested within the other in the next section of the `layoutMinis()` handler (Listing 5.22). The first one loops through all of the words for the given round and is performed

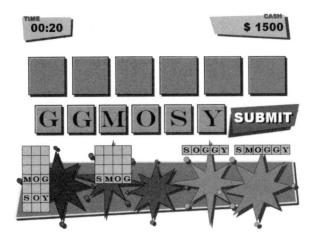

FIGURE 5.26 The mini chips are placed dynamically.

once for each viable word. The second, inner loop traverses through each of the blocks in a given word (Listing 5.23). Because the blocks need to be numbered sequentially, a special variable, tIndex, is iterated up by one every time the inner loop runs. This will be used to give each block in the round its own unique name.

LISTING 5.22 The layoutMinis() Handler

```
function layoutMinis():Void {
    this.focusEnabled = true;
    Selection.setFocus(this);
    var tMini = 0;
    var tBlocks = 0;
    var hexi;
    var tIndex = 0;
    var tColumn;
    var tWordCount = (_level0.tActiveWords.length);
    var tWord;
    var p6 = -1;
    var p5 = -1;
    var p4 = -1;
    var p3 = -1;
    _level0.pClipList = Array();
    _level0.pClipList.splice(0, _level0.pClipList.length);
```

The clip is given a name that combines with the number from tIndex, and that name is ultimately stored in a list of names so that the miniclips for any given word may be accessed later (Listing 5.23).

LISTING 5.23   The layoutMinis() Handler

```
for (tMini; tMini<tWordCount; tMini++) {
    tBlocks = 0;
    tWord = (_level0.tActiveWords[tMini]);
    for (tBlocks;
    tBlocks<_level0.tActiveWords[tMini].length; tBlocks++)
    {
        tIndex++;
        var theClipName = "babyBlock"+tIndex;
        this.attachMovie("ins_babyChip", theClipName,
        this.getNextHighestDepth());
```

The attachMovie command requires three arguments. The first is the name of the movie clip that you want to import. Note that this clip must be linked for access via ActionScript (Figure 5.27).

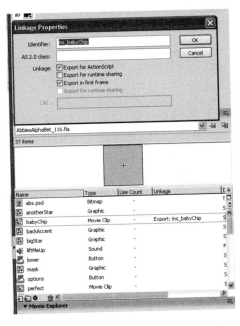

FIGURE 5.27   Movie clips must be linked before using attachMovie().

To prepare a movie clip for attachment in Flash, simply right-click on the clip in the library (F11 opens the library). From the drop-down context menu that appears, choose Linkage. The Linkage Parameters window will open. You will need to assign a linked name to the movie clip and choose Export for ActionScript and Export in first frame. The name you assign to the movie clip here will be the name you use in your code to provide the first argument for the `attachMovie` handler.

The second argument for the handler is the name that will be assigned to the instance in your movie. This is the name you will use internally to refer to this instance of the movie clip. The last argument is the depth at which you want the clip to appear. Generally this is on top of everything else, so it usually makes sense to simply use the `getNextHighestDepth()` function to return the position of the new top level instance. This will put your clip on top of everything else.

The next section of the `layoutMinis` handler creates a text field in the new movie clip instance and then sets the text and text style of that new instance (Listing 5.24). It makes the field display text in the right font and the right size and finally adds the name of the clip to the list of clips. Before moving on, the column is calculated, based on the word length.

LISTING 5.24   The `layoutMinis()` Handler

```
var label:TextField =
_level0[theClipName].createTextField(("tx"+theClipN
ame),
1, -12, -14, 24, 24);
label.text = "";
label.selectable = false;
var my_fmt:TextFormat = new TextFormat();
my_fmt.bold = true;
my_fmt.font = "Engravers MT";
my_fmt.size = 20;
label.setTextFormat(my_fmt);
_level0.pClipList.push(theClipName);
tColumn = (tWord.length);
```

The last section of this handler uses a case or switch statement to evaluate a property and respond to different clips differently (Listing 5.25). These clips have to be placed dynamically on the screen. The switch statement makes it possible to essentially say, "Hey make two rows of three letter words, eight words deep. Do the same with four-letter words, and then give five- and six-letter words one column each."

This is a little clunky, but ultimately it's faster to set it up this way so that the blocks will reliably print out on the screen in good positions and the little baby words will look good with everything else on the screen. The column is evaluated by the switch, and then it searches for the case that matches a given column width. Within each column the handler gets the appropriate clip and then sets it into the correct position, first horizontally and then vertically. At first, for three- and four-letter words this is placed in the left column of each, then if the block is obviously an instance of the ninth or greater words for that type, the group is moved to the right column and the height is reduced to compensate and move it back to the top of the second row.

Also at this point the startposition and number of cells in a word are stored to lists that will be used to determine which words (and characters) go with which movie clip instances.

LISTING 5.25 The layoutMinis() Handler

```
switch (tColumn) {
case 3 :
    _level0[theClipName]._x = (20+(tBlocks+1)*25);
    p3 = p3+1;
    _level0[theClipName]._y =
    (380+(Math.floor(p3/3)*25));
    if (p3%3 == 0) {
        _level0.pRoundWordStartList.push(tIndex-1);
        _level0.pRoundWordCountsList.push(tWord.length);
    }
    if (p3>=8*3) {
        _level0[theClipName]._x = (120+(tBlocks+1)*25);
        var t3 = p3-24;
```

```
            _level0[theClipName]._y =
            (380+(Math.floor(t3/3)*25));
        }
        break;
    case 4 :
        _level0[theClipName]._x = (220+(tBlocks+1)*25);
        p4 = p4+1;
        _level0[theClipName]._y =
        (380+(Math.floor(p4/4)*25));
        if (p4%4 == 0) {
            _level0.pRoundWordStartList.push(tIndex-1);
            _level0.pRoundWordCountsList.push(tWord.length);
        }
        if (p4>=8*4) {
            _level0[theClipName]._x = (340+(tBlocks+1)*25);
            var t4 = p4-32;
            _level0[theClipName]._y =
            (380+(Math.floor(t4/4)*25));
        }
        break;
    case 5 :
        _level0[theClipName]._x = (458+(tBlocks+1)*25);
        p5 = p5+1;
        _level0[theClipName]._y =
        (380+(Math.floor(p5/5)*25));
        if (p5%5 == 0) {
            _level0.pRoundWordStartList.push(tIndex-1);
            _level0.pRoundWordCountsList.push(tWord.length);
        }
        break;
    case 6 :
        _level0[theClipName]._x = (600+(tBlocks+1)*25);
        p6 = p6+1;
        _level0[theClipName]._y =
        (380+(Math.floor(p6/6)*25));
        if (p6%6 == 0) {
            _level0.pRoundWordStartList.push(tIndex-1);
            _level0.pRoundWordCountsList.push(tWord.length);
        }
        break;
```

```
default :
    break;
    }
        }
    }
}
```

You will find the prototype version of the game on your CD-ROM as AbbiesAlphaBet_117.fla found in the Tutorials\05media folder on the CD-ROM. A few changes have been applied since the earlier versions. There have been some graphical adaptations; for example, the buttons on the launch page have been altered to better match the color scheme. The background boxes have also been adapted on this page. These are still the same boxes, but the envelope tool was used to alter the group of boxes, applying curves to the outer edges of the overall background shape and twisting those edges to give it a more whimsical look (Figure 5.28).

FIGURE 5.28   The envelope tool was used to modify the box background.

An enterFrame event function was added to the movie to facilitate animated effects on the score box that displays the available cash. Adding an enterFrame event handler makes it possible to run an effect every time the playback head enters a frame. This means the dollar values in the Cash Available box could be rolled up by increments rather than just popping in dollar amounts. The result is that money earned is a more noticeable occurrence. The player sees the money rolling in and therefore is more aware that certain actions yield a monetary payoff.

Code was also added to this version to provide players with visual feedback when they quickly uncover either a five- or six-letter word (Figure 5.29). The player is shown a Speed Bonus! pop-up box for two seconds after earning this bonus. Additional points are awarded for speed bonus answers.

FIGURE 5.29 The Speed Bonus popup box appears for two seconds.

Another pop up, Perfect!, is displayed when a player successfully completes all of the words in the round before the clock expires. Bonus points, based on the amount of time left on the clock, are awarded for successfully solving the puzzle before the clock expires (Figure 5.30).

FIGURE 5.30   The Perfect game pop up.

In the end the prototype for *Abbie's AlphaBet* was created in a little over one week. About 30 people were able to test the software, and feedback was integrated into game design every day based on formal and informal feedback and testing. As feedback was received, ideas were ranked for importance, and those that fell at the top of the list (generally those required to make the game playable without obvious bugs) were implemented first.

This process is consistent with a general RAD approach. Some features remain unimplemented, and those will likely be implemented before the game is presented to potential distributors and portals. Each of the more than 100 versions of the game saved during development has been included for your perusal on the companion CD-ROM. You might find it useful to scan some of these to see how the game progressed over time.

SUMMARY

Rapid application development, or *RAD,* is an approach to software development often adopted in some form by casual game developers. It allows developers to include their potential customers in the design and development process and to consider the opinions of consumers as they create the game. RAD is not the perfect approach to every situation, but it is very often a good way to get an edge over other developers by increasing productivity as you create your game.

The game developed in this chapter is a good example of the way RAD development can help you quickly generate a functional prototype to evaluate how successful the gameplay experience will be. If after testing a game like this, you find that the target audience is dissatisfied with the experience, you've only invested a week and can easily reexamine the problems. If you had spent years on such a project, your overhead for changes would be enormous.

Part

II

Understanding the Market and the Business Model

6 Games in the Market

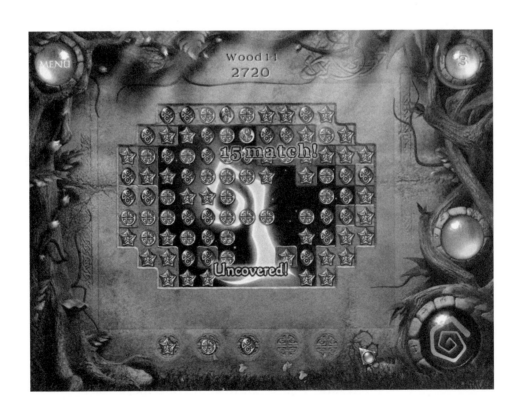

In This Chapter

■ Popular Genres
■ Appeal and Limitations
■ Professional Practice: Brian Robbins & the Casual Future

One distinct aspect of the casual games market is that the genres (types) of games that are distributed within the industry are fairly narrowly defined. *Conversion rates* on casual games are very low, and a healthy dose of the profits are generated by advertising. People like to find their favorite kind of game quickly and easily. This chapter describes the most popular genres of casual games and explains the qualities that typify games in each classification. Qualities common to all of the games in the market are also described. Finally, the question of future directions for the casual games market is addressed. An interview with Brian Robbins, casual game developer and cofounder of the International Game Developers Association Casual Games Special Interest Group reveals a vision of potential expansion of the current market through community evolution and multiplayer online experiences.

In this chapter you will learn how to:

■ Identify the major genres of casual games
■ Identify the qualities of the different genres
■ Design games that bridge genres
■ Design games that innovate by evolving features and qualities of a genre
■ Compare and evaluate the qualities of games
■ Understand professional practice related to genre choice, innovation, and feature design

The International Game Developers Association (IGDA) is the preeminent organization of professional game developers. The organization is composed of chapters throughout the world and presents the Game Developers Choice awards in association with the Game Developers Conference.

POPULAR GENRES

It isn't terribly difficult to figure out which genre is hot and which genre is not when it comes to casual games. Remember that it is all about the money and pay a visit to any of the major distribution portals. You'll find the games organized into common types or genres of casual games. The most common of these are puzzle, card, arcade, action, strategy, and word games. Sometimes word games don't even make the cut and action and arcade are often combined into one category. Puzzle games are almost always listed first, and among the puzzles, the match-three dynasty reigns supreme.

The match-three games are all descendents of the fill the cup tradition made popular by *Tetris*. The basic motif in this group of games is that players must identify or create a match of three or more like-colored objects in order to clear the board or empty the cup. These games generally provide some sort of clock against which the player competes to make as many matches as possible within a given time period.

The arcade games and action or shooter genre hearken back to the classic arcade titles of the 1980s and 1990s. They are generally similar to arcade classics, involving targeting, shooting, battling, and/or navigating via a main player character. Unlike their actual ar-cade cousins, these games generally don't have complex screens or screen movement but tend to stick to single-image or -location en-vironments to simplify the player's experience. It is also common to find puzzles that mimic the multipiece jigsaw puzzles (lots of assem-bly required) that you might remember from your grandmother's kitchen table. Simple strategy games and simulations have been growing more and more common in the industry, with titles like *Diner Dash* fast becoming household names. Card games remain a significant mainstay, and surveys suggest that they are some of the most popular options for online play.

MATCH-THREE DYNASTY

Any game or puzzle that requires the player to match sets of on-screen tokens belongs in the powerful and addictive match-three dy-nasty. These are all essentially matching games that require the player to create like-sets—usually like colored sets. Games of this type have dominated the casual games industry for the past several years. The major leaders in the category were *Collapse* and *Bejeweled*. Both have enjoyed tremendous popularity and longevity and both are fundamentally match-three–style games.

In *Collapse* layers of blocks rise from the bottom of a cup, and players identify groups of adjacent blocks of the same color. If the player clicks on a block amid a cluster of more than two blocks, all of the adjacent blocks of that color are removed from the board. The basic game mechanic is intensely, surprisingly addictive, and the subsequent variations in *Collapse 2* and *Collapse 3* gathered even more fans to the game. There have been many variations in recent years that are similar in style and game play. One that is particularly appealing is Sandlot Games' *Glyph* (Figure 6.1). There is no ques-tion about it; *Glyph* is a gorgeous game. With a particularly well-designed progress map and mini-game sequence, *Glyph* combines the match-three mechanics with jigsaw and musical pattern match-ing challenges.

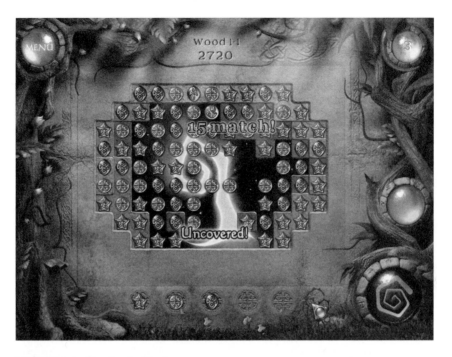

FIGURE 6.1   The basic *Glyph* game screen. All *Tradewind Legends, Westward,* and *Glyph* properties are trademarks, registered trademarks, or copyrights owned exclusively by Sandlot Games Corporation. All Rights Reserved.

In *Bejeweled* the matching is done by switching the position of one token on the screen (a jewel in this case). If the switch results in a sequential match of three or more tokens, the tokens are removed and points are awarded. Variations make the switching differ, the new tokens appear from different directions, and the look and feel of the game differs. The paradigm is very common, with similar games such as Ignition Entertainment's *Zookeeper* appearing on the Nintendo DS. Many of the more recent ones have added barrier crushing as an internal limit or untimed meter that gives the player a short-term goal and in essence lends the game a stress free (or stress reduced) end of session point.

How many games are there in this category? You'll go cross-eyed counting. A limited survey found about 30 such variants already available via common download portals. There are many, many games in this genre. They tend to be very similar, probably so that the players can easily learn the variations in the new game.

Most portals feature jigsaw and other puzzles in addition to the match-three genre. These include a substantial number of variants that, while puzzles, generally don't require much serious thought to complete. Some of the jigsaw puzzles are astonishingly well executed. They frequently allow players to customize the jigsaw-playing interface and even allow players to vary the number of pieces and replace images with their own photographs.

ARCADES AND SHOOTERS

Zuma and *Luxor* are among the most popular titles in this genre. In the tradition of *Snood* and *Breakout*, each is a basic shooting and targeting game that encourages players to shoot a ball at a target to create matched sets of balls. Games in this category are generally timed and usually elicit an excited response. They tend to be a bit more stressful to play and can be faster paced than games in the puzzle category (though there are certainly puzzles that are just as energizing).

Breakout-style games (games that feature breakable blocks that are targeted and destroyed using a paddle to deflect a bouncing ball or balls) are generally assigned to this category. Just as it is often difficult to put specific labels on films and books, it is often difficult to put specific labels on games. Many games have some aspects that make them good candidates for this category but also might be assigned elsewhere. In some cases portals will list the games in multiple categories when they feel it will increase sales opportunities. Other puzzles are rooted in Tanagrams, sequence-order games, and even number and logic puzzles.

WORD AND TRIVIA

A dominator in the word game market since its introduction has been *Bookworm*. This charming game broke onto the scene tickling just the right funny bone for fans of word manipulation puzzles and heavily addictive *Tetris*-style cup-draining puzzles. The game requires players to empty a cup full of lettered tiles by making words from adjacent letters on the tiles. Aided by a brilliantly simple and remarkably clear feedback system, players click letters one at a time to make words. The game found its niche with a rare combination of addictiveness and intrinsic rewards. Word games often suffer from severe onscreen clutter, and the result is limited appeal based on in-game screenshots.

Both word and trivia games have a substantial appeal for the primary demographic. Our target female is likely to enjoy both word and trivia games. While this is not the largest genre, it is a significant one. Perhaps the most important consideration developers face in this arena is the problem of ease of use. Like card games, word games can have complex and convoluted rules. One recent release, *Pat Sajak's Wheel of Fortune*, responds to this limitation by adding recorded step-by-step instructions the first time a player encounters the game. Trivia games have a similar need, though years of classroom testing provide a pretty solid format for most trivia games, enabling multiple-choice–style selection. While the interfaces vary, all of these games provide clear, easy access to the game, and virtually all encourage ongoing play by giving the player hints and other advantages to keep stress from mounting.

STRATEGY AND SIMS

You can usually spot a strategy or simulation game because it has *Tycoon* in the title. *Fish Tycoon, Lemonade Tycoon, Coffee Tycoon, Diner Dash,* and others allow the players to put themselves in a simulation of a real-world experience. Some such simulations are physics-based simulations of objects in motion, such as air-blowing simulations in which the player tries not to pop the bubble or ball-rolling simulations such as golf or bowling. In other cases the games are more focused on strategy. In *Plantasia,* for example, the player tends a garden, while in *Fish Tycoon* you work to manage and maintain a stock of fish. In the popular *Diner Dash* the player works to keep the customers happy, feeding them and clearing tables to earn tips.

MAHJONG, CARD, AND BOARD GAMES

A very popular genre in today's casual game market is *Mahjong* (*sparrow* in Chinese). This is a nineteenth-century Chinese game of skill and strategy. The original was a four player game played with tiles, but computer variants are generally intended for single players (*Mahjong Solitaire*). The playing pieces are specially decorated domino tiles featuring characters that are designed to be matched. These can be copies of the standard Mahjong deck of tiles or variations featuring all sorts of images.

For this reason, the game is often coupled with puzzle games in casual game portals. Because it probably evolved from Chinese domino and card games, it might be more correctly placed with card and board games. The game is so popular today that many portals are now dedicating a special classification just for Mahjong.

One of the most popular game genres is the *card game*. Probably extensions of ancient dominos, today's playing cards are based on those designed in France during the fourteenth century. Card games have been popular since their invention—probably about one thousand years ago in Central Asia. An extremely popular card game, solitaire, made the leap onto the personal computer. Microsoft packaged a free version of the game with early operating systems, and it is often called the first successful casual game. A mainstay of office secretaries worldwide, the game provided a quick distraction from the worries of the office.

Even before Microsoft solitaire, video poker had made an appearance. Card games have always been popular. Computer-based card games provide a channel for individuals to play the games even when they have no opponents to play with. This has always been the case with solitaire but is now also the case with multiplayer card games that can be played either against the computer or against other individuals communicating via the Internet.

Some innovation has been seen in this arena, but for the most part, the conventions of early card games have been followed. Most provide simple interfaces that focus almost exclusively on the cards. The emphasis is absolutely on instant recognition and facilitating the player's desire to have a familiar game experience.

APPEAL AND LIMITATIONS

Within the lifetime of any media form, there is a tendency to begin with a tremendous base. The form generally courts the support of the broadest possible audience. The materials that are distributed within the new media form are often as benign as possible. In early radio the term *potted-palm music* was used to describe this sort of bland neutrality that dominated the airwaves, encouraging everyone to listen often and without any concern that they might be offended or bothered by any of the entertainment. This is hardly the way you would describe radio today.

It is, however, the way you would describe the casual games industry today. The games have a strikingly benign, harmless quality. They are aimed at the broadest possible audience and rarely contain any material that could be considered in any way edgy or offensive. The games are clearly classified and designed to provide the most convenient, easy-to-use access for their audience. Portals have devoted enormous amounts of energy, time, and resources into making the acquisition of the games as simple, reassuring, and pleasant as is possible. All of these efforts are directed at an audience that is just beginning to learn the traditions and conventions of the media. Over time, people will become more accustomed to the basic conventions and concepts of the industry, and there will be more room for developers to make dramatic changes to the way that these problems are addressed. In the short term, some basic concepts can guide developers to success in the creation of casual titles: (1) stick to the available genres, (2) ensure that the player's experience is convenient and easy, and (3) make choices that facilitate the *escapist* experience of your intended audience.

STICK TO THE GENRE

One of the first questions a producer or acquisitions editor at one of the major portals will ask is, "What genre is the game?" They are considering whether or not they can sell your game just as much as they are considering whether or not it is a good game. A significant number of really great games go undistributed largely because they are not marketable within the constraints of these genres. That breakthrough idea in gameplay is as big a curse as it is a blessing, and it may even be all curses if you cannot find a way to distribute the game once it is finished, just because it uses a gameplay mechanic that is unfamiliar to the casual audience.

Of course, the bulk of casual games that go undistributed are just not well enough produced. You won't be making a successful casual title in your basement overnight. It takes considerable time and resources to produce a slick, clean, finished title. A 30-second Web game will probably not draw any serious distribution offers. It's fine to create games that contain elements of more than one of the major genres, and it may even be all right to create something that moves beyond a genre if it clearly remains a casual game.

This does not mean you should attempt to simply clone or copy an existing game within a genre. First, you'll lose the respect and support of a very kind and helpful community of game developers if you start cranking out copies of their games. You will also do yourself a significant disservice. Most of the fun of developing games is in creating your own gameplay ideas and experiences. Even within a very established genre, you can always think of some new ideas that modify or evolve the game to give customers a new experience. Your contributions should also not be trivial. Changing the tokens but copying exactly the mechanics and layout of an established game is not a serious attempt at innovating in a genre. Let your narrative concepts help determine the way your games are designed and played, and you are unlikely to be guilty of cloning another title.

THE IMPORTANCE OF EASE

Ultimately casual game players are looking for a hassle-free experience. They sat down at the computer to escape. The goal is to find a reality escape through the entertainment you designed. The last thing anyone wants when they sit down to relax and escape their problems is to fight with a dysfunctional computer. They don't know how to play your game unless (1) the game is identical or similar (at least in controls) to some other game they've already played or (2) the game teaches them (effortlessly) how to play. It is in this vein that casual games all fall within common genres.

Players can easily find the kind of game that offers them a familiar and satisfying escape. They launch their browser, find a portal, and surf straight to the genre they like. The games within that genre should all provide them with the sort of satisfaction that they crave, and ideally they'll like the game enough to pay for the upgrade.

PROFESSIONAL PRACTICE: BRIAN ROBBINS & THE CASUAL FUTURE

Brian Robbins has worked on a variety of casual game titles from the earliest years of the industry. He has contributed to over one hundred commercial titles in the *advergaming* and casual gaming arenas. Brian has worked with Fuel Industries, Game Trust, Clever-Media, and Worlds Apart Productions (now SOE Denver). In addition to his significant experience as a game developer, Brian was a cofounder of the International Game Developers Association's (IGDA) Casual Games Special Interest Group (SIG). Through the SIG he strives to provide the community with a common base to work from via whitepapers, wikis, and other resources that provide constantly updated information about the state of the industry to the members of the community.

Partridge: *Brian, you've been actively observing the state of the casual games industry since its inception. Do you have any predictions about the likely direction the industry will take in the near and not-so-near future?*

Robbins: While I don't think that low conversion rates mean that downloads are a broken model, there is certainly room for new ways to monetize consumers. In the very near future we're going to see a lot more portals building their catalog of Web-based titles and incorporating community features into otherwise single-player games. The industry is going to have to realize that the long-term value in this space is in creating a better experience for the player—one that makes them want to keep coming back to the same site or portal.

→

In the longer term, we are definitely going to see a rise in new payment methods. There will be a lot more games with item-based sales, where the initial game is free or close to it, and players pay for items that enhance or expand the experience. We've seen this model for years in the Asian MMO [massive multiplayer online] marketplace, and it's just starting to catch on in North America.

Partridge: *The problems presented by multiplayer games supported by multiple portals have been substantial (portals don't want to invite customers to learn more about competing sites, unrestricted speech creates opportunities for undesirable user comments, and economic models become difficult to pin down). How do you see the role of community evolving in the casual games industry?*

Robbins: Online communities made possible by an increasingly social Web are going to become an increasingly present aspect of casual games. Right now, that community is limited to global leader-boards or chat that appears around Web-based demos. I think we're going to start to see much more real community features become a standard in downloadable titles too. So far, nobody seems to have figured out how to do this right, but I think it's just a matter of time. The long-term stickiness of community is too important to leave behind.

I also see community playing a larger role in the actual design of the game through user-generated content. Sites like *Kongregate* which reward developers for making games the community enjoys, and *Pjio* which allows for an extremely low barrier to entry for game developers to get onto a portal and achieve a fair share of the revenue generated. This is going to change the way many players experience games. With no approval process to go through, we'll see games with a lot less polish, but much more unique gameplay.

$\rightarrow$

Partridge: *With such small conversion rates on downloadable casual games, do you have any recommendations for developers to maximize their profits within the casual games industry?*

Robbins: Developers need to make sure they know what they are giving away in the contracts they sign. A good game will find an audience and will be able to reach a lot of consumers. It is rarely worth it to sign away everything just to get that initial exposure. Fight to get a share of the advertising revenue, and a share of every other bit of revenue that your content generates, but also remember that publishers and portals aren't automatically the enemy. There is a lot they can provide if you work with them, but you need to make sure that the risk/reward is monetized fairly.

Developers should also look to take advantage of all the revenue models they can. Downloadable sales work very well for quite a few games, but in the coming years there are going to be many more ways to make money from casual games. The most successful developers will be the ones that take advantage of every reasonable opportunity they can.

Partridge: *What kinds of support mechanisms exist for developers just getting started in the casual games industry? Do you have any recommendations for new casual game developers?*

Robbins: One of the biggest reasons this space has evolved so much is the openness and collaborative nature of the entire community. There are a very significant number of people who realize that the casual games business doesn't have to be cutthroat and that it is in all of our best interests to continue sharing our best practices with each other. When we all collaborate to make our products and methods better, the result will be a much bigger and stronger marketplace for everyone to profit from.

$\rightarrow$

I would recommend that anyone serious about the industry should get involved with groups like the IGDA's Casual Games SIG, the Casual Games Association, and any other local developer groups that might exist. I guarantee that the more you contribute to these types of endeavors the more you will get out of them in return.

SUMMARY

Casual games tend to fall into several well-defined classifications or genres. Distributors and portals use these classifications to determine both how to sell the game and as a factor influencing whether or not they will carry the game. Each of the major classifications contains games that are easy to use and facilitate the players' desire to escape from their daily stresses.

The state of casual games may well be in flux. As computer users learn more and more about the conventions of computer games, casual games will probably become more and more complex to provide adequate challenges to entertain their audience.

7 Audience

In This Chapter

■ Demographics
■ Professional Practice: Adriano Parrotta, Emotion & Audience

Who is your audience? Most likely it is a 40-year-old woman with an interest in travel, pets, and gardening. But your audience is ultimately diverse, and the broader your game's appeal, the more likely you are to be able to sell your game via a diverse array of distribution outlets. In this chapter you'll learn more about the demographics of your target audience in order to better understand who plays casual games and, perhaps even more importantly, who buys them.

In this chapter the apparent tastes of casual game purchasers are described, as are the expectations of the typical casual game player. Patterns that are geared toward mass appeal in the market are identified. Finally, Adriano Parrotta, from Oberon Media, describes the role of demographics in the casual games industry.

In this chapter you will learn:

■ What are the key demographics of the casual games industry
■ How can you leverage those demographics and broaden your audience
■ What is involved in appealing to the core demographic
■ How industry insiders feel about casual game appeal and core audience
■ How to create games that innovate given the core demographic

DEMOGRAPHICS

We know that the average casual game purchaser is a forty-something on a broadband connection. She sits down to play more than once a day on average and she sticks to it for at least an hour when she does. She favors puzzles and/or card games.

What about the rest of the market? We also know that many, many times more people download and play casual games than those who buy them. This fundamental problem, the failure to monetize the download of a game, remains unsolved in the casual games arena. The consumer says, "Why buy the game when the fun is free?" The developer says, "Fifty thousand people played my game last month and I didn't recover enough to pay the light bill." The most dramatic offenders are young audiences. They'll spend a fortune on entertainment every week but wouldn't dream of dropping $20 to pay for a downloaded game. The industry is clearly in an entrepreneurial stage of development as companies search wildly for business models that improve the profit margin and broaden the target demographic.

Much of the evolution of casual games thus far has focused on targeting the games toward this females-over-40 demographic and improving the quality of the games. Investigations are also well under way that explore expanding the audience and making profits off a broader group of players. Clearly, advertising is a serious option for generating income, but much of the advertising thus far has involved creating "branded" games (or advergames) that celebrate the company or product and place the advertising in so prominent a role that players are immediately "wise" to the ploy.

We know that millions of people of all ages are downloading and playing games on the Internet. It isn't clear yet what the best method will be for converting this audience into a paying audience. Chances are good that the eventual model will combine all of the existing models, and if advertising-supported game distribution is going to perform competitively, it will need to clearly demonstrate that it has an impact within a given demographic and that industry can use that demographic appeal to target marketing efforts at potential consumers.

WHO WILL PLAY YOUR GAMES?

The audience for your games may not be as clear as women in their 40s. You may find that you are developing games that appeal to a different audience, and eventually there may be a clearer distribution outlet (or advertising-funded outlet) for your game. At this point, the typical casual game is likely to emphasize the women-over-40 demographic, or at least appeal to a broad enough audience that this target audience is included.

Significant evidence suggests that the data regarding women playing casual games are seriously skewed by the fact that (1) kids have their moms buy them games online and (2) several surveys show that young people are the major demographic on a wide array of casual games sites. The audience numbers seem to vary significantly from one portal to the next, with sites like Nick.com drawing a decidedly younger audience than PopCap, for example.

Assuming that the primary audience is women, the next logical question is how might that change the style and approach you take for your games? Acclaimed interface design visionary Brenda Laurel might be the first to have investigated this question. Laurel conducted early experiments for Interval Research Corporation in virtual reality and interface design. At the same time, Laurel and research associate Rachel Strickland were fascinated by the role played by gender in video games. Laurel worked with investors to launch the upstart game company Purple Moon in the 1990s, which released several girl-friendly games. She posited that girls would migrate toward technology more readily if they were exposed to games that interested them. Basically, Purple Moon found that girls were more interested in social interaction and narrative than blood, guts, and mayhem.

These principles are easily extended to women in the casual games demographic. Women are not generally attracted to shooting games or violence. People in this demographic often have some fear or uncertainty regarding the technology. The market group is often more interested in social experience and escape than in competition or battle.

WHY WILL THEY PLAY YOUR GAMES?

For the most part, you have about 1–5 square inches of graphics and 50 words to convince potential customers to play your game. Most portals allow you to use a small graphic (about 2 × 3 inches) and a couple of small icons to advertise your game (see Figure 7.1). You will generally provide a couple of small icon-sized graphics, or *bugs*, that will be visible if a player looks for more information about your game (Figure 7.1).

FIGURE 7.1   Very little is shown to get players to download. © Reflexive Entertainment. All Rights Reserved.

On the landing page most games get only a small graphic and limited bit of text to convince players to download. If the opening image is enough to elicit a response, the player will often be taken to a detail page, which shares more information about the game (Figure 7.2).

Generally the detail page will feature three very small thumbnails of screenshots along with small graphics and a more detailed description of the game. The players are more likely to download your game if the topic interests them and fits within their expectations and if they feel confident that playing the game will be similar to another game they enjoyed. By far the biggest factor influencing your game's success will be the length of time that it remains above the fold (in the top three to six games listed on the site). These prime listings are reserved for new launches and games that are particularly popular. Your game will need near-instant popularity to catch and hold this position for any length of time.

FIGURE 7.2 The detail page gives more info, but not much.

UNDERSTANDING MASS APPEAL

A mass medium is a technology-enabled communication channel, such as a book, radio, or television, that enables communication to a large group of people. The Internet-enabled personal computer is a mass medium. Casual games are a type of media delivered via that medium. The particularly interesting and pertinent information that is revealed by seeing this similarity between casual games and television shows or films is that it is possible to see patterns in the life cycle of every major mass medium since the book. Most notably, each begins its life as a new experimental technology and then enters an entrepreneurial phase wherein people try to make it profitable. The medium then enters a stable phase where profits can be reliably generated. Finally the medium is replaced or pressured by new media, and in order to continue to compete, it enters a demassification phase. During this phase the medium diversifies and attempts to appeal to niche audiences based on narrowly defined demographics.

ANTICIPATING DEMASSIFICATION

Some futurists have pointed to the increasing rates of new technology adoption and suggested that we are fast approaching a point of singularity, a moment in time at which new innovations will appear faster than we as a society can adapt to them. In a similar vein, it is easy to see evidence of all four phases of growth existing simultaneously in this industry that is only a few years old. Regardless of the timing, one thing is reasonably certain: the market will demassify.

At that point, matching your game's appeal to the right demographic will become absolutely imperative. Success or failure will absolutely hinge on finding the right audience, advertising to that audience, and then delivering a satisfying game experience to that audience.

PROFESSIONAL PRACTICE: ADRIANO PARROTTA, EMOTION & AUDIENCE

Adriano Parrotta is a developer partner manager at Oberon Media, a leading publisher and distributor of casual games. His job is to locate casual games and build relationships with the developer community. Before working at Oberon Media, Adriano worked as a facilities designer and project manager for a large insurance company, but his passion has always been with videogames. According to Parrotta, "This job allows me to be in direct contact with the developers that run the casual games industry, and by helping them become successful it helps grow this industry even further."

Partridge: *How should developers respond to the dominance of women in the demographic of casual game consumers when creating new games?*

Parrotta: The game development industry, whether it is casual games or core games, is mainly run by men. This really makes it difficult to tap into the tendencies that women have toward videogames. Developers need to make more effort to realize what women want out of their games. We often see games that try too hard to appeal to the female demographic, but they miss the mark entirely by focusing on the superficial aspects. This only serves to alienate your potential audience, as people do not like being portrayed by stereotypes. There have been too many examples of this in the casual games space.

Developers must get into the psyche of their potential audience. There are many books and articles out that have varying opinions on what the differences between men and women are. For example, one main distinction between the male and female audience is that men tend to gravitate towards games that are destructive (first person shooters, real

$\rightarrow$

time strategy combat games), whereas women tend to gravitate towards games that are constructive (simulation games,
puzzle games). While this is not a hard wall, there is always
crossover within these two categories. In doing any analysis
of the sales of games relative to the two demographics, you
will find this distinction bears out.

Partridge: *What is the role of emotion in games, and the potential of emotional appeal to expand the market?*

Parrotta: Emotion within video games can appeal to untapped markets, which includes women and people that
don't traditionally consider videogames as a form of entertainment. Emotion is what draws the player into the game
world. The reason why people watch movies and read
books is to experience the emotion that goes along with the
story. Movies that convey a love story create a distinctly different emotion than suspense movies. Video games are just
starting to tap into these emotions on a grand scale. Emotion
in video games is created by thoughtfully melding the story,
control, sound, and visuals to create a captivating experience
for the game player, and if you are able to get all of these elements working together, then you will be able to successfully
convey whatever emotional effect you are hoping to have on
the player. By putting some emotional appeal behind your
games, you stand a better chance of luring the nongamers
into the market, and by continually providing this sort of
emotionally driven content you have a better chance of holding their interests going forward.

Diner Dash is an extremely popular game within the casual game space. This game is a good example of how emotion can be brought into the gameplay in order to achieve a
connection with the player. The emotional connection in
the game is brought about by a few different design features.

$\rightarrow$

One of the main emotion triggers is the story itself, with the main character quitting her job as a stock broker to become a small business owner. Many people can connect with this idea, and it becomes a motivator for the player to progress through the game. Another is the use of emotion as an actual gameplay mechanic. The player must balance the need to accomplish things with the need to keep their customers happy. As the customers get more upset by waiting around, your tip money goes down and eventually they leave the restaurant. By the on-screen characters showing this sort of dynamic emotion, it elicits a response by the player as well.

Action games aren't the only genres that benefit from emotion. Puzzle games can achieve an emotional response from the player, thus driving the connection with the game. An example of this would be the game *Lumines*. This puzzle game was able to thoughtfully incorporate music in order to create this connection. The music changes dynamically with every action the player makes on screen. The entire theme changes from level to level, keeping the player hooked to see what comes up next. As you can see from these examples, emotion within games can be achieved under any circumstance. It just takes further planning and forethought in order to achieve the emotion you desire throughout the game.

Partridge: *You see an enormous number of games, including a significant number that don't make the cut for distribution. What advice would you give to developers working to craft their games for this market?*

Parrotta: The casual games market has come a long way over the last couple of years. There are many categories that are heavily populated and it may be hard to come into some of the established genres and be successful by merely creating a similar game that has been doing well in that

$\rightarrow$

space. The game that really gets noticed is the game that adds something new to the genre. I encourage everyone to create the games that they want to make, because we must keep the industry going by encouraging creativity, but it is important to push genres forward with your new games. Another thing to keep in mind is that the games that have been the most successful recently are the ones that have either created their own genres or done something so drastically different within the existing genre that they stood out and were noticed by the casual games audience.

Being truly creative and doing something that has never been done before is exceedingly difficult, but can bring to you a large payoff if it becomes the next big hit within the industry. Having said that, it is also important to realize that this is a growing industry that is always looking for new content, and that we are more than happy to take a look at your game at any stage of development in order to help with the direction of the game and to make it more successful. No matter what, you should never be discouraged from showing your game to a leading publisher or distributor. You never know what the reaction might be, and even if it is a negative reaction, it can only serve to help you create a better game in the end.

Partridge: *With the industry growing so rapidly, and with so many new options available to the new developer, what is something that they should look out for?*

Parrotta: Understanding the contracts you sign is probably the most important thing facing developers getting into the industry. We are currently working to expand the casual games market as widely as possible with new initiatives and outside-the-box thinking. The industry will probably be very different in two years than it is today. It is important for developers to take advantage of every opportunity

→

available to them within the industry. There have been stories of developers signing unfavorable contracts that have limited their ability to take advantage of the fantastic growth that this industry is experiencing. My advice to combat this would be for the developers to read through all their contracts and understand the implications of what they are signing. It is a shame when a developer signs a contract that they feel is beneficial up front only to learn that they are limited in what they can do within the market. There are great opportunities to be had within the casual games industry, and my feeling is that what is best for the developer is best for the industry.

SUMMARY

The audience for casual games is quite broad and growing steadily. It includes virtually anyone who uses a computer and who enjoys an occasional escape. The audience continues to grow by attracting new players from those who feel somewhat intimidated or overwhelmed by hard-core games. Purchasers of downloadable games are still most likely to be women over 40, but the audience is expanding, and it is likely to continue to broaden.

While we can identify the core qualities of a likely purchaser, targeting those qualities in a trivial way is not likely to appeal to a potential customer. They will probably find the effort transparent and ignore it. Industry insider Adriano Parrotta points out the growing potential of emotion and narrative to capture an audience and provide longevity for a brand or series of games. Parrotta also echoes the words of many industry experts when he challenges developers to innovate and create games that meet the needs of casual gamers but manage to stretch genres or create entirely new ones.

8 The Business Model

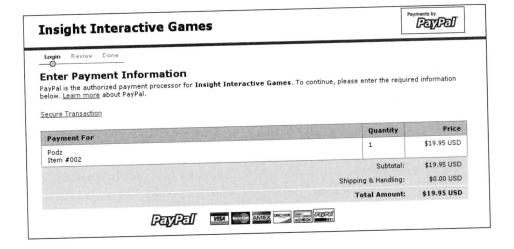

Insight Interactive Games   Payments by **PayPal**

Login Review Done

Enter Payment Information

PayPal is the authorized payment processor for **Insight Interactive Games**. To continue, please enter the required information below. Learn more about PayPal.

Secure Transaction

Payment For	Quantity	Price
	1	$19.95 USD
Podz Item #002		
	Subtotal:	$19.95 USD
	Shipping & Handling:	$0.00 USD
	Total Amount:	**$19.95 USD**

PayPal VISA MasterCard AMEX DISCOVER eCHECK PayPal

In This Chapter

■ Downloadable Casual Games
■ Alternative Distribution Paths
■ Professional Practice: Andy Phelps on Image and Community

Common business practices in the casual games industry are surprisingly well established given the very short time the industry has had to develop procedures and define norms. Casual game delivery systems may be easily divided into three basic categories. The mechanism that dominates (at least in our perception) is the downloadable casual game using a digital rights management (DRM) installation and wrapping device to handle the financial transactions. Embedded in this model is a growing tradition of advertising-supported online demos that provide a taste of the game without time limits and sometimes with limited features.

The other *alternative* distribution options for casual games include a growing number of delivery systems, many of which are also growing in popularity. Overseas flights are beginning to carry casual games on the backs of passenger seats as an option to in-flight movies, and more and more casual games are appearing on handheld game devices. Casual games delivered on CD-ROM are still sold in computer and office supply stores and via personal handheld devices such as cell phones and PDAs.

In this chapter you will learn:

■ How casual games are bought and sold
■ Various publication and distribution options
■ How to prepare games for distribution

- How to submit games to distribution agents and portals
- How to embed games with optional parameters to facilitate demonstration modes
- Professional practice related to contract negotiation and delivery

DOWNLOADABLE CASUAL GAMES

The most common model for casual games today is the downloadable casual game. In many ways this is the logical descendent of conventional shareware. Early shareware used a slightly less evolved model for documenting, promoting, and distributing titles, but it still involved selling individual titles for a reasonable price via Internet download.

Shareware is computer software that is generally sold after a brief demonstration period. In some cases the demonstration period is enforced, and the software ceases to function after a period of time. In other cases the software continues to function but reminds (or nags) the user to pay for the software after the clock has expired. Early shareware actually preceded the Internet. The first shareware applications were passed freely among friends and computing groups. Copying the software was encouraged, and the programs encouraged people to send in $10–$25 if they wanted to stay informed about new features or versions of the software.

The same problems of limited user familiarity that plagued early game adoption are the problems that dominated early attempts to sell the games and encourage players to download them. This is a common paradigm problem in new media. When radio was initially adopted, people had expectations of free content. The mental picture for the customer is "I paid for this expensive radio. The entertainment should be included," so the manufacturer gets the cash and the content producers are left to fend for themselves. If people were apt to expect free stuff with their $40 radio, imagine how they feel today with their $2,000 computer system. Fortunately, this mental construct wanes over time, and people become more willing to pay for highly desirable content.

Today developers can go it alone (creating their own DRM solutions) or work within the system (delivering games via portals such as Real Arcade and Yahoo). In either case an executable version of the software will be created. In both cases you will want to develop some strategies for marketing your game.

Going it Alone

One option casual game developers sometimes pursue is complete independence. It is possible to create your own DRM solution and embed it into your game so that you control every element of the *up-sell* process. The game may then be uploaded to shareware distribution points online such as upload/download.com or Tucows for mass availability, and if it is popular, you could end up selling some copies of your game.

> A purchase of the license for unlimited use of the software is often referred to as an *upsell* or *conversion* in the casual games industry. Conversion rates are very low, with most developers and distributors reporting that hit games convert about 2% of the time and successful games convert as little as 1% of the downloads into sales.

Essentially the game is programmed with a timer that writes the total amount of time spent playing into the system registry or some other location on the player's computer. This is often as simple as encrypting the current time on the host computer and storing the value. Then the time at various intervals (the end of a round or on exit of game) can be checked again and compared. When the time limit is reached, players are generally taken to a Web site where they may purchase the game online (Figure 8.1).

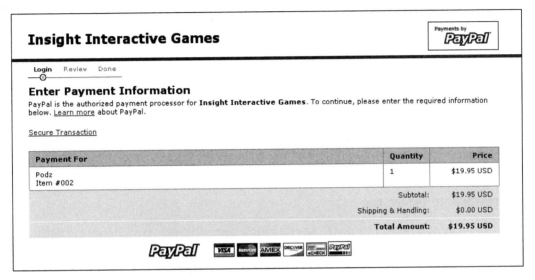

FIGURE 8.1   A typical internal upsell mechanism uses PayPal for purchasing.

If the developer chooses to handle sales internally, they stand to earn a larger percentage of the profits, but they sacrifice a substantial amount of promotion and marketing. Using a major portal or distributor can mean huge audiences, and the higher downloads mean more units sold. Using a general shareware distribution mechanism can yield an audience, but the competition for that audience's attention is much broader, and the downloads aren't anywhere near as high as they are with a game distributor or portal. Some developers, however, have found that it is possible to make their own sites, and consequently DRM solutions, Internet destinations for game players. Notably, PopCap, iWin, Oberon, and Reflexive have all managed to turn brand recognition into market share by luring game players to their proprietary Web sites.

Most developers eventually need to be able to integrate proprietary digital rights management solutions into their games and to allow DRM wrappers to envelope and manage their upsell. Ultimately the basic concerns behind your decisions regarding the DRM will be guided by reputation and credibility. Even a few mediocre but well promoted games create visibility for your brand. People need to trust the companies they deal with, especially when giving credit card information online. Even a great game is unlikely to engender trust among potential customers if they've never heard of any of the parties handling their money. If, however, they already own a game from a company, they are more likely to buy direct the next time.

Your choices then are essentially, write your own serial generator and issue serials in response to online payments through a trusted banking system such as PayPal, or integrate a commercial DRM wrapper into your game.

UNDERSTANDING THE SYSTEM

When working with portals and distribution providers, a DRM wrapper is usually provided. Generally you will be asked to provide the distributor with a fully functional, unrestricted version of the game. The portal or distributor will then wrap your game in their DRM. The DRM will usually provide compression and setup utilities for your game as well as upsell reminders and timeout notification. In some cases the DRM will even provide download assistance.

From a purely practical standpoint, there are logical steps to working with a distribution partner:

1. Once your game is finished, including beta testing and standard functions such as pause, sound control, screen resolution resetting, custom icons, and save and load features, submit your game to one of the prospective distributors.

It is customary to sign a nondisclosure agreement (NDA) at some point in the process. Many distributors will ask for an NDA prior to initial submission. There is no way to absolutely guarantee that you aren't sending that great idea into the hands of someone who would steal it, other than the fact that your idea is probably not really worth anything. If it really is a great idea, then you're probably good for more, making you a more

valuable commodity than the game. Few businesses are willing to risk their reputation for a quick property theft, so try to avoid paranoia about sending your idea or game to them. Also, don't be too quick to assume that someone has stolen your genius idea. People tend to have similar thoughts, especially given exposure to a common cultural experience, so it isn't unusual for more than one person to have an idea for a game that seems similar to another.

2. If you are offered a contract, the portal or distributor will give you explicit instructions for final preparations for your game.
3. If you aren't offered a contract, ask for advice. The producer will usually tell you exactly why they don't like your game. Don't be offended. Just listen and then act on the feedback. They aren't likely to be wrong, but you are. Do your best to fix the problems and then resubmit the game to the next distributor on your list.

There are many different portals and distributors. Each has different tastes, styles, and audiences. Nonetheless, as you are first learning the ropes, it is very possible that you will produce a game that just won't fit on any of the major portals. Make another game or substantially revise the one you already made if you find that the game is rejected by several distributors. You'll learn to make better games and you'll earn a reputation as a serious developer.

Once you have your first distribution contract, there are many new concepts to understand. First, you will be paid royalties for the downloads that are turned over into actual sales. The rates on royalties vary from 20 to 50% for most games. Compare these to the 5–10% common for CD-ROM games, and they look generous, but given the low turnover rates, this is still difficult for most developers to swallow. The truth is that the portals are absolutely the key to success, and at least at first you'll need to accept just about anything in order to get your game out there.

Some portals will offer incentives for listing only with them, in the form of a higher percentage for royalties. Some will have special programs, such as clubs, that can earn you a bit of extra revenue.

Some have advertising programs associated with online versions of the games, though not all pay you anything for the advertising they generate based on your game. It is wise to follow several steps before signing such a contract.

- See a lawyer.
- Work carefully through every aspect of the contract.
- Ensure that you legally own every element of your game.
- Make sure you have incorporated or otherwise protected yourself from litigation.
- Carefully check to make certain that your work does not infringe upon the work of others.

Once a deal is in place, your game will be added to the collection available via that portal. You will generally either receive regular statements from the distributor or will be able to access information about your game's turnover rates online. There is also a public entity that tracks sales statistics based on data from several of the major distributors.

> Game-sales-charts.com tracks the weekly and monthly top-10 lists in the casual games industry. The site includes charts of the latest top sellers from as many as 17 portals and seeks to provide an independent report of the success of games in the industry in order to promote sales.

If your game's conversion rate is above 1%, congratulations. It's time to move on to the next title. If it isn't, move on to the next game anyway. They can't all be hits. Every game you distribute increases your brand identity and adds to your wisdom about meeting the demands of the market. It may take considerable practice to master these concepts, but you are bound to get better if you ask questions and listen to the feedback with an open mind.

Conversion rates are the most important factor in the promotion, marketing, and portal position of casual games. The games with the highest conversion rates will get the most prominent position on the portals, the most marketing, and the broadest distribution. Games with low conversion rates will rapidly fade into relative oblivion. This doesn't mean that games with low profiles and low conversion rates are ignored. Such games will still see thousands of players, but the opportunities for games with low conversion rates are not nearly as good as those for high conversion rate games. This is a populist meritocracy, wherein the games that sell the most copies (are the most popular) will get the most time, energy, money, and clout invested back into them.

ALTERNATIVE DISTRIBUTION PATHS

A growing number of casual games are being distributed via alternative paths. One notable path growing rapidly over the past year has been the handheld game and PDA/cell phone market. Games have also appeared in airline seats and on cereal boxes. Casual games are sometimes distributed via CD-ROM and are finding their way into magazines.

FROM AIRPLANES TO HANDHELDS

The available platforms for casual games have grown substantially over the past few years. Passengers on Northwest Airlines overseas flights can now play *Bejeweled* if they'd rather amuse themselves with a casual game than a movie. Casual games easily satisfy the desire for a quick escape of the typical overseas air traveler. They also satisfy that need for people just looking for a quick escape from boredom in daily encounters. People waiting for a ride, a meeting, or a class enjoy spending that time with a simple amusement. The Northwest Airline games are mounted on a Unix system and make use of a simple controller integrated into a wired remote.

Casual games are appearing on a variety of handheld devices using Windows CE and on Nintendo's DS™ handheld game system.

The handheld games for Nintendo DS have been exceptionally popular, featuring the massively popular *Brain Age* and *Big Brain Academy*, which appeal to people who want a quick, rewarding, easy-to-learn, and addictive game experience. Given the success of these games in these locations, it is reasonable to expect continued growth. Likely extensions are more games on television (yes, there are already many delivered via digital cable) as well as games on trains, in restaurants, and perhaps even in refrigerators. As the cost of digital interaction continues to decrease, it even becomes conceivable that one day soon casual games will adorn the sides of cereal boxes or the handles of shopping carts, encouraging children to settle down and focus on the distraction, freeing parents to do their shopping.

CONVENTIONAL CD PUBLICATION

Conventional publishers are migrating rapidly to get on the casual games bandwagon. The process of pursuing publication deals with traditional CD-ROM publishers is similar to that of working with distributors. A couple of options for this sort of publication are Encore and Cosmi. Encore is the leading publisher of third-party software in North America, selling 3.8 million software units in 2006. Cosmi sold nearly 2.8 million. With software available in stores ranging from Office Depot® to Wal-Mart®, these companies provide you with access to the general public. Submission processes vary from publisher to publisher.

Casual games are also appearing on CDs in cereal boxes, along with associated toys, and in the backs of various magazines. Collections of casual games are especially popular.

PROFESSIONAL PRACTICE: ANDY PHELPS ON IMAGE AND COMMUNITY

Andy Phelps is the Director of Game Design and Development at the Rochester Institute of Technology. Andy's work in games programming education has been featured in the

→

New York Times, CNN.com, *USA Today*, National Public Radio, and a host of other places. Andy is a guru in the Flash and Director Development communities, with several techniques published at the Adobe Developer Center, the Director Online User's Group, and *MX Developer's Magazine* (now the *Web Developer's Journal*), and has recently turned his focus to M.U.P.P.E.T.S, a community-based development environment for students learning computer-development skills.

Partridge: *Recent public reports that a major studio invested $700,000 in the development costs for a casual game beg the question, do slick graphics and effects matter? Does a game have to look good to be good?*

Phelps: It's a misnomer when people talk about how "graphics aren't necessary." They are usually making the argument that gameplay is important—which it is—but that doesn't mean that ugly, second-rate presentation is acceptable. When I hear this argument from students, they almost invariably refer to *PAC-MAN*, which had (by today's standards) some fairly rudimentary graphics. This plays right into my trap—remember the version of the game for the Atari home console? It was ugly, and I hated it. I'd go to the mall to plug quarters into the arcade, because it was slick and colorful instead of grayscale and stretched all out of its aspect ratio. Another more current example is the comparison between *World of Warcraft* (*WoW*) and *Everquest II* (*EQII*).

Proponents will argue about how *EQII* spent too much of its development on graphics and not enough on gameplay, and that *WoW* is a much better game in terms of playability and feeling involved. The complete fallacy there is that obviously Blizzard took the look and feel of *WoW* very seriously—it's a beautiful game, and the artwork is amazing!

$\rightarrow$

Partridge: *Are there special implications for graphics in the casual games arena, where the player has a chance to experience the game for an hour before they make that purchase decision?*

Phelps: Well the first obvious consideration is that the size of the content is so significantly reduced. Shipping the user a bunch of preexisting content via disk and then downloading on top of that base is very different than all-Web delivery (either browser play or bundled download). Casual games typically have much tighter constraints in terms of content size. Also, because of the budgets involved and the size of the team (casual games are developed by far fewer people on a team-size basis), you just can't afford to be as in-depth and build everything in the world from scratch. This leads to development choices where the use of preexisting engines and code bases are very prevalent. This is a tack we are taking with one of our current projects, the Director–Flash 3D Interface (DF3DI), which seeks to put an ActionScript API overtop of the Shockwave 3D core so that developers more familiar with Flash can author some "true 3D" content quickly and import assets with prebuilt loader technology and XML bindings (*http://andysgi.rit.edu/andyworld10/df3di/*).

Prebuilt engines often have a certain "look" that they are good at reproducing, so you see that look a lot given the products people are producing the content with. Occasionally something will really stand out and represent an artistic style more so than the underlying tool, and to me these are really special pieces. As you note in the question, a lot of casual games use the "try before you buy" model—this means the graphics have to stand up and captivate interest enough that someone will choose to download it, the content will be small enough that the download isn't excessive, and that they will stand up over time enough that people want to invest in

→

the game. They can't replace gameplay (of course), but they had better augment it.

Partridge: *Many developers have predicted that the next frontier for casual games is in multiplayer and community-based games. Are there any general truths about virtual communities that you learned working with M.U.P.P.E.T.S. that developers can apply to their multiplayer games?*

Phelps: The Multi-User Programming Pedagogy for Enhancing Traditional Study (M.U.P.P.E.T.S.) project has taught us a great deal on a number of fronts. First and foremost, as soon as you start working with a virtual community, you have to be actively involved with them from the beginning to the end. Not so much as a day goes by where there isn't some question from the community we dig into and try to support. Quality involvement, good communication (and good communication software) build good experiences. It sounds very trite to say, and a lot like common sense, but I'm always amazed when I surf at the way some games can't seem to connect with their own player communities.

The next thing I would say is that a lot of first-time developers getting into multiuser drastically underestimate the complexity of the applications. Having three working clients in a back room of an office complex doesn't mean it will deploy well. Thorough testing and load-balancing are essential, but are often overlooked by people wanting to do their "first multiplayer game." I think the number of places that are equipped to really build a massively multiplayer casual game are relatively small. It really is hard. What will spring up first is wave upon wave of small group play games and/or head-to-head duels. These are doable now, and can be a lot of fun online.

Finally, and perhaps most frustratingly, is the age-old development lesson that everything is your fault. When we

→

deployed our system the first time, we invariably had systems we couldn't possibly have imagined that people wanted to run it on, and to this day we have users that issue us scathing feature requests. The things that have saved us thus are: a robust content pipeline, a reconfigurable and highly modifiable code base, and, most importantly, incredibly patient and intelligent faculty and students. Patience and perseverance are as important as being a good developer in that sense—the number of times you want to quit a multiuser community-driven project is nonzero.

Partridge: *You work with students every day who are headed for careers in the games industry. Do you have any advice for young developers considering a career in the field?*

Phelps: Certainly. First and foremost, if your interest is games, then find ways to connect everything else you are doing to games. When I was in high school and then while getting my undergraduate degree, I thought a lot of the things I was studying weren't very important. English. History. Civics. I wanted to be an artist, and I would basically draw all day and didn't care about much else. But looking back, this was incredibly short-sighted: how can you build a good world if you don't understand History? How can you create political intrigue without understanding both English (or the language you are writing in) and governmental structure? Building good games means telling good stories, and I blew a lot of my education thinking that the underpinnings of story weren't important.

The relevance of things like math and physics to game development is obvious—but in fact almost every academic discipline has impact on the construction of games. The best developers are the ones that can synthesize their every experience into the creation of new and interesting worlds: ignoring parts of this world is unlikely to produce success in synthesizing your own.

$\rightarrow$

Eventually I did wise up, and realized a number of things. The first is that you can't do everything yourself—no matter how good you are. The games industry is rough, everyone wants to be there, and you have to prove yourself. Brushing everyone else off and trying to "go it alone" is the worst possible strategy, particularly if your skills make you a strong programmer, but not a strong artist or storyteller (or vice versa). Teamwork, communication, and a winning personality are as important as your skill in building games—and this takes time working with other people to develop. So many young people that want to do games think the way to do that is to isolate themselves in a closet and program, when nothing could be further from the truth.

Finally, I make every one of my students happy by telling them that if they want to develop games, they have to play games. Play a lot of games. Don't just play one type of game over and over. Branch out and play lots of different genres on lots of different platforms. Analyze them. Pick them apart. What makes this part of a game fun? If you hated this part or that game, why? What did or didn't work? Keep a journal of what you play, what you liked, what you didn't, how you think it might have been built, and your overall experiences. Games are built by game developers, not by players. You can become a developer by dissecting the form, creation, craft, and style of the medium, but not by necessarily getting high score or level sixty. Invariably, some people who think they want to do games really just want to play them—if you are passionate about wanting to play games, the above doesn't even seem like "work."

Partridge: *Were there any people or things that strongly influenced your growth into a programming and graphics guru?*

Phelps: I would be remiss if I didn't thank my fellow faculty and my students at the Rochester Institute of Technology

→

for all their help and support in several of my projects, my wife Ashley for her tireless support of a crazy professor that devoted his life to games and entertainment, and my children, Emma and Kalan, the gamers of the future (or whatever else they want to be). Also many thanks to the Director games community, of which I am one very small part, from Hopper-Ex to DirGame-L to Tom Higgins, Darrel Plant, Barry Swan, Lucas, Dean Utian, James Newton, Noisecrime, Ullala, Zav, and all the rest that I haven't singled out by name. I've really enjoyed being a part of the community over the years, and appreciate all the help that it gives to its members. It is a great group.

SUMMARY

The most common business practice in the casual games industry is the try-before-you-buy model, descended largely from earlier conventions of shareware. Generally these try-before-you-buy games use DRM wrappers for installation and wrapping. The DRM handles the financial transactions as well. Advertising-supported online demos that provide a taste of the game, without the time limits and sometimes with limited features, are often used in conjunction with the try-before-you-buy model.

Alternative distribution options for casual games include a growing number of delivery systems, many of which are also growing in popularity. Casual games are appearing on the backs of airline seats, on PDAs, and on handheld game consoles. They are gaining popularity on cell phones and even appear in magazines.

9 Distributors and Portals

In This Chapter

■ The Major Distributors and Portals
■ Developer Distributors

The next obvious step for a casual game developer is game submission. In this chapter you'll find an overview of the distributors and portals who facilitate casual game publishers by hosting their games on portals. As you learned earlier, the distribution portal is the primary mechanism by which casual games are distributed.

Several third-party distributors host major portals. They each have slightly different audience demographics and game adoption policies and practices. In this section you'll learn how to submit your game for consideration by these portals and why you might choose to list a game with one portal over another. Keep in mind that many submissions to portals, about 86–92%, are rejected. If you included submissions initially rejected but eventually adopted in that figure, the number might well be even higher. Submitting a game is by no means a guarantee of acceptance.

These rejections, however, include a substantial number of games that simply aren't stable, thoroughly tested, or appropriate for the casual games market. Making the right match for your game requires research and diligence. The distributors will often provide specific rationale for a refusal, so you are given a mechanism for improving your game's appeal.

In this chapter you will learn:

- How to reach a distribution agreement with a portal or distributor
- How to submit games to distribution agents and portals
- Who the major distributors are and how their audiences differ
- How to improve your game based on feedback from rejected submission
- An understanding of professional practice related to game submission

THE MAJOR DISTRIBUTORS AND PORTALS

Most estimates suggest that the casual game industry will reach more than a billion dollars in annual sales during the next year. In an industry only about five years old, that is an amazing figure. The growth rate has risen significantly every year, and there is good reason to suspect that the industry might be at the base of a shockingly profitable exponential growth curve that is only now beginning to rise.

The hub of sales thus far has been the online portals hosted by game companies, distributors, and publisher/distributor teams. These sites have the advantage of absurdly high traffic. The largest are reporting as many as 40 million unique visitors each month. Any way you slice it, that's a huge audience, and the potential to turn those visits into profit is significant.

In this section you'll find descriptions of each of the major casual game distributors, including an overview of their game submission standards and audience demographics.

REALARCADE

RealArcade is likely the largest of the distribution portals online (*gamedevs.realarcade.com*). The company reports over 1 million downloads a day, with online sales exceeding $2 million. They provide significant global reach with localized sites around the world in several languages.

Their downloadable collection includes about 250 games, and their audience fits the profile, with about 70% female and most between 30 and 60 years of age. Submissions are taken online, and responses are generally quite prompt (1–2 weeks.) Real recently acquired GameHouse, so they now have in-house development. This sort of vertical integration is typical and can be expected with all of the major distributors eventually.

SHOCKWAVE.COM

Actually Atom Entertainment, this growing network of major entertainment aggregators made headlines recently when it was purchased by Viacom for $200 million. The acquisition of content producers by Viacom or any of the other mega-corporations that have created the modern climate of media conglomeration is nothing new, but the acquisition of Web-based content producers is a fairly recent phenomenon.

Atom is one of many companies that will not sign an NDA to review your game. This doesn't mean they are out to pirate your game. In many such companies, people get sued because a game they create is similar to something they reviewed. This is usually an absurd connection amounting to a frivolous lawsuit, but the costs of litigation are high. Accepting your submission is a high-risk proposition for a company, and if they sign an NDA and you do get mad, they have less protection.

They accept email submissions but require a format found on the developer FAQ page. The fact that their collection includes many alternative titles and their business model seems to benefit more from advertising suggests that their core audience may be younger. Atom reports that the core Shockwave.com demographic is only 54% female and their age spread is much more even, with only about 10% deviation over any age group 18–55+. They also run AddictingGames which skews even more heavily male and skews much younger, with nearly 40% of the audience below 24 years old.

MSN Games

Microsoft Network Games does not accept submissions directly. They work with distribution partners Oberon Media, RealNetworks, and SkillJam. The partner of primary interest if you are making downloadable casual games is Oberon. It is important to note that a deal with Oberon does not necessarily mean a game on MSN Games. Each MSN Games site around the world has different management, and each one will decide independently whether or not to take the game from the Oberon feed.

The demographic of players on the MSN Games site is predominantly female (66%), and predominantly middle aged (69% ages 25–54), with 41% college graduates and nearly 30% engaged in professional or managerial careers. The overwhelming majority have broadband connections, most access the Web from home, and most access the Web every day. Sixty-two percent have made an online purchase in the past 30 days.

Pogo

Pogo is a subdivision of Electronic Arts. Like MSN, Pogo uses Oberon to acquire a library of downloadable games. Developers submit their games to Oberon, and if Pogo wants to pick them up, they may. Pogo has an enormous base of online game players who visit the site to play online games and may or may not download games as a result.

Arcade Town

Arcade Town takes online game submissions via a form (*http://www.arcadetown.com/contact.asp*). Just use the drop-down menu for game developer submissions.

Try Media

One gateway to Yahoo is this Macrovision subsidiary. Some of the distribution portals will only work with the larger companies and through distribution partners like Try Media, which produces the digital rights management software Active Mark. Following in the vertical integration tradition, Try Media serves as a potential outlet for distribution as well as a resource for creating and embedding a custom upsell mechanism.

DEVELOPER DISTRIBUTORS

One common method used by communication businesses to maximize their profit potential is known as vertical integration. The basic phenomenon involves the integration of the production unit (the game publisher) with the distribution arm (the portal). It doesn't take much to understand that this will maximize the company's profits. Ultimately, if the company can produce adequate entertainment using internally contracted artists, rather than externally solicited contracts, more of the profits will go to the company. If you are a company, this is a great idea. Whether developer or distributor you stand to maximize your profits. Many of the major producers of casual games rapidly realized that they could turn their brand recognition into portal competition by moving customers from third-party portals to their own in-house portals.

They also are able to sell and distribute other companies' titles, creating a substantial base of revenue, even from games that they didn't publish, and effectively cashing in on their reputation.

OBERON GAMES

Oberon Games has one of the largest networks of portals of any of the distributor/aggregators. Oberon also produces games. Oberon makes games available to partners, and then the partners choose whether or not to adopt the games to their collection. Oberon accepts submissions via email (*developers@oberon-media.com*).

BIG FISH GAMES

Big Fish, probably the second-largest portal today, provides games to a variety of portal partners, most notably, Viacom and NBC, which translates into sites like Nickelodeon, Nick Jr., and Neopets®. The developer/distributor provides marketing and distribution solutions for publishers. Games are accepted at *submissions@bigfishgames.com*.

REFLEXIVE ARCADE

Reflexive aggregates and distributes games directly and via numerous portal partners. Reflexive also produces some of the most visually stunning casual games in the world. Reflexive accepts submissions at *submitgame@reflexive.com*.

POPCAP GAMES

PopCap develops and distributes games through their own portal and through distribution partners. One of PopCap's unique contributions is the PopCap Framework, a collection of resources used to build games that PopCap has made available to casual game developers. The framework is a set of C++ libraries that provide basic access to standard game features.

PopCap provides the framework and accepts online game submissions via their developer site (*developer.popcap.com*).

iWIN

iWin accepts online submissions of games as well as treatments and concept documents. They do publishing deals as well as act as a distributor/portal (email: *youwin@iwin.com*).

SUMMARY

Casual game developers generally work with one or more distributors or portals to make their games available to the public. A good idea is to submit your game to one portal at a time, listening carefully to the response. If a game appears to be immediately successful, you might want to shop it around a bit to see if you can get competitive bids from more than one portal or distributor, but don't overplay that hand. You'll find that people don't much like being played off one another, and profit margins are thin enough—and the industry small enough—that this is not a game you should play idly.

There are several third-party distributors who host major portals in addition to several game publishers who host their own portals. Each has different audience demographics and game adoption policies and practices. You can submit your game for consideration by these portals and in accordance with individual practice. You'll want to consider why you might choose to list a game with one portal over another. About 90% of submissions are rejected, but even if your game is rejected you'll probably receive valuable feedback that can help you strengthen your game or create a new, more appropriate game.

About the CD-ROM

The CD-ROM included with *Creating Casual Games for Profit and Fun* includes all of resource files necessary to complete the tutorials in the book. It also includes the images from the book in full color, and demos for you to use while working through the tutorials and exercises.

CD FOLDERS

IMAGES: All of the images from within the book in full color. These files are set up by chapter and named by the figure number.

TUTORIALS: All of the files necessary to complete the tutorials in the book. These files are all in common formats and are set up in chapter folders.

DEMOS: We have included a demo of Flash Jester's Jugglor and Meliora's Magic Res Xtra.

The first is a Flash wrapper. It is an application designed to extend Flash's reach by creating an executable file that bridge's Flash's access to the operating system.

The second is an unlimited version of the Meliora Magic Res Xtra. This extension for Adobe Director allows the applications that you make to alter the color depth and screen resolution of the computers on which they run.

SYSTEM REQUIREMENTS

- Windows 98/NT/2000
- Pentium Processor+
- CD/HardDrive
- 64 MB RAM
- 20 MB free disk space

- Mac OS 10+
- CD/HardDrive
- 64 MB RAM
- 20 MB Free HardDrive Space

You will need Adobe Flash and Adobe Director to work with these resource files. Both are available as free demos from the Adobe website. *Note that exe files will not function on a Macintosh and hqx files will not function on Windows.

INSTALLATION

To use this CD, you just need to make sure that your system matches at least the minimum system requirements. Each demo has it's own installation instructions and you should contact the developer directly if you have any problems installing the demo. The images and tutorial files are in .tiff, .fla, .dir, .swf, and .exe file formats.

Index